T0139105

Understanding White-Collar Crime

A Convenience Perspective

Understanding
White-Collar Crime
A Convenience Perspective

Petter Gottschalk

CRC Press
Taylor & Francis Group
Boca Raton London New York

CRC Press is an imprint of the
Taylor & Francis Group, an **informa** business

CRC Press
Taylor & Francis Group
6000 Broken Sound Parkway NW, Suite 300
Boca Raton, FL 33487-2742

© 2017 by Taylor & Francis Group, LLC
CRC Press is an imprint of Taylor & Francis Group, an Informa business

No claim to original U.S. Government works

Printed on acid-free paper
Version Date: 20160512

International Standard Book Number-13: 978-1-4987-6887-0 (Hardback)

Library of Congress Cataloging-in-Publication Data

Names: Gottschalk, Petter, 1950- author.
Title: Understanding white-collar crime : a convenience perspective / Petter Gottschalk.
Description: Boca Raton, FL : CRC Press, 2017. | Includes bibliographical references and index.
Identifiers: LCCN 2016013703 | ISBN 9781498768870 (alk. paper)
Subjects: LCSH: White collar crimes. | Commercial crimes. | Crime--Sociological aspects. | Criminology.
Classification: LCC HV6768 .G6876 2017 | DDC 364.16/8--dc23
LC record available at https://lccn.loc.gov/2016013703

**Visit the Taylor & Francis Web site at
http://www.taylorandfrancis.com**

**and the CRC Press Web site at
http://www.crcpress.com**

Printed and bound in the United States of America by Publishers Graphics, LLC on sustainably sourced paper.

Contents

Author

Petter Gottschalk is professor in the Department of Leadership and Organizational Behavior at BI Norwegian Business School in Oslo, Norway. He teaches courses on financial crime investigations and characteristics of white-collar criminals.

Dr. Gottschalk received the MBA degree in Operations Research at Technical University of Berlin in Germany, and the MSc degree in Systems Simulation at Thayer School of Engineering, Dartmouth College and Massachusetts Institute of Technology in the United States. He completed the doctoral degree in Strategy Implementation in the United Kingdom at Brunel University.

He has been president and chief executive officer at several companies including ABB Datacables and Norwegian Computing Center.

Dr. Gottschalk has published extensively on knowledge management, information technology management, police investigations, police misconduct, fraud examinations, white-collar crime, and corruption. Recently, his research has concentrated on developing convenience theory to explain white-collar crime.

Dr. Gottschalk is a popular speaker at universities and conferences all over the world. In recent years, he has been teaching in New Haven, Connecticut, New York, Orlando, Trinidad and Tobago, Hungary, and many other locations.

Introduction

This book deals with the topic of white-collar crime and considers the role of convenience in explaining its occurrence. It puts forward convenience as a theoretical explanation that underlies existing theories and research on white-collar crime.

Convenience seems present in all three dimensions of crime: economic dimension, organizational dimension, and behavioral dimension. Convenience in white-collar crime implies savings in time and effort by privileged and trusted individuals to solve a problem, where alternatives seem less attractive, and future threats of detection and punishment are minimal. The proposed theory of convenience in white-collar crime emerges as an integrated explanation in need of more theoretical work as well as empirical study. This book presents ideas that are grounded in the existing literature, and these ideas represent a novel perspective: They answer questions that are not adequately explained by the existing literature or provide different answers to "how…?," "why…?," and "when…?" questions.

Ever since Sutherland (1940) coined the term white-collar crime, there has been a debate who to include in and who to exclude from this category of criminals. For example, Brightman (2009) argues that personal computers and the Internet allow individuals from all social classes to buy and sell stocks and engage in similar activities that were once the bastion of the financial elite. Benson and Simpson (2015) find this insufficient as an argument to include virtually any nonviolent act committed for financial gain regardless of one's social status into the term white-collar crime, since the definition of white-collar criminal involves a breach of trust. Because scholars tend to disagree, white-collar crime is in need of additional theory.

Scholars seem to agree that while circumstances have changed over the years, the definition of a white-collar crime has to be both offense-based and offender-based. The offense-based perspective is concerned with financial crime for economic gain. The offender-based perspective is concerned with the role, profession, and position enabling the offender to commit crime. Thus, a white-collar criminal is a privileged person committing financial crime (Gottschalk and Rundmo, 2014).

While this book applies a convenience perspective to understand white-collar crime, Benson and Simpson (2015) apply an opportunity perspective to understand white-collar crime. In the terminology applied in this book, opportunity is an important element and prerequisite in making financial crime convenient for the white-collar criminal. Opportunity is an opening and a possibility to commit criminal acts as a means to reach an organizational or a personal goal. When criminal opportunity is attractive as a means to fulfill one's desires, rational actors will choose it.

As discussed in convenience theory in this book, opportunity is a distinct characteristic of white-collar crime and varies depending on the kinds of criminal involved (Michel, 2008). An opportunity is attractive as a means of responding to desires (Bucy et al., 2008). It is the organizational context where the white-collar criminal is a professional that provides the offender an opportunity to commit financial crime and conceal it in legal organizational activities. While opportunity in the economic dimension of convenience theory is concerned with goal achievements (such as sales and bonuses), opportunity in the organizational dimension is concerned with criminal activities (such as corruption and embezzlement).

Benson and Simpson (2015: 76) use the term *opportunity* to describe the organizational dimension, and they argue that without an opportunity, there cannot be a crime.

> What exactly is a criminal opportunity? According to routine activity theory, criminal opportunity comprises two elements: a suitable target and a lack of capable guardianship. A target can be a person or some kind of property. What makes a person or a piece of property suitable as a target for crime? That depends on a lot of factors. Without exploring all of them, we can identify some of the main considerations. (…) Property becomes attractive to an offender if it is portable, valuable, and fungible. The importance of value for property offenders is obvious. (…)
>
> The other component of a criminal opportunity is capable guardianship, or rather the lack of capable guardianship. You may think of capable guardianship as a big strong person who can defend you or your property, but the term guardianship is meant to be interpreted in a much broader way. It is just a convenient figure of speech. By capable guardianship, we mean anything that can either physically

prevent the offender from getting to the target or that can make the offender decide it is too risky to go after the target. Guardianship takes two main forms: blocking access and surveillance.

Blocking occurs when potential offenders have no access to passwords for electronic transactions, and when they are denied participation at travel and in meetings where sensitive information and knowledge are being exchanged. Surveillance occurs when potential offenders can be observed or otherwise detected either while committing the crime or afterward. Surveillance increases the likelihood that the offender's actions will be noticed, and, accordingly, the offender faces an increased risk of being caught. The opportunity is thus reduced.

References

Benson, M.L. and Simpson, S.S. (2015). *Understanding white-collar crime—An opportunity perspective*, New York: Routledge.

Brightman, H.J. (2009). *Today's white-collar crime: Legal, investigative, and theoretical perspectives*, New York: Routledge, Taylor & Francis Group.

Bucy, P.H., Formby, E.P., Raspanti, M.S. and Rooney, K.E. (2008). Why do they do it?: The motives, mores, and character of white collar criminals, *St. John's Law Review*, 82, 401–571.

Gottschalk, P. and Rundmo, T. (2014). Crime: The amount and disparity of sentencing—A comparison of corporate and occupational white collar criminals, *International Journal of Law, Crime and Justice*, 42, 175–187.

Michel, P. (2008). Financial crimes: The constant challenge of seeking effective prevention solutions, *Journal of Financial Crime*, 15 (4), 383–397.

Sutherland, E.H. (1940). White-collar criminality, *American Sociological Review*, 5, 1–12.

chapter one

Convenience theory of white-collar crime

Extracting the concept from marketing theory (Farquhar and Rowley, 2009), convenience in white-collar crime relates to savings in time and effort by privileged and trusted individuals to reach a goal. Convenience here is an attribute of an illegal action. Convenience comes at a potential cost to the offender in terms of the likelihood of detection and future punishment. In other words, reducing time and effort now entails a greater potential for future cost. "Paying for convenience" is a way of phrasing this proposition.

Convenience benefits and costs

Convenience is the perceived savings in time and effort required to find and to facilitate the use of a solution to a problem or to exploit an opportunity. Convenience directly relates to the amount of time and effort that is required to accomplish a task. Convenience addresses the time and effort exerted before, during, and after an activity. Convenience represents a time and effort component related to the complete illegal transaction process or processes (Collier and Kimes, 2012).

People differ in their temporal orientation, including perceived time scarcity, the degree to which they value time, and their sensitivity to time-related issues. Facing strain, greed, or other situations, an illegal activity can represent a convenient solution to a problem that the individual or the organization otherwise find difficult or even impossible to solve. The desire for convenience varies among people. Convenience orientation is a term that refers to a person's general preference for convenient solutions to problems. A convenience-oriented individual is one who seeks to accomplish a task in the shortest time with the least expenditure of human energy (Farquhar and Rowley, 2009).

Three main dimensions to explain white-collar crime have emerged (Gottschalk, 2015b). All of them link to convenience. The first dimension is concerned with economic aspects, where convenience implies that the illegal financial gain is a convenient option for the decision-maker to cover needs. The second dimension is concerned with organizational aspects, where convenience implies that the offender has convenient access to premises and convenient ability to hide illegal transactions among legal transactions. The third dimension is concerned with behavioral aspects, where convenience implies that the offender has convenient justification and acceptance of their own deviant behavior.

This book reviews the state-of-the-art relating to white-collar crime and criminals by applying the economic, organizational, and behavioral dimensions. By combining these dimensions, an integrated explanation of white-collar crime emerges, which we label convenience theory. White-collar criminals have convenient access, and financial crime saves them time and effort to solve a problem related to making a personal or organizational profit. Convenience is a relative concept, where the ease of problem solving can cause future costs for the offender. Crime is committed if found suitable by the offender, and especially when no alternative is in sight.

Convenience comes at a potential cost to the offender in terms of the likelihood of detection, prosecution, and prison sentence. Other potential costs are damage to family and friendships, loss of job, loss of income, isolation from profession, depression, and other psychological problems.

The following chapters present convenience theory's three dimensions. But first we provide a general explanation of theory development.

Theorizing and theory development

Whetten (1989) suggests that a theoretical contribution starts by identifying factors (variables, construct, concepts) that should be considered as part of the explanation of the phenomenon. He then suggests the how-part, which is how these concepts are related to each other. He also suggests that a theory has to explain the underlying psychological, economic, or social dynamics that justify the selection of factors and the proposed causal relationships. This rationale constitutes the theory's assumptions—the theoretical glue that welds the model together.

Eisenhardt (1989) argues that researchers develop theory by combining insights into observations, text in the research literature, sensible reasoning, and experience. Convenience theory has developed this way.

Sutton and Staw (1995) argue that a theory has to meet some minimum standards. They argue that references, data, lists of variables or constructs, diagrams, and hypotheses or predictions are not theory. They assert that theory is the answer to queries of *why*. Theory is about the connections among phenomena, a story about why acts, events, incidents, and reactions occur. They argue that theory emphasizes the nature of causal relationships, identifying what comes first as well as the timing of such events. Strong theory, in their view, delves into underlying processes to understand the systematic reasons for a particular occurrence or nonoccurrence.

Weick (1995) commented on Sutton and Staw's (1995) definition of theory by stating that what theory is not, theorizing is. Products of the theorizing process seldom emerge as full-blown theories. Data, lists, diagrams, and hypotheses can be part of a theorizing process. The process of theorizing consists of activities like abstracting, generalizing, relating, selecting, explaining, synthesizing, and idealizing. While theorizing is a process, theory is a product.

DiMaggio (1995) as well commented on Sutton and Staw's (1995) definition of theory by stating that there is more than one kind of good theory. They mentioned theory as covering laws, theory as enlightenment, and theory as narrative. He argues that good theory splits the difference, and that theory construction is social construction, often after the fact.

A few years later, Weick (1999) argued that theorizing in organizational studies has taken on a life of its own. He found that researchers seem more preoccupied with intellectual fashions than with advancement of knowledge. He argues that so much research is irrelevant to practice.

Colquitt and Zapata-Phelan (2007) found that many academics support Sutton and Staw's (1995) definition of a theory in terms of relationships between independent and dependent variables. Theory is then a collection of assertions that identifies how they are interrelated and why, and identifies the conditions under which relationships exist or do not exist. From this perspective, a theory is primarily useful to the extent it has the ability to explain variance in a criterion of interest. Other scholars support DiMaggio's (1995) suggestion that theory is an account of a social process, with emphasis on empirical tests of the plausibility of the narrative as well as careful attention to the scope conditions of the account.

Theory is a way of imposing conceptual order on the empirical complexity of the phenomenal world. Theory does more than simply abstract and organize knowledge. Theory identifies and describes relations between concepts within a set of boundary assumptions and constraints. Some see theory as a means of knowledge accumulation. These are the empiricists. Some see theory as a means of abstraction. These are the rationalists. Some see theory as normative explanations, which is not to represent the phenomenal world as it is but, rather, to see the world as it might be. A fourth role for theory is to legitimate knowledge (Suddaby, 2014).

Theory offers an explanation of relationships between concepts within a number of assumptions and constraints, and theory challenges assumptions about a given concept. For example, Hærem et al. (2015) extend the concept of task complexity and present a number of new assumptions to challenge old assumptions of task complexity. Theory reflects the structure of a phenomenon's knowledge base in abstract terms, such as the phenomenon of white-collar crime in the presented convenience theory.

The term theory is applied differently in various fields. Economists view theory as a stringent derivation of results based on certain assumptions.

It may seem, for example, that B follows from A, without really knowing why, since one only has assumptions and hypotheses.

Michailova et al. (2014) support Weick's view that theory cannot improve until we improve the theorizing process, and we cannot improve the theorizing process until we describe it more explicitly. They challenge the view that interesting theorizing would be an outcome only of high-quality, sustained relationships in the field, as suggested by the why-only perspective on theory.

In the following, the general theory of white-collar crime—consisting of economical, organizational, and behavioral dimensions—the emphasis is on theory as an explanation. An explanation is a set of statements constructed to describe a set of facts which clarifies contexts, modes, causes, and consequences of those facts. This is in line with Whetten (1989) who argues that a theory is an explanation of a phenomenon. He suggests that a theory has to explain the underlying economic, social, and psychological dynamics that justify the selection of factors. This is also in line with Weick (1995) who argued that the process of theorizing consists of several activities including explanations. It is as well in line with Colquitt and Zapata-Phelan (2007) who emphasize a theory's ability to explain variance in criteria of interest. Strong theory, in Sutton and Staw's (1995) view, delves into underlying processes so as to understand the systematic reasons for a particular occurrence or nonoccurrence, which the following theoretical descriptions intend to do.

Explanation for understanding is thus the main focus of the following theory. We search for a better understanding of white-collar crime. We are certainly not the only ones (Benson and Simpson, 2015: 71):

> Just as with conventional crime, many theoretical approaches have been tried in the search for a better understanding of white-collar crime. The process of applying standard criminological theories to white-collar crime often involves "conceptual acrobatics." Theorists have to take ideas and concepts that were originally developed to apply to traditional forms of crime and tweak them to account for the special features of white-collar crime and the distinguishing characteristics of white-collar offenders.

An example of a theorist who takes ideas and theorizes them is Jacques (2014), who defines an idea as a statement about the nature of reality that people have said, written, or otherwise communicated. This is in line with Williams (2008), who argues that we must devote more attention to considerations of knowledge and knowledgeability in the study of white-collar crime. He suggests that we need to be concerned with the extent to which the power of organizations maintain and reproduce themselves, and that we need theory to help document white-collar offending in society impeded by a crisis of knowledge.

Eisenhardt (1989) argues that theory development should include real cases and empirical evidence. She argues that there must be an intimate link between theory and empirical reality. Her argument is in line with those who include hypotheses testing as part of theory construction.

However, in this book we define theory in terms of its core and do not include the empirical side of research. We conclude by providing the following definition of theory as applied in this book to white-collar crime. *A theory is a systematic explanation of a phenomenon in reality. A theory is assumptions about relationships in practice. A theory combines insights from observations, previous research, hypotheses, and own reasoning. A theory emerges by abstraction, relationships, selection, simplification, and generalization.*

With this definition in mind, convenience theory might be classified as a middle-range theory rather than as an abstract theory. It was Merton (1968) who introduced middle-range theory as opposed to grand and abstract theory. Abstract theory as argued by Parson is an all-inclusive systemic effort to develop unified theory (Kang, 2014). Merton suggests that middle-range theory pushes our boundaries of knowledge for a specific phenomenon, while abstract theory includes everything and is thus impossible to evaluate or test in reality. Middle-range theory focuses on an interesting and relevant phenomenon in society—such as white-collar crime—to improve our understanding of and generate insights into behaviors, conditions, and patterns. Middle-range theory should enable development of models and hypotheses about the phenomenon.

Davis (1971) argues that an interesting theory is one that denies certain assumptions of their audience. Sandberg and Alvesson (2011) and Alvesson and Sandberg (2011, 2012) are on the same track by suggesting that theory construction should challenge assumptions. Theorists should challenge dominant assumptions in existing research. One of the dominant assumptions in white-collar crime research is differential association, which argues that criminal behavior is learned. Convenience theory in this book challenges this assumption and suggests that white-collar crime is not learned.

Alvesson and Sandberg (2011) define theory as a statement of relations among concepts within a boundary set of assumptions and constraints. They develop problematization as a methodology for generating research questions, which they argue will lead to more interesting and influential studies. The alternative to problematization is gap-spotting, which tends to provide researchers with a shared—and to a large extent taken-for-granted—norm for generating research questions from existing theory. Alvesson and Sandberg (2012) argue that there is a shortage of high-impact research in management studies because they are mainly based on gap-spotting. The two authors repeat their suggestion of prob-lematization rather than gap-spotting from a third research article two years earlier (Sandberg and Alvesson, 2011).

Social economic conflict in society

One of the peculiar aspects of white-collar crime is that the privileged and powerful punish their own. Bystrova and Gottschalk (2015) phrased the question: Why does the ruling class punish their own?

Social conflict theory suggests that the powerful and wealthy in the upper class of society define what is right and what is wrong (Petrocelli et al., 2003; Siegel, 2011). The rich and mighty people can behave like "rob-ber barons" because they make the laws and because they control law enforcement (Chamlin, 2009; Haines, 2014; Kane, 2003; Sutherland, 1940, 1949; Veblen, 1899; Wheelock et al., 2011). The ruling class does not con-sider white-collar offenses as regular crime, and certainly not similar to street crime (Hagan, 1980; Lanier and Henry, 2009a,b; Slyke and Bales, 2013).

Nevertheless, crime by individuals in the elite tends to be prosecuted if crime is detected and evidence of wrongdoing is present (Brightman, 2009; Gottschalk and Rundmo, 2014; Seron and Munger, 1996), as long as they are not too powerful (Pontell et al., 2014) and do not have too excellent defense attorneys (Gottschalk, 2014). This theory section addresses the fol-lowing research question: Why does the ruling class punish their own?

Social conflict theory views financial crime as a function of the conflict that exists in society (Siegel, 2011). The theory suggests that class conflict causes crime in any society, and that those in power create laws to protect their rights and interests. For example, embezzlement by employees is as a violation of law to protect the interests of the employer. However, it might be argued that an employer must and should protect its own assets. Bank fraud is a crime to protect the powerful banking sector. However, in the perspective of conflict theory one might argue that a bank should have systems making bank fraud impossible. If an employee has no opportu-nity to commit embezzlement, and if a fraudster has no opportunity to commit bank fraud, then these kinds of financial crimes would not occur, and there would be no need to have laws against such offenses. Law enforcement protects powerful companies against counterfeit products, although they should be able to protect themselves by reducing opportu-nities for the production of counterfeit products.

Social conflict theory holds that laws and law enforcement are used by dominant groups in society to minimize threats to their interests posed by those whom they perceive as dangerous and greedy (Petrocelli et al., 2003). Crime is defined by legal codes and sanctioned by institu-tions of criminal justice to secure order in society. The ruling class secures order in the ruled class by means of laws and law enforcement. Conflicts and clashes between interest groups are restrained and stabilized by law enforcement (Schwendinger and Schwendinger, 2014).

According to social conflict theory, the justice system is biased and designed to protect the wealthy and powerful. The wealthy and powerful can take substantial assets out of their own companies at their own discretion whenever they like, although employed workers in the companies were the ones who created the values. The superrich can exploit their own wealth that they created as owners of corporations as long as they do not hurt other shareholders. Employees have no right to object. It is no crime to take out values from your own enterprises and build private mansions for the money. This is no crime by the owners. Even when the owners just inherited the wealth created by earlier generations, they can dispose freely of it for private consumption. Similarly, top executives who are on each other's corporate boards grant each other salaries that are 10 or 20 times higher than regular employee salaries. As Haines (2014: 21) puts it, "financial practices that threaten corporate interests, such as embezzlement, are clearly identified as criminal even as obscenely high salaries remain relatively untouched by regulatory controls." Furthermore, sharp practices such as insider trading that threaten confidence in equities markets have enjoyed vigorous prosecution, since the powerful see them as opaque transactions that give an unfair advantage to those who are not members of the market institutions.

Marxist criminology

Karl Marx, who analyzed capitalism and suggested the transition to socialism and ultimately to communism, created the basis for social conflict theory. Capitalism is an economic system in which persons privately own trade, industries, firms, shops, and means of production and operate these enterprises for profit. Socialism is an economic system characterized by cooperative enterprises, common ownership, and state ownership. Communism is a socioeconomic system structured upon the common ownership of the means of production and characterized by the absence of social classes.

Marxist criminology views the competitive nature of the capitalist system as a major cause of financial crime (Siegel, 2011). It focuses on what creates stability and continuity in society, and it adopts a predefined political philosophy. Marxist criminology focuses on why things change by identifying the disruptive forces in capitalist societies, and describing how power, wealth, prestige, and perceptions of the world divide every society. The economic struggle is the central venue for the Marxists. Marx divided society into two unequal classes and demonstrated the inequality in the historical transition from patrician and slave to capitalist and wage worker. It is the rulers versus the ruled. Marx also underlined that all societies have a certain hierarchy wherein the higher class has more privileges than the lower one. In a capitalist society where economic resources equate to power, it is in the interest of the ascendant class to maintain economic stratification in order to dictate the legal order (Petrocelli et al., 2003).

When economic resources equate to power, then conflict and competition between groups will occur for scarce resources such as education, housing, and jobs. Dominant groups can reduce the threat of other groups in the competition for resources through social control and criminal punishment (Wheelock et al., 2011).

In Marxist criminology, capitalism is a criminogenic society, that is, a society that has a tendency to produce criminality. Capitalism is a system of economic production in which power is concentrated in the hands of a few, with the majority existing in a dependency relationship to the powerful (Lanier and Henry, 2009b: 259):

> This class-based economic order is maintained by a criminal justice apparatus that serves the interests of the wealthy at the expense of the poor. Those who challenge this system of production are destined for social control, especially if they are seen as a serious threat to the system.

Another German theorist was Max Weber, who wrote about classes in society, economic exploitation of people, political repression, and conflict within society. Neither Marx nor Weber wrote extensively about theories of crime or criminal behavior, but their theoretical perspective served as a good basis for conflict theory. Economic inequalities advance to assume disproportionate power in society and lead to social conflict.

Laws and law enforcement

Conflict theory provides an explanation of crime, since it is concerned with social inequality, class and racial differences, and the power used by the ruling class through its criminal justice apparatus. Conflict theorists see inequality based on differences in wealth, status, ideas, and religious beliefs. Not only do capitalist societies generate vast inequalities of wealth, but also those who own the wealth, who control large corporations and financial and commercial institutions, influence those who have political power to get the laws they want (Lanier and Henry, 2009b).

Conflict theory is a perspective in criminology that emphasize the social, political, or material inequality of a social group (Seron and Munger, 1996), that draw attention to power differentials, such as class conflict. Crime stems from conflict between different segments of society fueled by a system of domination based on inequality, alienation, and justice. Crime is harm that comes from differences in power (Lanier and Henry, 2009a).

Conflict is a fundamental social process. Society is largely shaped by the competing interests of social groups who struggle for dominance in order to enact or maintain a social structure most beneficial to them (Petrocelli et al., 2003: 2):

> Conflict theory asserts that the relative power of a given social group dictates social order in that powerful groups not only control the lawmakers, but also the law enforcement apparatus of the state. In essence, laws are made which serve the interests of the privileged, and the police are used to suppress and control any segment of society that poses a threat to the status quo.

According to conflict theory, economic inequalities and repression lead to deviant behavior. Laws, law-breaking, and law enforcement are factors that evolve from and contribute to social conflicts and strengthen the dominant position of powerful individuals. Laws tend to penalize behavior of certain classes, and not individuals, due to the fact that it is the more powerful classes that are in a position to pronounce certain actions as illegal. The ruling class is faced with the decision of which values to enforce when making laws. Criminal law plays the role of a social control mechanism. Certain types of conduct are prohibited, and certain kinds of sanctions are imposed for their infringement. The ruling class in society has the power to define certain behavior as deviant, while the ruled class might be of a differing opinion about what is right and what is wrong. Criminal laws are established mainly for the protection and development of the institutions of capitalism. Through laws, the powerful class exercises its power and controls the resources.

An example is alcohol versus drug laws. Alcohol is legal, while drugs are illegal in most capitalist societies. Hagan (1980) argues that the reason why the prohibition of narcotics outlasts the prohibition of alcohol is that historically the use of different drugs has been associated with minority groups, whereas alcohol has been a socially acceptable intoxicant used by members of the middle and upper classes. Drug laws are specifically, if not explicitly, targeted at looser groups in society. As a result, alcohol prohibition was eventually repealed, while drug laws are still in force.

In addition to laws and law breaking, sanctioning of laws in terms of law enforcement is a factor that evolves from and contributes to strengthen the dominant position of the ruling class. Even if some of the misconduct and offenses by members of the ruling class are determined by law as white-collar crime, law enforcement is often reluctant to investigate and prosecute the criminals. They may be too powerful with friends in key positions (Pontell et al., 2014). Furthermore, the size of the police force is typically larger for policing the lower classes. As an example, Norwegian police has two national units for investigations of violent crime and financial crime, respectively. While the National Criminal Investigation Service has 700 employees, the National Authority for Investigation and Prosecution of Economic Crime and Environmental Crime has only 140 employees. Thus, combatting financial crime has only 20 percent of the resources available to combatting street crime. As stated by Chamlin (2009: 546), "crime control practices are disproportionately responsive to the concerns and fears of the more powerful segments of society."

Kane (2003) studied the relationship between the size of the police force and minority population on the precinct level in New York City. The study shows that the police force increased when minority population fractions increased. The study supports the minority group-threat hypothesis that the percentage of black and Latino populations in U.S. cities can predict variations in municipal police resources. Specifically, the study found that increases in the percentage of Latino populations of precincts can predict changes in police deployment, and the link between Latino populations and police deployment is nonlinear. This leads to police perception of the area as an offense space, and they tend to choose aggressive policing in the area.

Sanctioning of laws enables the dominant economic class to pressure a domestic order that allows its interests to be promoted and maintained. Economic stratification is so important to the ruling class that they will pressure legislators to enact repressive measures intended to control groups considered volatile and threatening (Petrocelli et al., 2003). Conflict theory of crime control contends that the political state functions to further the distinctive interests of the most powerful segments of society. Within the context of crime control, this means suppressing illegal activities of out-group members that particularly endanger social elites or violate their behavioral norms (Chamlin, 2009).

Law enforcement targeted at white-collar criminals is nonaggressive and often discrete not only because of the upper class affiliation. Another reason is white-collar defendants' ability to recruit top defense lawyers who apply symbolic defense in addition to substance defense, as well as information control, in their work for white-collar clients (Gottschalk, 2014). It is well known that having a well-qualified and possibly famous attorney increases one's chances of a favorable outcome in any legal dispute. Some individual white-collar offenders avoid criminal prosecution because of the class bias of the courts (Tombs and Whyte, 2003).

When white-collar criminals appear before their sentencing judges, they can correctly claim to be first-time offenders. According to Slyke and Bales (2013), theory and empirical research often have agreed that white-collar offenders benefit from leniency at the sentencing stage of criminal justice system processing. Croall (2007) argues that the term "crime" is contentious, as many of the harmful activities of businesses or occupational elites are not subject to criminal law and punishment but administrative or regulatory law and penalties and sanctions. Therefore, very few white-collar criminals seem to be put on trial, and even fewer higher-class criminals are sentenced to imprisonment. Another reason for the low prosecution and conviction rate for white-collar criminals is the extraordinary broadly and fuzzy defined offenses in criminal law for white-collar crime (Hasnas et al., 2010).

Reasons for punishing their own

Reason 1: Reduce Conflict. Since white-collar crime is crime by the wealthy and powerful, it seems to contradict social conflict theory. There are no reasons why the wealthy and powerful would like to see laws that turn their own actions to regular criminal offenses. When Sutherland (1940, 1949) first coined the term "white-collar crime," there were indeed reactions in the audience of upper-class people. They asked why one should define actions by privileged individuals of the influential classes as crime at the level of street crime by ordinary criminals. According to Brightman (2009), Sutherland's theory of white-collar crime first presented in 1939 was controversial, particularly since many of the academics in the audience perceived themselves to be members of the upper echelon in American society. The audience was the American Sociological Association where Sutherland gave his address and first presented his theory of white-collar crime. What Podgor (2007) found to be the most interesting aspect of Sutherland's work is that a scholar needed to proclaim that crime of the upper socio-economic class is in fact crime that should be prosecuted. It is apparent that prior to the coining of the term "white-collar crime," wealth and power allowed many persons to escape criminal liability.

Veblen's (1899) sociological study of the "leisured classes" and their rapacious conspicuous consumption had an influence on Sutherland's (1940, 1949) research. Josephson (1962) who coined the term "robber barons" in the 1930 was also an influential scholar at that time. Therefore, Sutherland's work on white-collar crime seems to fit with conflict theory, where he might have seen a need to reduce the level of conflict in society by defining obvious unjustified misconduct by privileged individuals as regular crime. This is in line with Arrigo and Bernard (1997), who apply conflict theory to explain initiatives for more prosecution of white-collar criminals. Seron and Munger (1996: 187) quoted, "The plain fact is that in a new stage of capitalism, class divides as ruthlessly as it did in the age of the Robber Barons."

Reason 2: Government Influence. Another reason for starting to define capitalists and other persons of respectability and high social status as regular criminals when they abuse their powers for personal or organizational profit is the need of governments to gain some kind of control over the business sector and the market economy. Business and professional elites had achieved political influence beyond what most democratic governments found acceptable. Even worse, some enterprises were so powerful that they became almost untouchable for government interventions. They were "too powerful to fail, (and) too powerful to jail" (Pontell et al., 2014).

Criminological attention on the activities of business enterprises and other organizations, their creativity and power, remains in a conflict with political influence of business executives, capitalists, and members of the professional elites. Haines (2014: 20) discusses corporate fraud as an example, where she argues:

> Criminalization of corporate fraud deflects attention to one of these actors, the business and its directors, without clear recognition of the role played by government itself.

Haines (2014) argues that governments critically, in close consultation with the professions, "enact legal and regulatory reforms that engender confidence in both the accuracy of accounts and materiality of money while also further institutionalizing their underlying ambiguities". Hence, even as governments are excited to sanction corporate criminals with more vigor, they are at the same time implicated in the creation of corporate criminals. Corporate fraud implies that there has been a criminal misrepresentation of a financial or business state of affairs by one or more individuals for financial gain, where banks, shareholders, and tax authorities are among the victims. Yet, misrepresentation is a matter of opinion rather than accuracy. For example, estimating values of products in stock is no exact science. If nobody wants to buy products in stock, they have no value. While governments work at arm's length through external auditors, law enforcement is reluctant to prosecute unless misrepresentation of the value of a business is completely out of range.

Reason 3: "Our" Laws. A third reason for the prosecution of the wealthy and powerful is that their own laws did not intend to target members of their own class. The lawmakers had others in society in mind. Caught by surprise that members of their own class violate their own laws leads the ruling class to turn laws against their own allies. When those allies demonstrate nonconforming and deviant behavior, others in the ruling class take on the task of prosecuting deviating members of the elite. "As we are reminded today, those who make the laws don't have the right to break the laws," Richard Frankel, the specialist agent in charge of the Criminal

Division of the New York office of the Federal Bureau of Investigation, said at a news conference.

FBI held its news conference as Sheldon Silver, the speaker of the State Assembly in New York, faced prosecuted for corruption. State prosecutors charged Silver with having exploited his position as one of the most powerful politicians in the state of New York to obtain millions of dollars in bribes and kickbacks. Prosecutors accused Silver's law practice of being a fiction where the sources of large payments of bribes were hiding (Rashbaum and Kaplan, 2015: A24). Silver was arrested in Manhattan on a five-count indictment in January 2015. U.S. attorney Preet Bharara alleged that the Manhattan democrat used New York's ethics laws to hide his scheme—allowing him to become wealthy off his position in power (Spector, 2015).

Silver resigned a few weeks later as speaker (McKinley, 2015). At the same time, Malcolm A. Smith, a former majority leader of the New York State Senate, was convicted of federal corruption charges including bribery, wire fraud, and extortion (Vega, 2015).

Reason 4: Deviant Behavior. A fourth reason might be disappointment within the ruling class. The ruling class in society faces decisions over which values to enforce. When individuals in their own upper-level class violate some of these values, then the majority defines it as a crime. Those who violate values of fair competition among capitalists and market access, for example, are potential criminals, even if they belong to the same class as those condemning them.

President George W. Bush's connections to Enron and CEO Kenneth Lay were well documented in major American newspapers. However, when Enron emerged as a deviant organization with a bad apple CEO, Lay and other top executives were prosecuted. Lay died of a heart attack before his conviction (Bendiktsson, 2010).

Reason 5: Crime Victims. A fifth and final reason might be the victim of crime. If the victim of white-collar crime were another person in the upper class, then the ruling class would like to protect that person. Victimization of upper-class members by other upper-class members can be considered a crime. Upper-class members need protection against deviant individuals in their own class. It is an inter-group conflict in the dominant class (Wheelock et al., 2011). Maybe Madoff can serve as an example. Rich Jews placed their money in Madoff's investment fund with the promise and expectation that the rate of return would be extraordinarily good. Instead, they lost their money. Wealthy people were victims of Madoff's Ponzi scheme. The government had to sanction such behavior by Madoff, and he received a record prison sentence of 150 years (Ragothaman, 2014).

In a study of convicted white-collar criminals in Norway, the distribution of victims was as follows (Gottschalk, 2015a): (1) employers, (2) banks, (3) tax authorities, (4) customers, (5) shareholders, and (6) others.

Employers belong to the elite themselves, while banks and tax authorities are powerful institutions in societies. Customers may be weak victims, while shareholders who become victims of insider trading can be a quite powerful group in collaboration with the stock exchange.

Theoretical model

Our discussion of several reasons why the ruling class punish their own can be framed into a theoretical model as illustrated in Figure 1.1. The dependent variable is the likelihood of white-collar crime prosecution, which can be defined at both a national jurisdiction level and an individual person level. Here it is at the national jurisdiction level in society. The likelihood of white-collar crime prosecution increases in society according to the following propositions.

> *Proposition 1*: Growing social conflict from financial crime by upper socio-economic class members increases the likelihood of white-collar crime prosecution.
>
> *Proposition 2*: Deteriorating government influence and control over the business sector increases the likelihood of white-collar crime prosecution.
>
> *Proposition 3*: Lacking conformity to laws by the ruling class among upper socio-economic class members increases the likelihood of white-collar crime prosecution.

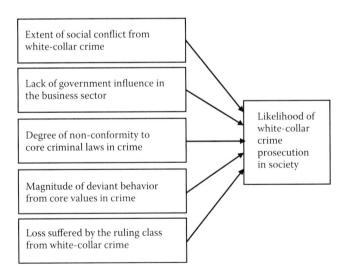

Figure 1.1 Research model for predictors of white-collar crime prosecution from social conflict theory.

Proposition 4: Deviating behavior from ruling class values among upper socio-economic class members increases the likelihood of white-collar crime prosecution.

Proposition 5: Victimization of ruling class members and their interests by white-collar criminals increases the likelihood of white-collar crime prosecution.

Both propositions 3 and 4 are concerned with class obedience in terms of upper-class expectations to their own members.

In addition to these five reasons derived from social conflict theory, there are a number of other factors influencing the likelihood of white-collar crime prosecution in society. For example, the extent of laws and law enforcement are of importance.

Conflict theory approach

Conflict theory is an interesting approach to our understanding why most still do not consider white-collar crime as a regular kind of crime similar to street crime. In terms of neutralization theory (Bock and Kenhove, 2011), it is possible to explain the lack of guilt feeling among many convicted white-collar criminals with their perception of not having done anything wrong (claim to entitlement) and with their perception that laws are wrong (legal mistake).

Reiman (2007: 112) argues that the criminal justice system functions from start to finish in a way that makes certain that the offender at the end of the road in prison is likely to be a member of the lowest social and economic groups in society:

> For the same criminal behavior, the poor are more likely to be arrested; if arrested, they are more likely to be charged; if charged, more likely to be convicted; if convicted, more likely to be sentenced to prison; and if sentenced, more likely to be given longer prison terms than members of the middle or upper classes.

Based on conflict theory, there is no reason why members of the elite should arrest, charge, convict, and sentence themselves. In fact, behavioral economics dating back to Adam Smith's book *The Theory of Moral Sentiments* can explain why it is instinctively relevant to express sympathy with white-collar criminals, which again is reflected in laws and statutes. As Ashraf et al. (2005: 141) express it, we humans tend not to have sympathy with poor people, but rather with rich people, that is, "contrary to the sensible notion that one should sympathize with those less fortunate than oneself, Smith argued that there is a natural tendency to experience sympathy for the great and rich." Smith explained in 1759 human sympathy for rich people in misconduct in the following way: "What pity we think, that anything should spoil and corrupt so agreeable a situation." That is, we have sympathy with and feel pity for white-collar individuals who are "victims" of their own crime. Instinctive irrationalities can give extreme consequences in terms of who we accept and respect, and those we despise and dislike—despite identical actions by both groups of people.

In this theory section on conflict theory, the following research question was phrased: Why should the powerful punish their own? Five answers have emerged: (1) reduce the level of conflict between rich and poor in society; (2) increase government control over the business sector; (3) avoid those making the laws breaking the laws; (4) punish those who do not behave according to elite values; and (5) punish those upper-class members that victimize other upper-class members.

In conclusion, conflict theory is an interesting approach to our understanding why most still do not consider white-collar crime as a regular kind of crime similar to street crime. In terms of neutralization theory (Bock and Kenhove, 2011), it is possible to explain the lack of guilt feeling among many convicted white-collar criminals with their perception of not having done anything wrong (claim to entitlement) and with their perception that laws are wrong (legal mistake).

References

Alvesson, M. and Sandberg, J. (2011). Generating research questions through problematization, *Academy of Management Review*, 36 (2), 247–271.

Alvesson, M. and Sandberg, J. (2012). Has management studies lost its way? Ideas for more imaginative and innovative research, *Journal of Management Studies*, 50 (1), 128–152.

Arrigo, B.A. and Bernard, T.J. (1997). Postmodern criminology in relation to radical and conflict criminology, *Critical Criminology*, 8 (2), 39–60.

Ashraf, N., Camerer, C.F. and Loewenstein, G. (2005). Adam Smith, Behavioral Economist, *Journal of Economic Perspectives*, 19 (3), 131–145.

Bendiktsson, M.O. (2010). The deviant organization and the bad apple CEO: Ideology and accountability in media coverage of corporate scandals, *Social Forces*, 88 (5), 2189–2216.

Benson, M.L. and Simpson, S.S. (2015). *Understanding white-collar crime—An opportunity perspective*, New York: Routledge.

Bock, T.D. and Kenhove, P.V. (2011). Double standards: The role of techniques of neutralization, *Journal of Business Ethics*, 99, 283–296.

Brightman, H.J. (2009). *Today's white-collar crime: Legal, investigative, and theoretical perspectives*, New York: Routledge, Taylor & Francis Group.

Bystrova, E.G. and Gottschalk, P. (2015). Social conflict theory and white-collar criminals: Why does the ruling class punish their own? *Pakistan Journal of Criminology*, 7 (1), 1–15.

Chamlin, M.B. (2009). Threat to whom? Conflict, consensus, and social control, *Deviant Behavior*, 30, 539–559.

Collier, J.E. and Kimes, S.E. (2012). Only if it is convenient: Understanding how convenience influences self-service technology evaluation, *Journal of Service Research*, 16 (1), 39–51.

Colquitt, J.A. and Zapata-Phelan, C.P. (2007). Trends in theory building and theory testing: A five-decade study of the Academy of Management Journal, *Academy of Management Journal*, 50 (6), 1281–1303.

Croall, H. (2007). *Victims, crime and society*. Los Angeles: Sage Publications.

Davis, M.S. (1971). That's interesting, *Philosophy of the Social Sciences*, 1, 309–344.

DiMaggio, P.J. (1995). Comments on "What Theory is Not," *Administrative Science Quarterly*, 40, 391–397.

Eisenhardt, K.M. (1989). Building theories from case study research, *Academy of Management Review*, 14 (4), 532–550.

Farquhar, J.D. and Rowley, J. (2009). Convenience: A services perspective, *Marketing Theory*, 9 (4), 425–438.

Gottschalk, P. (2014). *Financial crime and knowledge workers: An empirical study of defense lawyers and white-collar criminals*, New York: Palgrave Macmillan.

Gottschalk, P. (2015a). *Fraud examiners in white-collar crime investigations*, Boca Raton, FL: CRC Press, Taylor & Francis Press.

Gottschalk, P. (2015b). *Internal investigations of economic crime—Corporate case studies and regulatory policy*, Boca Raton, FL: Universal Publishers.

Gottschalk, P. and Rundmo, T. (2014). Crime: The amount and disparity of sentencing—A comparison of corporate and occupational white collar criminals, *International Journal of Law, Crime and Justice*, 42, 175–187.

Hagan, J. (1980). The legislation of crime and delinquency: A review of theory, method, and research, *Law and Society Review*, 14 (3), 603–628.

Haines, F. (2014). Corporate fraud as misplaced confidence? Exploring ambiguity in the accuracy of accounts and the materiality of money, *Theoretical Criminology*, 18 (1), 20–37.

Hasnas, J., Prentice, R. and Strudler, A. (2010). New directions in legal scholarship: Implications for business ethics research, theory, and practice, *Business Ethics Quarterly*, 20 (3), 503–531.

Hærem, T., Pentland, B.T. and Miller, K.D. (2015). Task complexity: Extending a core concept, *Academy of Management Review*, 40 (3), 446–460.

Jacques, S. (2014). The quantitative-qualitative divide in criminology: A theory of ideas' importance, attractiveness, and publication, *Theoretical Criminology*, 18 (3), 317–334.

Josephson, M. (1962). *The robber barons: The classic account of the influential capitalists who transformed America's future*, Orlando, FL: Harcourt.

Kane, R.J. (2003). Social control in the metropolis: A community-level examination of the minority group-threat hypothesis, *Justice Quarterly*, 20 (2), 265–295.

Kang, N. (2014). Towards middle-range theory building in development research: Comparative (historical) institutional analysis of institutional transplantation, *Progress in Development Studies*, 14 (3), 221–235.

Lanier, M.M. and Henry, S. (2009a). Chapter 3: Conflict and radical theories, in: *Essential criminology*, 3rd ed. Boulder, CO: Westview, Member of the Perseus Books Group.

Lanier, M.M. and Henry, S. (2009b). Chapter 10: Capitalism as a criminogenic society—Conflict, Marxist, and radical theories of crime, in: *Essential Criminology*, 3rd ed. Boulder, CO: Westview, Member of the Perseus Books Group.

McKinley, J. (2015). Settlement in suit against ex-lawmaker, *The New York Times*, Friday, February 6, page A20.

Merton, R. (1968). *Social theory and social structure*, New York: The Free Press.

Michailova, S., Piekkari, R., Plakoyiannaki, E., Ritvala, T., Mihailova, I. and Salmi, A. (2014). Breaking the silence about exiting fieldwork: A relational approach and its implications for theorizing, *Academy of Management Review*, 39 (2), 138–161.

Petrocelli, M., Piquero, A.R. and Smith, M.R. (2003). Conflict theory and racial profiling: An empirical analysis of police traffic stop data, *Journal of Criminal Justice*, 31 (1), 1–11.

Podgor, E.S. (2007). The challenge of white collar sentencing, *Journal of Criminal Law and Criminology*, 97 (3), 1–10.

Pontell, H.N., Black, W.K. and Geis, G. (2014). Too big to fail, too powerful to jail? On the absence of criminal prosecutions after the 2008 financial meltdown, *Crime, Law and Social Change*, 61 (1), 1–13.

Ragothaman, S.C. (2014). The Madoff debacle: What are the lessons? *Issues in Accounting Education*, 29 (1), 271–285.

Rashbaum, W.K. and Kaplan, T. (2015). U.S. says assembly speaker took millions in payoffs, abusing office, *The New York Times*, Friday, January 23, pages A1 and A24.

Reiman, J. (2007). *The rich get richer and the poor get prison*, 8th ed. Boston: Allyn and Bacon, Pearson Publishing.

Sandberg, J. and Alvesson, M. (2011). Ways of constructing research questions: Gap-spotting or problematization, *Organization*, 18 (1), 23–44.

Schwendinger, H. and Schwendinger, J. (2014). Defenders of order or guardians of human rights? *Social Justice*, 40 (1/2), 87–117.

Seron, C. and Munger, F. (1996). Law and inequality: Race, gender…and, of course, class, *Annual Review of Sociology*, 22, 187–212.

Siegel, L.J. (2011). *Criminology*, 11th ed. Belmont, CA: Wadsworth Publishing.

Slyke, S.R.V. and Bales, W.D. (2013). Gender dynamics in the sentencing of white-collar offenders, *Criminal Justice Studies*, 26 (2), 168–196.

Spector, J. (2015). Lawmaker accused in graft scheme, *USA Today*, Friday, January 23, page 4A.

Suddaby, R. (2014). Editor's comments: Why theory? *Academy of Management Review*, 39 (4), 407–411.

Sutherland, E.H. (1940).White-collar criminality, *American Sociological Review,* 5, 1–12.

Sutherland, E.H. (1949). *White collar crime*, New York: Holt Rinehart and Winston.

Sutton, R.I. and Staw, B.M. (1995). What theory is not, *Administrative Science Quarterly*, 40, 371–384.

Tombs, S. and Whyte, D. (2003). Scrutinizing the powerful: Crime, contemporary political economy, and critical social research. In S. Tombs and D. Whyte (Eds.), *Unmasking the crimes of the powerful*, New York: Lang, pp. 3–48.

Veblen, T. (1899). *The theory of the leisure class: An economic study of institutions*, New York: Macmillan.

Vega, T. (2015). Ex-state senate chief is guilty of bribery, *The New York Times*, Friday, February 6, page A20.

Weick, K.E. (1995). What theory is not, theorizing is, *Administrative Science Quarterly*, 40, 385–390.

Weick, K.E. (1999). Theory construction as disciplined reflexivity: Trade-offs in the 90s, *Academy of Management Review*, 24 (4), 797–806.

Wheelock, D., Semukhina, O. and Demidov, N.N. (2011). Perceived group threat and punitive attitudes in Russia and the United States, *British Journal of Criminology*, 51, 937–959.

Whetten, D.A. (1989). What constitutes a theoretical contribution? *Academy of Management Review*, 14 (4), 490–495.

Williams, J.W. (2008). The lessons of 'Enron'—Media accounts, corporate crimes, and financial markets, *Theoretical Criminology*, 12 (4), 471–499.

## chapter two

Economical dimension in convenience theory

The first dimension of convenience theory is the economical dimension. In this chapter, this dimension is first explained. Thereafter, some aspects of the economical dimension are explained in more detail.

Economical profit in crime

White-collar crime is profit-driven crime based on economic opportunities and threats. As argued by Naylor (2003), transfers of property occur by free-market exchange or fraud; and these transfers involve redistribution of wealth and distribution of income. Fraud is illegal procurement of a private asset or means of advantage through deception or through the neglect of care for the interests of an asset required by duty. In particular, fraud includes heterogeneous forms such as misappropriation, balance manipulation, insolvency, and capital investment abuse (Füss and Hecker, 2008).

Profit-driven crime occurs both because of threats and opportunities. Threats can come from loss-making business and special market structure and forces. Economic power available only to certain corporations in concentrated industries, but not to others, may generate criminal conduct. The threat of losing in a bankruptcy what owners already had created can cause executives to rescue and save the company by illegal means. An entrepreneur, who has spent all his time building the enterprise, might be unable to let it disappear. The intention is to protect economic interests of the corporation (Blickle et al., 2006). Threats can come from a monopoly, where potential competitors have the choice of either committing crime or joining the monopoly (Chang et al., 2005). Financial gain is a requirement for survival in all markets (Brightman, 2009).

Profit-driven crime because of opportunities includes opportunities for large contracts, subsidiaries abroad, extra personal bonus, personal promotion, and improved reputation. Bribing government officials abroad can secure establishment of local presence in oil and gas, while the executive can receive a personal bonus for goal achievement. Opportunities can also be found in private life, where the white-collar criminal has the opportunity to acquire a summer house and a bigger boat. Opportunity is here defined as a possibility to reach an organizational or personal goal. Later in the organizational dimension of convenience theory, we will use the term opportunity in the sense of a possibility to commit white-collar crime.

The economic model of rational self-interest considers incentives and probability of detection (Welsh et al., 2014). Human behavior finds motivation in the self-interested pursuit of pleasure and the avoidance of pain (Hirschi and Gottfredson, 1987). The rational choice model finds support in an empirical study by Bucy et al. (2008), who identified a number of motives for white-collar crime. According to their study, greed is the most common reason for white-collar criminal acts (Hamilton and Micklethwait, 2006). Money and other forms of financial gain is a frequent motivator documented in many studies. Criminals pursue desired goals, weigh up likely consequences, and make selections from various options. When criminal opportunity is attractive as a means to fulfill one's desires, rational actors will choose it. Goldstraw-White (2012) defines greed as socially constructed needs and desires that can never be completely satisfied. Because participating in crime is a rational choice, crime rates will be lower where levels of punishment are more certain and/or more severe (Pratt and Cullen, 2005). Rational choice theorists have generally adopted the position of standard economic theory's notion of revealed preferences. However, Kamerdze et al. (2014) argue that affects and individual affective states play a role in one's utility functions and are thus relevant for rational choice theory because they have an impact on mediating cognitive processes.

The Russian-American psychologist Abraham Maslow developed a hierarchy of human needs. Needs start at the bottom with physiological need, need for security, social need, and need for respect and self-realization. White-collar crime is mainly concerned with the top two levels in terms of status and success. This is different from street crime, which is often concerned with food, clothes, and other basic needs. According to the database with 405 convicted white-collar criminals in Norway, few if any seem to have had a basic need motivation. Rather, almost all seem concerned with status, profit, success, self-realization, and respect from others (Gottschalk, 2015a,b,c).

Another well-known motivation researcher is Fredrick Herzberg who made a distinction between hygiene factors and satisfiers. Satisfiers include achievement, recognition, work itself, responsibility, promotion, and growth. According to his motivation theory, dissatisfaction can be prevented by improvements in hygiene factors such as pay and benefits, but these improvements will not alone provide motivation.

If the criminal considers the criminal opportunity convenient in terms of current gain (profit) relative to future cost (punishment), and the criminal would like to avoid additional time and effort to solve the problem, then convenience theory suggests that white-collar crime will be committed. White-collar crime is not offenses of passion. They are not spontaneous or emotional, but calculated risks for a convenient solution to a challenge or problem by rational actors. As argued by Agnew (2014: 2), "crime is often the most expedient way to get what you want," and "fraud is often easier, simpler, faster, more exciting, and more certain than other means of securing one's ends."

While the economic model of rational self-interest considers incentives and probability of detection (Welsh et al., 2014), Agnew's (2014) theory of social concern and crime suggests that crime can also be committed when people have more considerations for others than for their own interests.

Profit-driven crime is more likely in organizations motivated by ambitious economic goals. The pursuit of ambitious goals tends to accept a greater variety of means to reach goals (Jonnergård et al., 2010). One of the means available to executives is financial crime. Goal achievement by financial crime can imply both corporate crime and occupational crime, since a criminal may be promoted and paid a bonus after goal achievement.

Profit-driven crime is less likely in organizations that are not in the business of making money. We can expect that there is less white-collar crime in public sector organizations compared to private sector organizations. In Norway, only 7.7 percent of convicted white-collar criminals worked in the public sector. Gottschalk and Smith (2016) explain the low fraction of public sector criminals by public service motivation theory, which argues that individuals enter into privileged positions in the public sector for other reasons than profit and financial success.

Profit-driven crime and markets

In conformity with the managerial perspective in business literature which highlights the role of managers as agents in deciding enterprise strategies and operations (Lopez-Rodriguez, 2009), as well as leading the activities required to implement corporate priorities, managers can develop and implement both legal and illegal strategies. Managers' perceptions and interpretations determine their commitment to certain goals over other goals (sub-goals). The goal of business enterprises is to make a profit, which can be achieved both legally and illegally. Strong and ambitious goal-orientation in competitive markets can lead to a strategic choice of white-collar crime.

Profit-driven crime by both legal and criminal business enterprises should be understood mainly in economic rather than sociological or criminological terms. The amounts involved can be staggering (Menon and Siew, 2012). In an attempt to formulate a general theory of profit-driven crime, Naylor (2003) proposed a typology that shifts the focus from actors to actions by distinguishing between market crime, predatory crime, and commercial crime.

Leonard and Weber (1970: 408) argued that too little attention has been paid to market forces as a reason for criminal behavior:

> Insufficient attention has been focused by sociologists on the extent to which market structures—that is, the economic power available to certain corporations in concentrated industries—may generate criminal conduct.

Market integrity is concerned with the integrity of markets to reduce market forces as a reason for criminal behavior. The concept of market integrity tends to imply many statements, such as low levels of crime, efficiency in law enforcement, fairness in competitive markets, access to information for market participants, effective regulation and prevention of financial crime, and confidence among market actors. The concept of market integrity suggests that the extent of market integrity can be measured in terms of the following (Fodor, 2008):

- Market misconduct—measuring changes in the prevalence of dishonest activity.
- Efforts to educate, detect, and enforce—measuring changes in the enforcement and understanding of relevant laws and regulations.
- Effectiveness, efficiency, and fairness of market structures—measuring changes in the operational performance of markets.
- Perceptions of market integrity—quantifying changes in public confidence in the integrity of capital markets.

According to the concept of market integrity by Fodor (2008), a delicate interplay of perceptions, effective regulation, law enforcement actions, and extent of market misconduct determines the relative integrity of a given market over time. Inherent within this complex interaction of market forces are a series of checks and balances that suggest that market integrity may not be measured in absolute terms, but rather in a relative nature that could vary according to jurisdictions and environmental conditions.

Market integrity can be influenced by government regulation in both a positive and a negative direction. Deterioration in market integrity will occur if market actors feel the need to commit financial crime in order to adapt to new regulation regimes. An example can be found in European procurement rules, where corruption might be the only way of achieving commercial government contracts. Opportunities for both fraud and corruption could plausibly increase owing to new rules governing public procurement (Dorn et al., 2008).

Corruption is an example of profit-driven crime. The causes of corruption are complex. Corruption is often a symptom of other, deeper-seated factors, such as poorly designed economic policies, low levels of education, underdeveloped civil society, and the weak accountability of public institutions (Ksenia, 2008).

Motivation for corruption is to influence others. The concept of motivation is in line with the concept of reasoned action, where the intention of an individual is influenced by personal attitudes, social norms, and weighing up these two considerations (Woodbine and Liu, 2010: 29):

> These motivational factors emanate from the self (personal identity), the environment and the interaction of the two. Within organizational settings, the self could be studied using needs theory, while the environment can be studied using leadership theory.

Motivation involves personality and cultural factors that induce individuals to act in ways that neutralize the strong ethical controls of society. Specific cultural factors that lead to crime and criminal behavior include the desire to make a fast buck, the fear of losing what has already been made, defining competitive struggle as being positive rather than negative or selfish, differential association, and even the structure of the industrial economy such as market exchange and the use of money (Anguilera and Vadera, 2008). At the level of the individual, the process of differential association explains how normative conflict produces individual acts of crime (Matsueda, 1988). Differential association, which belongs to the behavioral dimension of convenience theory, suggests that criminal behavior is learned in association with those who define such criminal behavior favorably and in isolation from those who define it unfavorably (Sutherland, 1983).

Anguilera and Vadera (2008) make distinctions between procedural corruption, schematic corruption, and categorical corruption. Procedural corruption results from either the lack of formalized procedures or formal rules of business conduct in the organization, or from the violation of existing formal procedures, for personal gain. Schematic corruption is structured and present uniformly throughout the organization, and results due to the simultaneous involvement of multiple organizational levels in corrupt acts and at multiple points in time. Categorical corruption is the result of concentrated and delimited acts of corruption within the organization.

Exchange theory suggests that micro-level actors are involved in economic exchanges where white-collar crime might be the consequence of attraction, competition, differentiation, integration, and opposition (Hansen, 2009).

Rational choice by self-interest

The economic model of rational self-interest considers incentives and probability of detection (Welsh et al., 2014). Rational choice theory argues that it is indeed rational to be a criminal providing two conditions are satisfied: The potential profit is great and the likelihood of punishment is small (Lyman and Potter, 2007: 62):

> Rational choice theory suggests that people who commit crimes do so after considering the risks of detection and punishment for the crimes (risk assessment), as well as the rewards (personal, financial, etc.) of completing these acts successfully. On the other hand, persons who do not commit crime decide that completing the act successfully is too risky or not worth the benefits.

Rational choice theory suggests that people who commit crimes do so after considering the risks of detection and punishment for the crimes alongside the rewards of successfully completing criminal acts. Examples of this theory include a man who discovers that his wife is having an affair and chooses to kill her, her lover, or both; the bank teller who is experiencing personal financial difficulty and decides to embezzle funds from the bank to substantially increase her earnings; and an inner-city youth who decides that social opportunities are minimal and that it would be easier to make money by dealing crack cocaine (Lyman and Potter, 2007).

In economics, the rational choice approach implies that if the rationally expected utility of an action clearly outweighs the expected disadvantages resulting from the action, thereby leaving some net material advantage, then every person will commit the offense in question. One of the many suppositions of this theory is that people generally strive for enjoyment and fulfillment of desire for material goods (Blickle et al., 2006).

Weismann (2009: 627) applied rational choice theory to study normative ethical corporate behaviors:

> Rational choice theory as a basis for predicting corporate behaviors in the marketplace from an institutional perspective relies on two key assumptions. First, corporations will achieve regulatory compliance through an internal system of checks and balances, which can be relied upon by the regulators. Second, the least intrusion by regulators into internal corporate affairs provides the most efficient and effective means of corporate governance and internal control practices.

In organized crime, Shvarts (2001) suggests that rational choice theory can explain the growth of the Russian Mafia. Because of low income and financial difficulties at the individual level, combined with a corrupt police force, it seems rational to move into organized crime to improve the standard of living for members joining the criminal organization.

Rational choice theory suggests that humans are selfish, focused on achieving their own individual happiness as the highest moral purpose of rational existence. Altruism, in contrast, is thereby irrational and, therefore, determinative of undesirable outcomes. By placing others above oneself in altruism, one denies self-sufficiency, eschews personal happiness, and compromises individual rights. Here, sacrifice is the antithesis of rationality, where the individual surrenders the right to the wrong, good to evil. Self-interest is defended in the rational choice theory by contrasting it with irrational sacrifice (Barry and Stephens, 1998).

Rational choice theory finds support in an empirical study by Bucy et al. (2008), who identified a number of motives for white-collar crime. According to their empirical study, greed is the most common reason for white-collar criminal acts. Money and other forms of financial gain were found to be a frequent motivator. Criminals pursue desired goals, weigh up likely consequences, and make selections from various options. When criminal opportunity is attractive as a means of responding to desires, rational actors will choose it.

The economic model of rational self-interest considers incentives and probability of detection (Welsh et al., 2014). Rational choice theory argues that it is indeed rational to be a criminal provided that two conditions are satisfied: the potential profit is large and the punishment is small. Persons who do not commit crime decide that completing the act successfully is too risky or not worth the benefits.

Because participating in crime is a rational choice, crime rates will be lower where levels of punishment are more certain and/or more severe. Rational choice theory—by some labelled deterrence theory—assumes that offenders exercise rational judgment and are reasonably aware of the potential costs and benefits associated with criminal acts. This assumption translates generally into the proposition that aggregate crime rates in a region can be curbed by the crime-control activities of the criminal justice system in terms of increased costs and probable risk of detection (Pratt and Cullen, 2005). Deterrence theory is treated not as an economic theory but rather as a behavioral theory in our research, which we return to later in this book.

Utility theory suggests that a criminal will attempt to maximize the utility from criminal behavior. An expected utility maximizing criminal commits an illegal act and, if he or she is neither caught nor punished, his or her total wealth thereby increases by an amount x. His or her criminally enhanced total wealth, $w + x$, will be greater than his or her current wealth w. He is caught and punished with probability p and the punishment consists of a fine, z, which is less than or equal to his enhanced wealth, $w + x$. His personal assessment of any benefits to him of his criminal activity is described by a utility function linking p and z to w and x (Cain, 2009).

The rational choice theory adopts a utilitarian belief that the economical individual is a reasoning actor who weighs means and ends, costs and benefits to make a decision whether or not to commit white-collar crime. Consequently, the behavior of a benefit-maximizing actor can be influenced by modification of incentives. This can be done by closing gaps in criminal liability where more activities are defined as crime, and by increasing the sentencing range. Such measures will cause a decrease in crime rate, according to the theory. Furthermore, increase in detection rate will cause a decrease in crime rate (Hefendehl, 2010).

Rational choice by individuals can sometimes be explained by their actions and reactions to others' actions, where white-collar crime can be both an act of action as well as an act of reaction. This is often called game theory (Krebs et al., 2003: 2):

> Based on utility theory, game theory involves the mathematical representation of the decision making process in situations where the interests of two or more players are interconnected and interdependent. A player may be either an individual or a group that operates as a single decision making entity. Players in situations of uncertainty choose from a set of available actions called strategies, each of which offers a probability of producing a possible outcome. The choice a player makes is determined by the anticipated utility, viewed as an indication of the individual's beliefs and preferences that each alternative behavioral strategy is expected to produce.

Money laundering is a type of white-collar crime that has been studied by game theory (Araujo, 2010).

Cain (2009) argues that the general piece of evidence available is that criminals are more responsive to changes in the chance of being caught (p) than to changes in the consequence. Since it is sometimes said that punishment does not work, only the probability of being caught will influence the behavior in the desired direction. In certain cases, the consequence may influence the behavior in an undesired direction, whereby a crime with a longer sentence may stimulate the criminal. This is similar to a demand that increases when the price of the good increases (the Giffen effect).

Transaction costs in criminal activities

Transaction costs include efforts, time, and direct payments linked to search, development, negotiations, risks, management, and control of relationships with others. Transaction costs can reduce the profitability of white-collar crime and increase the likelihood of detection. Transaction costs occur when an offender has to deal with other individuals and organizations. White-collar criminals will attempt to minimize transaction costs and orient criminal activity toward offenses where transaction costs are low.

Transaction costs include both costs associated with conflicts and costs associated with misunderstandings (Wright, 2006: 58):

> Transaction costs apply both to legitimate business and to illicit enterprises. They include the costs of conflicts and misunderstandings that lead to delays, to breakdowns and to other malfunctions. They can include such things as the costs of incentives, of ensuring co-ordination and the enforcement of regulations, rules or customs. In the case of a criminal organization, controlling transaction costs is necessary to keep it protected from betrayal and from prosecution. This includes the need to protect the organization from informers and from others (such as law enforcement agencies) who threaten its profits and stability. For such organizations, the use of violence and coercion is often the most effective way of reducing transaction costs.

Wright (2006: 58) studied organized crime, and found that, for example, mafia groups consider transaction costs before criminal acts are carried out:

> Mafia groups consider the costs of each transaction in estimating the risk involved in their drug dealing operations. Betrayal of the group by informers leading to disruption of operations, seizure of drugs, and arrest of group members is the predominant transaction cost in such cases.

Violence and threats can be considered here both as transaction costs and as means to reduce transaction costs. By use of threats and violence, a criminal might expect that the victim will behave more in accordance with criminal expectations.

Transaction costs occur when someone leaks to the police, and when someone attempts whistleblowing, as the criminal has to increase efforts for cover up and hiding traces and paths. To keep someone silent, a white-collar criminal may have to bribe someone, and in such a situation the bribe can be considered a transaction cost.

An indication of transactions costs in white-collar crime is the number of individuals involved in crime. In our sample of 369 convicted white-collar criminals from 2009 to 2014 in Norway, there were 101 criminals who operated alone, thus causing no transaction costs. We can assume that a rising number of involved persons causes an increase in transaction costs. The distribution of involved persons as a measure of transaction costs was as follows: 101 criminals operated alone, 60 criminals operated in a group of 2 offenders, 63 criminals operated in a group of 3 offenders, 56 criminals operated in a group of 4 offenders, 25 criminals operated in a group of 5 offenders, 30 criminals operated in a group of 6 offenders, 14 criminals operated in groups of 7 offenders, and 8 criminals operated in a group of 8 offenders.

According to transaction cost theory, transaction costs are influenced by the extent of deviant behavior, the extent of deviant act, and general uncertainty in the environment. Opportunistic behavior by others can cause a rise in transaction costs for the criminal(s). Opportunism means following personal interests characterized by smartness and egoism. Opportunism includes behaviors such as lying, cheating, and stealing.

Transaction cost theory describes white-collar crime not in terms of activities but in terms of relationships. Hierarchy and market are two alternative forms of dealing with others. Hierarchy is based on power and influence, while market is based on demand and supply. Hierarchy can cause large transaction costs, if the criminal is not in complete control. Market can cause large transaction costs, if others ask for substantial fees to implement desired behavior.

Transaction costs will influence whether a white-collar criminal involves someone else in the crime. Costs will also influence the choice of who to involve in crime. Some crime types can be carried out alone, such as fraud, embezzlement, insider trading, and theft. Other crime types must involve at least one other person, such as corruption. Yet other types must involve several other persons, such as Ponzi schemes (Nolasco et al., 2013). A white-collar criminal will try to do as much as possible on his own if transaction costs are large.

Others who are causing transaction costs can be internal as well as external persons relative to the organization where the criminal has his home. They can be participants in crime, neutrals in crime, as well as victims of crime. Costs occur because of efforts, problems, and risks.

According to Henisz and Williamson (1999), transaction cost economics is a comparative contractual approach to economic organization in which the action resides in the details of transactions on the one hand and governance on the other. Given that all complex criminal contracts are unavoidably incomplete and that contract as mere promise—unsupported by credible commitment—is not self-enforcing (by reason of opportunism), the question for the criminal is which transactions should be organized how. Much of the predictive content of transaction cost economics works through the discriminating alignment hypothesis, according to which transactions, which differ in their attributes, are aligned with governance structures, which differ in their costs and competencies, so as to effect a (mainly) transaction cost economizing result. Implementing this requires that transactions, governance structures, and transaction cost economizing all be part of the criminal scheme.

Transaction cost economics concurs that the transaction is the basic unit of analysis and regards governance as the means by which order is accomplished in a relation in which potential conflict threatens to undo or upset opportunities to realize gains (Henisz and Williamson, 1999). The problem of conflict on which transaction cost economics originally focused is that of bilateral dependency. The organization of transactions that are supported by generic investments is considered easy: classical market contracting works well because each party can go its own way with minimal cost to the other. Specific investments are where the problems arise.

Williamson (1979, 1981) identified three types of transactions according to specificity. Nonspecific transactions have low asset specificity and are associated with the acquisition of commodities. Idiosyncratic transactions have high specificity. Mixed transactions have elements of both commodity and customization. Transaction specificity can be viewed alongside transaction frequency, a second major construct of transaction cost economics, which distinguishes occasional from recurrent transaction types. Recurrent transactions in crime increase the likelihood of detection, while at the same time unit transaction costs will drop.

Two frequency categories multiplied by three specificity types produces six discrete transaction classes. It can be argued that the market is better for all but two classes, which are both recurrent and idiosyncratic.

The third major determinant of transaction costs is uncertainty, compounded by the bounded rationality of humans and often associated with the complexity of the crime to be carried out. Uncertainty is recognized as a major determinant of transaction costs. Given the cognitive limits of human actors, complex arrangements in crime are unavoidably incomplete. Relational incompleteness poses problems when paired with the condition of opportunism—which manifests itself as adverse selection, moral hazard, shirking, sub-goal pursuit, and other forms of deviant behavior. Because human actors will not reliably disclose true conditions on request or self-fulfill all promises, contract as mere promise, unsupported by credible commitments, will not be self-enforcing (Williamson, 2000).

Transaction cost theory received attention in 2009 when Professor Oliver Williamson received the Nobel Prize in economics for his research on transaction cost economics. Williamson builds his theory on works by earlier Nobel Laureates such as Professors Herbert Simon and Ronald Coase. A core assumption in their work is that actors behave in an opportunistic way, which means that people explore and exploit opportunities at the costs of others. Furthermore, it is difficult, almost impossible, to foresee another person's attitude toward opportunistic possibilities. Therefore, some of the transaction costs occur because actors have to control each other to detect and prevent opportunism (Dibbern et al., 2008).

References

Agnew, R. (2014). Social concern and crime: Moving beyond the assumption of simple self-interest, *Criminology*, 52 (1), 1–32.

Aguilera, R.V. and Vadera, A.K. (2008). The dark side of authority: Antecedents, mechanisms, and outcomes of organizational corruption, *Journal of Business Ethics*, 77, 431–449.

Araujo, R.A. (2010). An evolutionary game theory approach to combat money laundering, *Journal of Money Laundering Control*, 13 (1), 70–95.

Barry, B. and Stephens, C.U. (1998). Objections to an objectivist approach to integrity, *Academy of Management Review*, 23 (1), 162–169.

Blickle, G., Schlegel, A., Fassbender, P. and Klein, U. (2006). Some Personality correlates of business white-collar crime, *Applied Psychology: An International Review*, 55 (2), 220–233.

Brightman, H.J. (2009). *Today's white-collar crime: Legal, investigative, and theoretical perspectives*, New York, Routledge, Taylor & Francis Group.

Bucy, P.H., Formby, E.P., Raspanti, M.S. and Rooney, K.E. (2008). Why do they do it?: The motives, mores, and character of white collar criminals, *St. John's Law Review*, 82, 401–571.

Cain, M. (2009). Is crime Giffen? *Journal of Financial Crime*, 16 (1), 80–85.

Chang, J.J., Lu, H.C. and Chen, M. (2005). Organized crime or individual crime? Endogenous size of a criminal organization and the optimal law enforcement, *Economic Inquiry*, 43 (3), 661–675.

Dibbern, J., Winkler, J. and Heinzl, A. (2008). Explaining variations in client extra costs between software projects offshored to India, *MIS Quarterly*, 32 (3), 333–366.

Dorn, N., Levi, M. and White, S. (2008). Do European procurement rules generate or prevent crime? *Journal of Financial Crime*, 15 (3), 243–260.

Fodor, B. (2008). Measuring market integrity: A proposed Canadian approach, *Journal of Financial Crime*, 15 (3), 261–268.

Füss, R. and Hecker, A. (2008). Profiling white-collar crime: Evidence from German-speaking countries, *Corporate Ownership & Control*, 5 (4), 149–161.

Goldstraw-White, J. (2012). *White-collar crime: Accounts of offending behaviour*, London: Palgrave Macmillan.

Gottschalk, P. (2015a). *Fraud examiners in white-collar crime investigations*, Boca Raton, FL: CRC Press, Taylor & Francis.

Gottschalk, P. (2015b). *Investigating financial crime—Characteristics of white-collar criminals*, Hauppauge, NY: Nova Science Publishers.

Gottschalk, P. (2015c). *Internal investigations of economic crime—Corporate case studies and regulatory policy*, Boca Raton, FL: Universal Publishers.

Gottschalk, P. and Smith, C. (2016). Detection of white-collar corruption in public procurement in Norway: The role of whistleblowers, *International Journal of Procurement Management*, in press.

Hamilton, S. and Micklethwait, A. (2006). *Greed and corporate failure: The lessons from recent disasters*, Basingstoke, UK: Palgrave Macmillan.

Hansen, L.L. (2009). Corporate financial crime: Social diagnosis and treatment, *Journal of Financial Crime*, 16 (1), 28–40.

Hefendehl, R. (2010). Addressing white collar crime on a domestic level, *Journal of International Criminal Justice*, 8, 769–782.

Henisz, W.J. and Williamson, O.E. (1999). Comparative economic organization—Within and between countries, *Business and Politics*, 1 (3), 261–277.

Hirschi, T. and Gottfredson, M. (1987). Causes of white-collar crime, *Criminology*, 25 (4), 949–974.

Jonnergård, K., Stafsudd, A. and Elg, U. (2010). Performance evaluations as gender barriers in professional organizations: A study of auditing firms, *Gender, Work and Organization*, 17 (6), 721–747.

Kamerdze, S., Loughran, T., Paternoster, R. and Sohoni, T. (2014). The role of affect in intended rule breaking: Extending the rational choice perspective, *Journal of Research in Crime and Delinquency*, 51 (5), 620–654.

Ksenia, G. (2008). Can corruption and economic crime be controlled in developing countries and if so, is it cost-effective? *Journal of Financial Crime*, 15 (2), 223–233.

Leonard, W.N. and Weber, M.G. (1970). Automakers and dealers: A study of criminogenic market forces, *Law & Society Review*, 4 (3), 407–424.

Lopez-Rodriguez, S. (2009). Environmental engagement, organizational capability and firm performance, *Corporate Governance*, 9 (4), 400–408.

Lyman, M.D. and Potter, G.W. (2007). *Organized crime*, 4th ed. Uppler Saddle River, NJ: Pearson Prentice Hall.

Matsueda, R.L. (1988). The current state of differential association theory, *Crime & Delinquency*, 34 (3), 277–306.

Menon, S. and Siew, T.G. (2012). Key challenges in tackling economic and cyber-crimes—Creating a multilateral platform for international co-operation, *Journal of Money Laundering Control*, 15 (3), 243–256.

Naylor, R.T. (2003). Towards a general theory of profit-driven crimes, *British Journal of Criminology*, 43, 81–101.

Nolasco, C.A.R.I., Vaughn, M.S. and Carmen, R.V. (2013). Revisiting the choice model of Ponzi and pyramid schemes: Analysis of case law, *Crime, Law and Social Change*, 60, 375–400.

Pratt, T.C. and Cullen, F.T. (2005). Assessing macro-level predictors and theories of crime: A meta-analysis, *Crime and Justice*, 32, 373–450.

Shvarts, A. (2001). The Russian mafia: Do rational choice models apply? *Michigan Sociological Review*, 15, 29–63.

Sutherland, E.H. (1983). *White collar crime—The uncut version*, New Haven, CT: Yale University Press.

Weismann, M.F. (2009). The foreign corrupt practices act: The failure of the self-regulatory model of corporate governance in the global business environment, *Journal of Business Ethics*, 88, 615–661.

Welsh, D.T., Oronez, L.D., Snyder, D.G. and Christian, M.S. (2014). The slippery slope: How small ethical transgressions pave the way for larger future transgressions, *Journal of Applied Psychology*, http://dx.doi.org/10.1037/a0036950.

Williamson, O.E. (1979). Transaction-cost economics: The governance of contractual relations, *The Journal of Law & Economics*, 22 (2), 233–261.

Williamson, O.E. (1981). The modern corporation: Origins, evolution, attributes, *Journal of Economic Literature*, 19 (4), 1537–1568.

Williamson, O.E. (2000). The new institutional economics: Taking stock, looking ahead, *Journal of Economic Literature*, 38 (3), 595–613.

Woodbine, G.F. and Liu, J. (2010). Leadership styles and the moral choice of internal auditors, *EJBO, Electronic Journal of Business Ethics and Organization Studies*, 15 (1), 28–35.

Wright, A. (2006). *Organised crime*, Devon, UK: Willan Publishing.

chapter three

Organizational dimension in convenience theory

The second dimension of convenience theory is the organizational dimension. In this chapter, this dimension is first explained. Thereafter, some aspects of the organizational dimension are explained in more detail.

Organizational opportunity in crime

Opportunity is a distinct characteristic of white-collar crime and varies depending on the kinds of criminals involved (Michel, 2008). An opportunity is attractive as a means of responding to desires (Bucy et al., 2008). It is the organizational dimension that provides the white-collar criminal an opportunity to commit financial crime and conceal it in legal organizational activities. While opportunity in the economic dimension of convenience theory is concerned with goals (such as sales and bonuses), opportunity in the organizational dimension is concerned with crime (such as corruption and embezzlement).

Aguilera and Vadera (2008: 434) describe a criminal opportunity as "the presence of a favorable combination of circumstances that renders a possible course of action relevant." Opportunity arises when individuals or groups can engage in illegal and unethical behavior and expect, with reasonable confidence (Haines, 2014), to avoid detection and punishment. Opportunity to commit crime may include macro and micro level factors. Macro level factors encompass the characteristics of the industries in which the business finds itself embedded, such as market structure, business sets of an industry, that is, companies whose actions are visible to one another, and variations in the regulatory environment (Aguilera and Vadera, 2008).

Benson and Simpson (2015) argue that many white-collar offenses manifest the following opportunity properties: (1) the offender has legitimate access to the location in which the crime is committed; (2) the offender is spatially separate from the victim, and (3) the offender's actions have a superficial appearance of legitimacy. Opportunity occurs in terms of those three properties that are typically the case for executives and other individuals in the elite. In terms of convenience, these three properties may be attractive and convenient when considering white-collar crime to solve a financial problem. It is convenient for the offender to conceal the crime and give it an appearance of outward respectability (Pickett and Pickett, 2002).

The organizational opportunity consists of two dominating aspects:

1. The white-collar criminal has an opportunity to commit and carry out financial crime because of a prominent position in the organization based on trust and power.
2. The white-collar criminal has an opportunity to conceal and hide financial crime because of a prominent position in the organization based on trust and power.

Opportunity is dependent on social capital available to the criminal. The structure and quality of social ties in hierarchical and transactional relationships shape opportunity structures. Social capital is the sum of actual or potential resources accruing to the criminal by virtue of his or her position in a hierarchy and in a network (Adler and Kwon, 2002).

White-collar crime in the organizational setting is characterized by task simplicity. A task is a combination of information and required actions leading to a result. Simplicity versus complexity is a characteristic of the task itself, the person or persons doing the task, the context in which the task is performed, and the behavioral pattern required to perform the task (Hærem et al., 2015).

Hærem et al. (2015) modeled task complexity as a network of events, where an event is an action performed by some actor at some moment in time. Simplicity of a criminal task increases as the network of events has fewer nodes and ties as well as more possible paths to the goal. Organizational design can influence complexity, and principles of organizational design such as modularity can reduce complexity and increase criminal simplicity. Financial crime tasks by white-collar criminals may be simple, while detection tasks by others may be complex. Thus, the relationship between crime complexity and detection complexity can be a fraction far below one as an indication of convenience.

The organizational dimension of white-collar crime becomes particularly evident when financial crime is committed to benefit the organization rather than the individual (Trahan, 2011). This is called corporate crime as opposed to occupational crime for personal benefit. Hansen (2009) argues that the problem with occupational crime is that it is committed within the confines of positions of trust and in organizations, which prohibit surveillance and accountability. Heath (2008) found that individuals who are further up the chain of command in the firm tend to commit bigger and more severe occupational crime. Corporate crime, sometimes labeled organizational offending (Reed and Yeager, 1996), on the other hand, is resulting from offenses by collectivities or aggregates of discrete individuals (Bradshaw, 2015). If a corporate official violates the law in acting for the corporation, we still define it as corporate crime. However, if he or she gains personal benefit in the commission of a crime against the corporation, we regard it as occupational crime. A corporation cannot be subject to imprisonment, and therefore, the majority of penalties to control individual violators are not available for corporations and corporate crime (Bookman, 2008).

An organization is a system of coordinated actions among individuals and groups with boundaries and goals (Puranam et al., 2014). An organization can be a hierarchy, a matrix, a network, or any other kind of relationship between people in a professional work environment. Rule-breaking and law-breaking seem sometimes necessary to ensure organizational flexibility and to reach business goals. Because rules and laws are formulated in abstract terms, they cannot precisely prescribe behavior in any situation. To act in novel situations sometimes demands breaking rules and laws in order to fit it to the organizational circumstance at hand (Eberl et al., 2015).

Corporate crime represents pro-organizational actions on the wrong side of the law. It demonstrates loyalty to the collective, while at the same time representing betrayal to the collective. Pro-organizational actions refer to voluntary tasks undertaken to benefit the organization including helping and solving problems and exploring possibilities. For example, white-collar criminals might "lie for their organization or submit fraudulent documents, thus benefiting the organization but hurting other stakeholders in a way that contradicts the mandates of the care/harm and fairness/cheating moral foundations" (Fehr et al., 2015: 197).

The loyalty-betrayal paradox is defined by a dedication to the in group and reflects such values as patriotism, self-sacrifice, and allegiance. It is a dysfunctional dedication. Dysfunctional network theory suggests that corporate crime emerges as a consequence of the dysfunction of value networks (Dion, 2009). Dysfunctional network theory as well as institutional theory argues that corporate crime occurs more frequently as a response to moral collapse in the environment (Scott, 2008).

In the Norwegian database of 405 white-collar criminals, 68 offenders (17%) committed financial crime on behalf of the organization as corporate criminals (Gottschalk, 2015c). Corporate crime represents integrity violation as well as lack of commitment to moral standards, as exemplified in the Siemens scandal in Germany. The corruption case of Siemens was the greatest bribery scandal in the history of German business, enabled by insignificant detection risk, lacking organizational rules, and lacking ethical culture (Eberl et al., 2015).

The organizational dimension of white-collar crime also becomes particularly evident when several persons in the business participate in crime (Ashforth et al., 2008), and when the organization generally is dominated by misconduct and an unethical culture (O'Connor, 2005), either it is occupational crime or corporate crime that is occurring. When several participants and sleeping partners are involved in crime, and the corporate culture almost stimulates violation of the law, then we label the organization as a rotten apple barrel or rotten apple orchard, as Punch (2003: 172) describes them:

> The metaphor of 'rotten orchards' indicates that it is sometimes not the apple, or even the barrel, that is rotten but the system (or significant parts of the system).

The empirical study of Norwegian white-collar criminals by Gottschalk (2015a) indicates that barrel criminals commit crime for a larger amount and are associated with larger organizations than apple criminals. In the database, there are 254 convicted white-collar criminals (63%) that belonged to rotten barrels (Gottschalk, 2015c).

Agency theory is a management theory often applied to crime, where normally the agent, rather than the principal, is in danger of committing crime. Problems arise in the relationship because of diverging preferences and conflicting values, asymmetry in knowledge about activities, and different attitudes toward risk. Agency theory describes the relationship between the two parties using the concept of work-based interactions. The agent carries out work on behalf of the principal in an organizational arrangement. Principal-agent theory holds that owners (principals) have different interests from administrators (agents), such that principals must always suspect agents of making decisions that benefit themselves, to the cost of the principals. For example, chief executive officers (CEOs) are suspects for cheating the owners (Williams, 2008), and purchasing managers are suspects of cheating their CEOs (Chrisman et al., 2007). Galvin et al. (2015: 163) found that "it is not uncommon to learn of individuals in positions of power and responsibility, especially CEOs, who exploit and undermine their organizations for personal gain."

In general, agency models view corruption and other kinds of financial crime a consequence of the principal's inability to prevent effectively the agent from abusing power for his or her personal gain (Li and Ouyang, 2007). However, the principal can just as well commit financial crime in the principal-agent relationship. For example, the chief financial officer (CFO) as an agent provides a board member with inside information, on which the principal acts illegally.

The organizational setting may prevent some white-collar criminals from prosecution. The company may be too big to fall, and the criminal too powerful to jail. For example, after the 2008 financial meltdown in the United States, people expected that the government would prosecute fraud in large financial institutions. Pontell et al. (2014: 10) assessed the reasons why there have been no major prosecutions to date:

> From a criminological standpoint, the current financial meltdown points to the need to unpack the concept of status when examining white-collar and corporate offenses. The high standing of those involved in the current scandal has acted as a significant shield to accusations of criminal wrongdoing in at least three ways. First, the legal resources that offenders can bring to bear on any case made against them are significant. This would give pause to any prosecutor, regardless of the evidence that exists. Second, their place in the organization assures that the many below them will be held more directly responsible for the more readily detected offenses. The downward focus on white-collar and corporate crimes is partly a function of the visibility of the offense and the ease with which it can be officially pursued. Third, the political power of large financial institutions allows for effective lobbying that both distances them from the criminal law and prevents the government from restricting them from receiving taxpayer money when they get into trouble.

Similarly, Valukas (2010) found no wrongdoing at Lehman Brothers, which went bankrupt because of mismanagement decision making.

Opportunity as a distinct characteristic of white-collar crime can be exemplified in a gender perspective. As long as a glass ceiling exists for most women in terms of promotion to top positions, women have less opportunity to commit white-collar crime. Therefore, we expect to find fewer female criminals than male criminals. This suggestion is supported in an empirical study of white-collar criminals in Norway, where the female fraction was only 7 percent and the remaining 93 percent were men (Gottschalk, 2015c).

In the organizational dimension, a business represents a platform for crime activities by white-collar criminals. While the criminal is at the individual level, the business is at the organizational level. Above the organizational level we find the state. In some countries, all three levels interact to create convenient opportunities for financial crime. The individual as a member of the elite enjoys power in the organization and influence in the surrounding society. In some countries, illicit collusion between states, organized criminals and white-collar criminals creates ample opportunities for financial crime. One category of financial crime is corruption, which Kupatadze (2015) found to be present in the post-Soviet region, showing the blurring of governments, organizations, and individuals. This is in line with institutional theory, which suggests that opportunities are shaped by individuals, groups, other organizations, as well as society at large (Bradshaw, 2015; van Donk and Molloy, 2008). Political corruption is often tolerated in state bureaucracies, since the leadership prefers political stability to the kinds of reforms required by anti-corruption that would investigate the elite. The new term "state oligarch" originated in 1990s Russia when a number of high-ranking government officials were installed in the boardrooms of major corporations. State corporatism improves white-collar crime convenience by lack of transparency and lack of accountability because fiscal and regulatory institutions are weak and elites do not favor institutions that would constrain their behavior (Kupatadze, 2015). While the ruling class in some countries prefers to punish their own for deviant behavior (Bystrova and Gottschalk, 2015), the ruling class in other countries prefers to protect their own for reasons of stability and mutual benefit.

Opportunity-driven financial crime

The theory of profit-driven crime suggests that financial crime is opportunity driven, where executives and managers identify opportunities for illegal gain (Gottschalk, 2015a,b). Opportunity is a flexible characteristic of financial crime and varies depending on the type of criminal involved (Aguilera and Vadera, 2008; Michel, 2008).

Opportunity for illegal profit is the basis for white-collar crime. Opportunity arises when individuals or groups can engage in illegal and unethical behavior and expect, with reasonable confidence, to avoid detection and punishment. Opportunity to commit crime may include macro- and micro-level factors. Macro-level factors encompass the characteristics of the industries in which the organization is embedded, such as the market structure, organizational sets of an industry, that is, companies whose actions are visible to each other, and variations in the regulatory environment (Aguilera and Vadera, 2008).

Opportunity theory suggests that an opportunity is attractive as a means of responding to desires (Bucy et al., 2008). White-collar criminals take advantage of positions of professional authority and power in their opportunity structures available within business for personal and corporate gain. When opportunity is attractive as a means of responding to desires, rational actors will choose it (Baird and Zelin, 2009; Huisman and Erp, 2013), based on a preference where disadvantages are outweighed by advantages. A desire can be based on greed, which is a socially constructed need that can never be completely satisfied (Goldstraw-White, 2012).

Benson and Simpson (2015) argue that many white-collar offenses manifest the following opportunity properties: (1) the offender has legitimate access to the location in which the crime is committed; (2) the offender is spatially separated from the victim, and (3) the offender's actions have a superficial appearance of legitimacy. Opportunity is represented in terms of these three properties that are typically the case for executives and other individuals in the elite.

Opportunity theory is concerned with situations emerging where there is a possibility for actors and groups to carry out illegal and unethical acts with little detection risk and low likelihood of punishment (Aguilera and Vadera, 2008). Opportunity theory suggests that where there is a criminal temptation, someone will explore and exploit the opportunity to make a profit, either for themselves as an occupational crime or for the company as a corporate crime. Aguilera and Vedera (2008: 434) describe the criminal opportunity as "the presence of a favorable combination of circumstances that renders a possible course of action relevant."

It is widely recognized that an important—if not the most important—cause of all crime is criminal opportunity. Without opportunity, there can be no crime. Opportunities are important causes of white-collar crime, where the opportunity structures may be different from those of other kinds of crime. These differences create special difficulties for control, but they also provide new openings for control (Benson and Simpson, 2015).

Huisman and Erp (2013) argue that a criminal opportunity has the following five characteristics: (1) the effort required to carry out the offense, (2) the perceived risks of detection, (3) the rewards gained from the offense, (4) the situational conditions that may encourage criminal action, and (5) the excuse and neutralization of the offense.

Opportunity is part of the fraud triangle, which argues that three conditions of fraud arise from fraudulent financial reporting (Ilter, 2009):

1. Incentives/pressures: Management or other employees have incentives or pressures to commit fraud.
2. Opportunities: Circumstances provide opportunities for management or employees to commit fraud.
3. Attitudes/rationalization: An attitude, character, or set of ethical values exists that allows management or employees intentionally to commit a dishonest act, or they are in an environment that imposes pressure sufficient to cause them to rationalize committing a dishonest act.

Thus, the risk of fraud is a combination of incentives/pressures, opportunities, and attitude/rationalization. Opportunity can be found in desirable profit in an accessible arena, while pressure and rationalization lead to the decision to commit crime. Pressure and rationalization are criteria in decision-making. Pressures are also present in the organization as well as in its competitive environment (Dodge, 2009).

The fraud examination process pays attention to the fraud hypothesis approach, which has four sequential steps (Ilter, 2009): analyzing the available data, developing a fraud hypothesis, revising it as necessary, and confirming it:

1. Analyzing the available data: An auditor gathers documentary evidence depicting all of the business.
2. Developing a fraud hypothesis: Based on what investigators discovered during analysis, a fraud examiner develops a hypothesis— always assuming a worst-case scenario—of what could have occurred. This hypothesis addresses one of the three major classifications of occupational (internal) fraud: asset misappropriations, corruption, or fraudulent financial statements.
3. Revising it as necessary: If, for example, the facts do not point to a kickback scheme, the fraud examiner will look for the possibility of a billing scheme. Although the two schemes have several common elements, the latter raises its own red flags.
4. Confirming it: Testing of the hypothesis by combining theoretical elements with empirical evidence.

Motivation is different from but at the same time linked to opportunity (Steffensmeier and Allan, 1996: 478):

> Motivation is distinct from opportunity, but the two often intertwine, as when opportunity enhances temptation. As in legitimate enterprise, being able tends to make one more willing, just as being willing increases the prospects for being able.

Opportunity arises out of certain jobs. For example, the opportunity to engage in health care fraud is obviously easier if one has a job in the health care system. Individuals who are in key positions and involved in networks based on trust have increased access to criminal opportunities. The opportunity perspective is important because these offenses usually require special business-related access to commit conspiracies, frauds, and embezzlement (Benson and Simpson, 2015).

Offenders take advantage of their positions of power with almost unlimited authority in the opportunity structure because they have legitimate and often privileged access to physical and virtual locations in which crime is committed, are totally in charge of resource allocations and transactions, and are successful in concealment based on key resources used to hide their crime. Offenders have an economic motivation and opportunity (Huisman and Erp, 2013); linked to an organizational platform and availability, and in a setting of people who do not know, do not care, or do not reveal the individuals with behavioral traits who commit crime. Opportunity includes people who are loyal to the criminal either as a follower or as a silent partner.

White-collar criminals make their money seem legitimate by creating a business environment of some sort in hope of not being scrutinized or caught. The environment serves as a cover to the illegal money making scheme. The one committing the crime feels invisible when he or she has the resources to commit crime. The criminal has the ability and chance to carry out the financial crime in secret.

Empirical research based on opportunity theory has studied the gender gap issue, where opportunity theory suggests that the reason for less female white-collar crime is because of lack of opportunity for women. Gender segregation and inequality in the workplace, it has been argued, limit women's access to opportunities to commit white-collar crime (Benson and Simpson, 2015; Dodge, 2009). Opportunity theory suggests that the female crime fraction will increase as access to opportunities increases as part of an emancipation process (Steffensmeier et al., 2013).

We have seen that opportunity theory suggests that as women's opportunities to commit white-collar crime increase, so will their deviant behavior, and the types of crime they commit will much more closely resemble those committed by men. However, in an old study by Hill and Harris (1981), they found no support for the suggestion that similar male-female criminal profiles emerge as opportunities for females expand.

The American dream suggests that everyone in America has an opportunity to become monetarily successful. High white-collar crime rate can be attributed to the commitment to the goal of material success as experienced in the American dream. It is caused by an overemphasis on success in exposed assets (Schoepfer and Piquero, 2006), and it is not matched by a concurrent emphasis on what means are legitimate for reaching the desired goal (Pratt and Cullen, 2005).

In our study of convicted Norwegian white-collar criminals, it seems that public sector executives have less opportunity to commit financial crime when compared to their colleagues in the private sector. In our study of corruption, the bribed person sees an opportunity to gain a profit by accepting the offer.

Although individuals with low self-control are not expected to commit crime at every opportunity, research has shown that low self-control is almost always a significant correlate of criminal and analogous behaviors (Piquero et al., 2010).

Agency relationships in crime

Agency theory has broadened the risk-sharing literature to include the agency problem that occurs when cooperating parties have different goals and division of labor. The cooperating parties are engaged in an agency relationship defined as a contract under which one or more persons (the principals) engage another person (agent) to perform some service on their behalf which involves delegating some decision-making authority to the agent (Jensen and Meckling, 1976). Agency theory describes the relationship between the two parties using the metaphor of a contract.

According to Eisenhardt (1989), agency theory is concerned with resolving two problems that can occur in agency relationships. The first is the agency problem that arises when the desires or goals of the principal and agent conflict and it is difficult or expensive for the principal to verify what the agent is actually doing. The second is the problem of risk sharing that arises when the principal and agent have different risk preferences. The first agency problem occurs when the two parties do not share productivity gains. The risk-sharing problem might be the result of different attitudes toward the use of new technologies, for example. Because the unit of analysis is the contract governing the relationship between the two parties, the focus of the theory is on determining the most efficient contract governing the principal-agent relationship given assumptions about people (e.g., self-interest, bounded rationality, risk aversion), organizations (e.g., goal conflict of members), and information (e.g., information is a commodity that can be purchased).

Agency theory has long been applied to crime, where normally the agent, rather than the principal, is in danger of committing crime. Problems arise in the relationship because of diverging preferences and conflicting values, asymmetry in knowledge about activities, and different attitudes toward risk. Agency theory describes the relationship between the two parties using the concept of work-based interactions. The agent carries out work on behalf of the principal in an organizational arrangement. Principal-agent theory holds that owners (principals) have different interests from administrators (agents), such that principals must always suspect agents of making decisions that benefit themselves, to the cost of the principals. For example, CEOs may always be suspected of cheating the owners, and purchasing managers may always be suspected of cheating CEOs (Chrisman et al., 2007).

In general, agency models view corruption and other kinds of financial crime as a consequence of the principal's inability to effectively prevent the agent from abusing its power for his or her personal gain. The main reasons for this inability are the principal's lack of information about the agent's work, lack of effective checks and balances, and ineffective enforcement and punishment for criminal executives (Li and Ouyang, 2007). However, crime can just as well be committed by the principal rather than the agent. For example, the CFO as an agent provides a board member with inside information, on which the principal acts illegally. Another example is the relationship between leader and follower in crime, where the leader is a principal while the follower is an agent, as presented earlier in this book.

Garoupa (2007) applied agency theory to criminal organizations. He models the criminal firm as a family business with one principal and several agents. He has an illegal monopoly in mind where it is difficult to detect and punish the principal unless an agent is detected. Furthermore, it is assumed that agents work rather independently so that the likelihood of detection of one agent is fairly independent from that of another. An example of such agents is drug dealers in the street with the principal being the local distributor. Another example would be agents as extortionists or blackmailers distributed across a city with the principal being the coordinator of their activities providing them with information or criminal know-how.

Gross (1978: 65) discusses criminals as agents for a criminal organization in the following way:

> Although organizations are here held to be criminogenic and although courts no longer exhibit much hesitation in charging the organization itself with crime, organizations of course cannot themselves act—they must have agents who act for them. Who will the persons be who will act for organizations in their criminal behavior?

Agency theory describes the relationship between two parties using the concept of a contract. It specifically addresses which issues affect the relationship. Agency theory is primarily used for situations where two parties enter into a contract, but the reasoning of the theory is also relevant when no formal contract is signed or what might be more relevant, the contract does not deal with issues brought forward by agency theory. An agency relationship arises whenever an individual or an organization is authorized to act for or on behalf of another individual or organization (Benson and Simpson, 2015).

Agents provide principals with some sort of specialized service based on the agent's expertise and training. They do things that principals may not have the ability, expertise, time, or willingness to do for themselves. Principals place their trust in agents and hope that they will act in their best interests (Benson and Simpson, 2015).

Problems arise when the two are not quite alike, if they differ in some way. The agency theory points to areas where the two parties may differ. They may at least be dissimilar in the following aspects:

1. Preferences: the participants may have conflicting values and attitudes.
2. Knowledge: the participants do not have the same knowledge, thus the relationship is characterized by asymmetry between parties involved.
3. Risks: the participants may have different attitudes toward risk, some may be risk willing, while others have risk aversion, that is, they dislike exposure to risks.

Deception is closely related to the abuse of trust. Abuses or violations of trust occur in agency relationships. Agents sometimes abuse trust placed in them by their principals. The relationship is unbalanced, and the agent's actions may be based on factors that the principal has no way of knowing about (Benson and Simpson, 2015).

Institutional moral collapse

It becomes more convenient to commit financial crime by white-collar criminals in organizations characterized by moral collapse. Institutional theory of moral collapse suggests that opportunities improve for white-collar criminals. For example, Bradshaw (2015) found criminogenic industry structures in the offshore oil industry.

Institutional theory contributes an understanding of organizational behavior that is influenced by individuals, groups, and other organizations, as well as society at large of which they are a part. The theory emphasizes how organizational structure and organizational culture are driven by norms, attitudes, and rules, which are common to most organizations in society. While organizational structure is characterized by design of positions in terms of job specialization, behavioral formalization, unit grouping, and unit size (van Donk and Molloy, 2008), organizational culture is characterized by accepted practices, rules, and principles of conduct that are applied to a variety of situations, as well as generalized rationales and beliefs (Barton, 2004).

Institutional theory applied to white-collar crime means that white-collar criminals find opportunity for and acceptance of illegal behaviors because of moral collapse generally in the organization.

Institutional theory

Institutional theory argues that business enterprises are much more than simple tools and instruments to achieve financial goals and ambitions.

The theory says that organizations are adaptable systems that recognize and learn from the environment by mirroring values in society. This reasoning is used to explain why business organizations tend to be similar in the same industry and the same nation and region (Kostova et al., 2008).

Moral collapse happens when organizations are unable to see that bright line between right and wrong. Seven signs of ethical collapse have been identified: (1) pressure to maintain those numbers, (2) fear and silence antidotes for fear and silence, (3) young ones and a bigger-than-life CEO, (4) weak board, (5) conflicts, (6) innovation like no other, and (7) goodness in some areas atones for evil in others.

Shadnam and Lawrence (2011: 379) apply institutional theory to explain moral decline and potential crime in organizations:

> Our theory of moral collapse has two main elements. First, we argue that morality in organizations is embedded in nested systems of individuals, organizations and moral communities in which ideology and regulation flow "down" from moral communities through organizations to individuals, and moral ideas and influence flow "upward" from individuals through organizations to moral communities. Second, we argue that moral collapse is associated with breakdowns in these flows, and explore conditions under which such breakdowns are likely to occur.

Shadman and Lawrence (2011: 393) formulated several research hypotheses, which imply that the likelihood of moral decline will vary depending on several circumstances:

- Moral collapse is more likely to happen in organizations that operate in moral communities in which flows of ideology are disrupted, either through a lack of commitment to formal communication mechanisms by community leaders or the disruption of informal communication networks by high rates of membership turnover.
- Moral collapse is more likely to happen in organizations in which structures and practices diminish the organization's capacity to absorb and incorporate morally charged institutions from the organization's moral community because the organization monopolizes the attention of its members and/or because the organization delegitimizes the morally charged institutions rooted in the moral community.
- Moral collapse is more likely to happen in organizations in which accusing individuals of misconduct creates significant social and

economic costs for the organization or the moral community within which it operates.

Moral collapse is more likely to occur in organizations to the degree that employment conditions undermine disclosure and/or work arrangements diminish the effectiveness of surveillance.

Institutional theory is mainly a sociological and public policy perspective on organizational studies. The theory sheds light on normative structures and activities. Institutional theory in public policy emphasizes the formal and legal aspects of government structures. Signs from organizations are observed as indications of values in organizational members. When activities are repeated in the same way and within the same structure, then those activities are institutionalized, and the sum of activities based on shared perceptions of reality can be defined as an institution (Hatch, 1997).

Institutional theory considers the processes by which structures, including schemes, rules, norms, and routines, become established as authoritative guidelines for social behavior. Institutional adaption is caused by political, cultural, and social influences. Behavioral patterns supported by norms, values, and expectations lead to cultural influence. A desire to equal others implies social influence. Normative institutional pressure is concerned with conformity, where deviance is disliked, disapproved, or even dismissed (Hatch, 1997).

In a study of factors leading to ethical and moral decline and collapse in large U.S. enterprises such as Enron and WorldCom, it was found that employees did indeed see ethical problems in illegal actions that were going on. But management governed the organization by a culture where alignment was awarded, while punishment was given to those who questioned corporate practice. When an organization collapse morally, it means that those in the organization have drifted into rationalizations and legalisms, and all for the purpose of getting the results they want and need at almost any cost. In Enron, top management told in an email why they were restructuring the company so frequently: "The basic business model is to keep outside investment analysts so confused that they will not be able to figure out that we don't know what we're doing".

Gross (1978) argued in his classical article on the theory of organizational crime that in a considerable number of areas of sociology, studies of crime and delinquency usually have a strong theoretical base. He suggested two important theoretical relationships. First, the internal structure and setting of organizations is of such a nature as to raise the probability that the attainment of the goals of the organization will subject the organization to the risk of violating societal laws of organizational behavior. Second, persons who actually act for the organization in the commission of crimes will, by selective processes, be associated with upward mobility in organizations, be likely to be highly committed to the organization and, for various reasons, be willing and able to carry out crime, should it seem to be required in order to enable the organization to attain its goals, to prosper, or at least, to survive.

Institutional theory is in line with dysfunctional network theory, in that organizations tend to mirror the basic elements of their environments. The largest business corporations can more easily absorb the negative impact of legal sanctions that certain governmental or regulatory agencies might impose on them. The largest business enterprises might have better lawyers and other resources, so that they are able to contend with legal pursuits in more effective and efficient ways. Microsoft versus the United States and Microsoft versus the European Union are typical examples. Therefore, laws and regulations tend to have a far less deterrent effect in the case of large business organizations (Dion, 2009).

Dysfunctional network theory

Dysfunctional network theory suggests that corporate crime emerges as a consequence of the dysfunction of value networks. A value network is the context within which a firm identifies and responds to customers' needs, solves problems, procures input, reacts to competitors, and strives for profit. Within this context, the firm may opt for deviant behavior, in line with their competitors in the industry. Dion (2009) argues that organizational culture makes it possible to adopt organizational purposes or objectives, which are basically deviant in comparison with social norms yet in line with the competition. Deviant purposes can be chosen when business corporations are trapped by doubtful, immoral, or disloyal means that are used by competitors. They could also be trapped by the business milieu as a social institution. Finally, they could be trapped by their own sector-based morality, which is oriented toward profit maximization.

Dysfunctional network theory makes clear that the mission of the business corporation cannot be isolated from three basic components inherent in any capitalistic system: making profits, responding to customers' needs, and reacting to competitors. Values in the value network have four basic meanings (Dion, 2009):

- Organizational values refer to what the company considers an ethical behavior or decision;
- Organizational values reflect the criteria that employees use when they must prioritize various alternatives of action;
- Organizational values determine the basic strategic decisions taken by top managers;
- Organizational values are the criteria that give guidance throughout the resource-allocation process.

Within the corporate culture, the tendency to commit financial crime is influenced by a number of factors. If the business corporation is experiencing poor financial performance, if the organization is large and unstable, and if the level of concentration in the market is high, then corporate crime is more likely to occur. According to Dion (2009), business corporations with greater power in the market tend to commit more illegalities.

Value networks define what companies can and cannot do. Value networks focus on values and attitudes from an ethical viewpoint. Competitors that are involved in given value networks contribute to defining the manner in which each enterprise in an industry can strive for profit. Dion (2009) argues that the capacity to convert corporate intangibles, such as corporate reputation, in a negotiable value could contribute to the prevention of corporate crime.

According to dysfunctional network theory, the way a given enterprise defines its strategies and justifies past choices of markets determines its perceptions of the economic value it assigns to alternative legal and illegal actions. Value networks constitute the cultural mix that explains how different strategic elements play a decisive role in the way an organization views ethical considerations. Organizations tend to mirror the basic elements of their environments.

Social network theory

Bruinsma and Bernasco (2004) used social network theory to describe and tentatively explain differences in social organization between criminal groups that perform three types of transnational illegal activities: smuggling and large-scale heroin trading; trafficking in women; and trading in stolen cars. Groups that operate in the large-scale heroin market tend to be close-knit, cohesive, and ethnically homogeneous. Groups active in the trafficking of women have a chain structure, while those that operate in the market for stolen cars are characterized by three clusters of offenders in a chain. Both groups are less cohesive than criminal groups in the large-scale heroin market. The differences in social organization between the three types of illegal activities appear to be related to the legal and financial risks associated with the crimes in question, and thereby to the level of trust required between collaborating criminals.

While white-collar crime is concerned with financial crime in legal business, it is nevertheless interesting to apply institutional theory to those who are in illegal business, such as criminal groups. Even criminal motorcycle gangs, for example, tend to mirror the basic elements of the environment to which they want to belong. Their moral collapse has been replaced by an attitude of being a 1 percent community outside the main community (Gottschalk, 2013).

Institutional theory has a long history. The general argument advanced was that formal organizational structure reflected not simply technological imperatives and resource dependencies, but also institutional forces, which included rule-like frameworks, rational myths, and knowledge legitimated through official learning. The theory emphasizes the privileged position of organizations as legitimate, dominant actors in modern societies (Scott, 2008).

Conspiracy theory

When institutional theory of moral collapse blames external forces for causing internal deterioration, it may be linked to conspiracy thinking. For example, one of the most widely held theories of organized crime today in the United States is known as the alien conspiracy theory. This theory blames outsiders and outside influences for the prevalence of organized crime in society. Over the years, unsavory images, such as well-dressed men of foreign descent standing in shadows with machine guns and living by codes of silence, have become associated with this theory. The alien conspiracy theory posits that organized crime (the Mafia) gained prominence during the 1860s in Sicily and that Sicilian immigrants are responsible for the foundations of U.S. organized crime, which is made up of 25 or so Italian-dominated crime families (Lyman and Potter, 2007).

Lyman and Potter (2007: 60) discuss this theory as follows:

> Although some skeptics insist that the alien conspiracy theory was born out of hysteria incited by the media, it has received considerable support over the years from federal law enforcement organizations, public officials, and some researchers. It has been argued, however, that federal law enforcement organizations have self-serving reasons to promulgate this theory: It explains their inability to eliminate organized crime, it disguises the role of political and business corruption in organized crime, and it provides fertile ground for new resources, powers, and bureaucratic expansion.

Lombardo (2002) has challenged the alien conspiracy theory as an explanation of the origin of organized crime in America; he reviewed the history of Black Hand (organized crime group) activity in Chicago in the early twentieth century, arguing that the development of Black Hand extortion was not related to the emergence of the Sicilian Mafia, but rather to the social structure of American society.

Generally, a conspiracy theory is an explanatory proposition that accuses others of having caused or covered up an illegal situation. The external environment is to blame. It is comfortable for people in an organization to assume that the moral collapse of the organization is caused by external factors.

Monopoly is a special kind of organizational situation where institutional theory can explain moral collapse. A monopoly exists when a specific enterprise is the only supplier of a particular commodity. Similarly, an oligopoly consists of a few entities dominating an industry. Potential business actors have no choice but to join the monopolistic enterprise or one of the oligopolistic enterprises (Chang et al., 2005).

Organized crime

Financial crime sometimes occurs as part of organized crime. Traditionally, a criminal organization is thought of as a monopolistic firm, and the theory of monopoly is predominantly used to analyze organized crimes. The monopolistic model implies that, on deciding to commit a crime, potential criminals have no other choice but to join the criminal organization. Chang et al. (2005) find this perspective to be less than exhaustive in terms of describing criminal behavior. They argue that the determination of the market structure for crime should be endogenous, something that has notable implications for the optimal crime enforcement policies and crime itself.

To exhume the conventionally neglected facts and provide a more complete picture regarding organized crime, Chang et al. (2005) developed a model in terms of a criminal decision framework in which individual crime and organized crime are coexisting alternatives to a potential offender. The model makes the size of a criminal organization a variable and explores interactive relationships between varying sizes of criminal organization, the crime rate, and the government's law enforcement strategies. Model runs showed that the method adopted to allocate the criminal organization's payoffs and the extra benefit provided by the criminal organization play crucial roles in an individual's decision to commit a crime and the way in which he or she commits that crime.

Socialization theory

Socialization theory argues that learning in the organization how to commit financial crime and getting to know persons in the criminal trade will increase the likelihood of white-collar crime (Lyman and Potter, 2007: 69):

> Many lower-class male adolescents experience a sense of desperation surrounding the belief that their position in the economic structure is relatively

fixed and immutable. As a result of failing to meet cultural expectations of achieving upward mobility, conditions become ideal for socialization functions such as recruitment, screening, and training for organized crime to occur at the community level.

Differential association theory (a social learning theory) proposes that a person associating with individuals who have deviant or unlawful mores, values, and norms learns criminal behavior. Certain characteristics play a key role in placing individuals in a position to behave unlawfully, including the proposition that criminal behavior is learned through interaction with other persons, as well as interaction occurring in small intimate groups (Hansen, 2009). Criminal behavior is learned in social association with deviant persons (Matsueda, 1988).

Matsueda (1988) argues that the theory of differential association, along with the concept of white-collar crime, was probably Edwin Sutherland's greatest legacy. The theory explains individual criminality with a social psychological process of learning crime within interaction with social groups. Criminal behavior is thus the result of learning an excess of activities favorable to crime. This is the differential association process.

Furthermore, Matsueda (1988) argues that Sutherland's attempt to explain aggregate crime rates across groups and societies is less well known. Here, he specified the theory of differential social organization to explain rates of crime with an organizational process of group dynamics. The crime rate of a group is determined by the extent to which the group is organized in favor of crime versus organized against crime. Moreover, the explanation of crime rates, differential social organization, is consistent with the explanation of individual acts of crime in terms of differential association.

Individuals embedded within structural units are differentially exposed to activities in favor of or opposed to delinquent and criminal behavior. Therefore, criminal associations and normative conflict vary across community types (Hoffmann, 2002).

Learning theories have been used to explain the onset of criminal activity. The body of research on learning theory stresses the attitudes, ability, values, and behaviors needed to maintain a criminal career (Lyman and Potter, 2007).

Double-bind leadership

There are various ways a leader in an organization can make subordinates and colleagues passive toward the leader's misconduct and crime. One approach is double-bind leadership that belongs to the dark sides of leadership. The theory of double-bind leadership suggests that mixed messages from a leader creates a double bind for a colleague or subordinate. Individuals are caught in double bind situations in organizational relationships when the criminal leader is expressing two orders of message and one of these denies the other. Individuals are unable to comment on the message being expressed to correct their discrimination in terms of which order of messages to respond to, since the situation in double-bind leadership is such that they cannot make a meta communicative statement (Hennestad, 1990).

An individual is not able to comment on the ambiguity of the message by being critical in an assessment of the consequences of double bind because it cements the ambiguity of the situation. A simple example of double bind is a child being exposed to signals of both love and hate from a parent. The child is trapped (Hennestad, 1990: 268):

> If the situation is defined as one of hate, the child could be punished for her reaction. On the other hand, if the child defines the signal as one of love, the reaction could be rejection of her affection.

A double bind is a dilemma in communication in which an individual receives conflicting messages, with one message negating the other. This creates a situation in which a successful response to one message results in a failed response to the other message, so that the person might be wrong regardless of response. The nature of a double bind is that the person is unable to confront the sender of messages with the inherent dilemma. The double bind theory is seen as part of the human experience of communication that involves intense relationships and the necessity to discriminate between orders of messages (Gibney, 2006).

The double bind theory can be applied to both individuals and organizations. A double bind organization is a social system where mixed messages are the rule rather than an exception. An organizational schizophrenia occurs in the organization, where mixed messages cannot be revealed, which has a negative effect on an employee's initiatives and learning situation. The result is a lack of authentic dialogue, which can freeze the horizon of meaning in the organization, thereby rendering infertile the soil of growth of vitality of organizational dynamics (Hennestad, 1990).

Glasø and Einarsen (2008) studied emotion regulation in leader-follower relationships. They found that negative emotions such as disappointment, uncertainty, and annoyance are typically suppressed, while positive emotions such as enthusiasm, interest, and calmness are typically expressed or faked. When leaders and followers referred to experienced or expressed emotions, the most highly scored emotions were "glad," "enthusiastic," "well," and "interested." The reported level of emotion regulation was higher for leaders than for followers.

According to Glasø et al. (2006), emotional control can be defined as a process in which individuals influence the emotions that they experience, when they arise, and how they perceive and express them. In this line of reasoning, people can modify their emotions and the emotional expressions connected with them. Emotional control in the workplace is called emotional labor or emotion work. Emotion work takes place in face-to-face or voice-to-voice interactions, and its purpose is to influence other people's perceptions, emotions, attitudes, and behavior.

Obedience theory has the potential to explain follower behavior. Obedience theory is related to the fraud triangle that consists of pressure, opportunity, and rationalization (Baird and Zelin, 2009; Hollow, 2014). The pressures to commit crime are often overt requests of management, but can also be based on perceptions from reward and incentive structures.

An even stronger argument for follower behavior can be found when obedience theory is linked to self-control theory. Self-control theory proposes that individuals commit crime because of low self-control. Except in rare cases of mass fraud such as the Enron scandal, not all elite individuals within a given organization or industry will commit crime. Hence, although the elite at the top of their profession and corporation differentially associate with the people of equal status in their own and other corporations, not all corporate elites commit crimes and behave in an overtly deviant manner (Hansen, 2009).

Leaders tend to be more domineering and assertive, and less social avoidant, distrustful, and exploitable than followers. Glasø et al.'s (2010) study shows that 30 percent of the leaders exhibit elevated profiles of personality characteristics regarding interpersonal problems, on a level comparable to that of a sample with psychiatric patients, thus indicating that severe problems may arise in social interactions between leaders and followers.

Leaders can employ different behaviors, actions, and practices that they direct at followers in order to make them cooperate. Bullying and harassment by leaders are examples of a practice reported to happen on a regular basis in many work organizations. Bullying and harassment are carried out deliberately to cause humiliation, offense, and distress (Hoel et al., 2010).

Dark sides of leadership are associated with counterproductive work behaviors, misconduct, and crime. At the same time, characteristics of followers can make the situation even worse. For example, narcissistic employees have been found to be less satisfied with their jobs. Narcissistic followers ruthlessly pursue aggrandizement of the individual self, even at the price of diminishing others and at the risk of sacrificing interpersonal bonds. Narcissistic followers tend to score their supervisors more negatively than non-narcissistic individuals (Mathieu, 2013). Narcissism is the psychological construct most associated with an orientation of self-love. The person has a sense of superiority, self-centeredness, entitlement, and a strong desire for authority and personal power (Galvin et al., 2015).

Negative consequences of narcissistic individuals in the workplace are mostly related to damages in interpersonal relationships. Followers high on neuroticism rated their leaders lower on positive leadership. Followers' perception of their leaders such as trust and satisfaction, fear and respect, influence their willingness to participate in misconduct (Salter et. al., 2009). Followers' belief in their leaders' behavior as morally right make followers experience shame and guilt when they fail to support their leaders' actions (Fehr et al., 2015).

The leadership trait perspective is an important intellectual tradition in leadership research. For white-collar criminals, we may find both light and dark sides of leader traits, although the dark sides may be the most prominent when white-collar criminals commit financial crime.

Judge et al. (2009) identified four dark side personality traits:

- *Narcissism* is a personality trait that is characterized by arrogance, self-absorption, entitlement, and hostility. Narcissists exhibit an unusually high level of self-love, believing that they are uniquely special and entitled to praise and admiration. As a self-regulatory defense mechanism against a grandiose yet shallow self-concept, narcissists tend to view others as inferior to themselves, often acting in insensitive, hostile, and self-enhancing ways. Narcissist leaders are more likely to interpret information with a self-serving bias and make decisions based on how those decisions will reflect on their reputations.
- *Hubris* exists when an individual has excessive pride, an inflated sense of self-confidence, and makes self-evaluations in terms of talent, ability, and accomplishment that are much more positive than any reasonable objective assessment would otherwise suggest. Leaders who carry an exaggerated sense of self-worth are likely to be defensive against most forms of critical feedback, and respond to negative feedback by questioning the competence of the evaluator and the validity of evaluation technique. When subordinates or peers disagree with hubristic leaders, these leaders deny the credibility and value of negative evaluations.
- *Social dominance* represents a preference for hierarchy and stability to achieve control. Dominant individuals tend to control conversations, put pressure on others, and demand explanations for otherwise normal activities. Dominating individuals tend to be prejudiced, power hungry, and manipulative.

- *Machiavellianism* is a term used to define a personality trait characterized by cunning, manipulation, and the use of any means necessary to achieve one's political ends. These kinds of leaders are concerned with maximizing opportunities to craft their own personal power.

Most CEO research has tended to take a rather one-sided view of leadership, emphasizing its positive and constructive aspects while avoiding its darker sides. A possible reason for this one-sided attention may be that leadership research has primarily focused on leader effectiveness, strategic thinking, and factors that contribute to optimal performance and results (Glasø et al., 2010). However, there are several dark sides of leadership that merit attention by researchers. One of the darkest sides of leadership is white-collar crime, where the CEO exploits criminal options for corporate and/or personal gain. This constitutes the main topic of our statistical analysis.

However, dark sides of leadership can be found in less severe forms. One example is bullying and harassment, which may or may not be linked to crime. Bullying and harassment by CEOs are reported to happen on a regular basis in many work organizations. Bullying and harassment at work may be defined as repeated behavior, actions and practices directed at one or more colleagues, which may be conducted either deliberately or unconsciously, but which are unwanted by the targets, causing humiliation, offense and distress, and which may interfere with job performance and/or cause an unpleasant working environment (Hoel et al., 2010).

The heroic perspective on leadership has been shown to be part of a frequently held romantic illusion of leadership, which, in turn, it has been argued, attracts people with narcissistic personality. Leadership positions prove tempting to narcissists because they provide legitimate exposure to attention from others, a sense of importance and power, and also as gratification in terms of the sense of entitlement that narcissists seem particularly prone to (Arnulf and Gottschalk, 2013).

Entrepreneurial theory can be applied to white-collar crime, whereupon we look at the dark side of entrepreneurialism. To understand entrepreneurial behavior by white-collar criminals, important behavioral areas include modus essendi, modus operandi, and modus vivendi. Modus essendi is a philosophical term relating to modes of being. Modus operandi is method of operating, which is an accepted criminological concept for classifying generic human actions from their visible and consequential manifestations. Modus vivendi represents the shared symbiotic relationship between different entrepreneurial directions (Smith, 2009).

Social disorganization

This perspective argues that structural conditions lead to higher levels of social disorganization—especially of weak social controls—in organizations and between organizations, which in turn results in high rates of crime (Pratt and Cullen, 2005). Rates of financial crime are not evenly dispersed across time and space in the private or public sector.

Social disorganization increases offenders' opportunities to commit financial crime without being detected. Offenders have unrestricted and legitimate access to the location in which the crime is committed without any kinds of controls. Offenders' actions have a superficial appearance of legitimacy also internally, since both legal and illegal actions in the organization are characterized by disorganization (Benson and Simpson, 2015).

Social disorganization theory argues that crime is a function of people dynamics in the organization and between organizations, and not necessarily a function of each individual within such organizations. Business enterprises experiencing rapid changes in their social and economic structures that are in a zone of transition will experience higher crime rates. Management mobility is another structural factor or antecedent that can be held to produce organizations that are socially disorganized. Conventional mechanisms of social control are weak and unable to regulate the behavior within organizations (Pratt and Cullen, 2005).

Especially in knowledge organizations where the hierarchical structure tends to be weak, social controls among colleagues are of importance to prevent financial crime. An unstable and disorganized unit will suffer from lack of knowledge exchange and collaboration to prevent and detect white-collar crime (Swart and Kinnie, 2003).

Structural antecedents include not only management instability and rapid organizational changes, but also external factors such as family disruptions and no intelligence about life outside work. Social disorganization can be found at the very top of organizations, where chief executives have created large business space for themselves without access from others. There are no ties allowing others to act collectively to fight problems (Pratt and Cullen, 2005).

Social control is an opposite of social disorganization. Social control theory argues that individuals will restrain from white-collar crime if society and the organization has processes that prevent them from doing so (Abadinsky, 2007: 22):

> Social control refers to those processes by which the community influences its members toward conformance with established norms of behavior. Social control theorists argue that the relevant question is not, Why do persons become involved in crime, organized or otherwise? but, rather, Why do most persons conform to societal norms? If, as control theorists generally assume, most persons

are sufficiently motivated by the potential rewards to commit criminal acts, why do only a few make crime a career? According to control theorists, delinquent acts result when an individual's bond to society is weak or broken. The strength of this bond is determined by internal and external restraints. In other words, internal and external restraints determine whether we move in the direction of crime or of law-abiding behavior.

Social control theory is also concerned with relationships between individuals controlled and those that perform controls (Tiwana and Keil, 2009: 13):

> We define attempted control as the extent to which a controller attempts to utilize a given control mechanism to influence controlee behavior. Attempted control therefore refers to the control mechanisms that the controller implements in a given project, independent of whether or how they are exercised. We define realized control as the extent to which the controller is able to successfully exercise a given control mechanism during the systems development process. An attempted control mechanism must be effectively exercised, or realized, for it to enhance systems development performance.

Corporate disorganization weakens the ability of social bonds to circumscribe delinquent behavior. In enterprises characterized by instability and heterogeneity, the likelihood of effective socialization and supervision is reduced. The impact of social bonds varies by type of organization and disorganized units negatively affect the ability of social bonds to reduce delinquent behavior (Hoffmann, 2002).

Social disorganization can be a result of one or more deviant cultures in the organization. Deviant culture theory argues that joining a criminal subculture in the upper class will increase the likelihood of white-collar crime (Lyman and Potter, 2007: 70):

> The subculture shares a lifestyle that is often accompanied by an alternative language and culture. The lower-class lifestyle is typically characterized by being tough, taking care of one's own affairs, and rejecting any kind of governmental authority.

Cultural deviance theories are based on the assumption that, for example, slum dwellers violate the law because they belong to a unique subculture that exists in lower-class areas. The subculture's values and norms conflict with those of the upper class on which criminal law is based (Lyman and Potter, 2007).

Social networks may play an important role in the incidence of white-collar crime. An example of social networks is people sharing a common religion, religious language, and history composed of stories of events, a homeland, and oppression. They may have ancestors who emigrated from the same regions in the world, and they may have settled in certain population clusters (Corcoran et al., 2012).

Follower obedience in organizations

Obedience theory has the potential to explain follower behavior in white-collar crime. Obedience theory is related to the fraud triangle that consists of pressure, opportunity, and rationalization. Obedience theory can be useful in explaining pressures and rationalizations providing the motives for individuals to commit acts of occupational fraud (Baird and Zelin, 2009: 1):

> Perceived need or pressure often comes from personal financial problems or living beyond one's means, but it can also come from direct pressure from someone in authority in the workplace and the threat of losing one's job for failure to go along with the boss's scheme. Obedience theory posits that individuals may engage in behaviors that conflict with their personal values and beliefs if they are subjected to pressures to obey someone in authority. According to this theory, the individuals rationalize this behavior by essentially placing full responsibility on the authority figure rather than taking any individual responsibility for the action themselves.

Obedience pressure is considered a form of social influence pressure, alongside two other types of social influence pressure: compliance pressure and conformity pressure (Baird and Zelin, 2009: 2):

> Compliance pressure is similar to obedience pressure, except that compliance pressure can come from one's peers as well as from superiors, while obedience pressure must come from an authority figure. Conformity pressure refers to pressure to conform to perceived or societal norms.

Of the three forms of social influence pressure, Baird and Zelin (2009) argue that obedience pressure can be especially potent owing to the power that persons in authority have over their subordinates. People within an organization quietly follow the orders of top executives and rationalize their actions by denying responsibility for their behaviors. The pressures to commit crime are often overt requests of management, but can also be based on perceptions from reward and incentive structures.

Authority can be defined as domination, where the probability is high that a certain specific command will be obeyed by a given group of persons. Authority assumes voluntary compliance or an interest in obedience. Obedience is an obligation that is formal and one follows it without regard to one's own attitude or lack of value of its content. It is often essential that the authority is believed to be legitimate, and there needs to be an immediate relation between command and obedience (Aguilera and Vadera, 2008).

Social bonding theory proposes that the presence of four key elements of belief, attachment, commitment, and involvement may lead to elite misdeeds based on the strength of the bonds formed between corporate "bad boys" (Hansen, 2009).

When a follower moralizes a leader's behavior, the behavior becomes a matter of right and wrong. Moralization refers to the process through which an observer confers a leader's actions with moral relevance. Positive moralization involves perceiving a leader's behavior as morally right. According to Fehr et al. (2015), followers experience feelings of shame and guilt when they fail to support these morally right actions and reject those who vocalize morals that contradict their own. Therefore, the moralization of a leader's actions may hold important implications for how a follower might subsequently behave by obedience.

Organizational systems failure

The organizational dimension of white-collar crime is especially obvious when crime is convicted in a setting where the rotten apple barrel metaphor is appropriate, and where the culture stimulates rather than prevents misbehavior by members of the organization. Ashforth et al. (2008) argue that it is comforting to assume that one bad apple or renegade faction within an organization is essentially responsible for crime that is all too prevalent. However, organizations are important to our understanding of crime because they influence the actions of their members. Therefore, both micro and macro views are important in order to understand crime.

Generally, a rotten apple is someone who persistently exhibits one or more of the following behaviors: withholding effort from others, expressing negative affect, or violating important interpersonal norms. Withholders of efforts ignore their responsibilities and ride free off the efforts of others. Behavioral examples of withholding effort include not doing something or not completing tasks. Expressing negative affect implies a negative mood or attitude. Personally negative individuals are more likely to exhibit an awkward interpersonal style, and they express pessimism, anxiety, insecurity, and irritation. Violating norms implies deviant behavior such as making fun of someone, saying something hurtful, making an inappropriate ethnic or religious remark, cursing someone, and publicly embarrassing someone (Felps et al., 2006). In our context of white-collar crime, a rotten apple is a person who commits financial crime individually.

It is certainly an interesting issue whether to view white-collar misconduct and crime as acts of individuals perceived as "rotten apples" or as an indication of systems failure in the company, the industry, or the society as a whole. The perspective of occupational crime favors the individualistic model of deviance, which is a human failure model of misconduct and crime. This rotten apple view of white-collar crime is a comfortable perspective to adopt for business organizations as it allows them to look no further than suspect individuals. It is only when other forms of group (O'Connor, 2005) and/or systemic (Punch, 2003) corruption and other kinds of crime erupt in a business enterprise that a more critical look is taken at white-collar criminality. Furthermore, when serious misconduct occurs and is repeated, there seems to be a tendency to consider crime to be a result of bad practice, and lack of resources or mismanagement, rather than acts of criminals.

The "rotten apple" metaphor has been extended to include the group level view of cultural deviance in organizations with a "rotten barrel" metaphor (O'Connor, 2005). Furthermore, Punch (2003) has pushed the notion of "rotten orchards" to highlight deviance at the systemic level. Punch (2003: 172) notes, "the metaphor of 'rotten orchards' indicate(s) that it is sometimes not the apple, or even the barrel, that is rotten but the *system* (or significant parts of the system)."

When the system is rotten, we can talk about systemic crime or systems crime (Punch, 2003: 172):

> ... in some way encouraged, and perhaps even protected, by certain elements in the system. .... "Systems" refers both to the formal system—the police organization, the criminal justice system and the broader socio-political context—and to the informal system of deals, inducements, collusion and understandings among deviant officers as to how the corruption is to be organized, conducted, and rationalized.

The systemic view is in line with the routine activity perspective, which argues that frequency of crime is highest where motivated offenders intersect in time and space with attractive targets that lack capable guardianship. Criminal events occur when motivated offenders have the opportunity to victimize property. Opportunities consist of attractive or suitable targets and a lack of capable protection against attacks. An organization characterized by potential offenders, potential targets, and absence of guardianship is associated with higher frequency of financial crime (Pratt and Cullen, 2005).

The theory of systems failure recognizes that systems never can take complete control over humans, and systems can never completely register what humans are doing. Systems failure is always possible if skilled white-collar criminals put sufficient effort into committing financial crime.

Furthermore, social contract theory assumes that ethical dilemmas in business overlay a universe of economic transactions involving actors whose ability to comprehend their moral implications is inherently limited, and thus creates and maintains an extent of social disorganization. Social contracts at macro and micro levels constitute the basis for analyzing how individuals and organizations fulfill ethical obligations through consent and through conformity to social norms (Barry and Stephens, 1998).

References

Abadinsky, H. (2007). *Organized crime*, 8th ed. Belmont, CA: Thomson Wadsworth.

Adler, P.S. and Kwon, S.W. (2002). Social capital: Prospects for a new concept, *Academy of Management Review*, 27 (1), 17–40.

Aguilera, R.V. and Vadera, A.K. (2008). The dark side of authority: Antecedents, mechanisms, and outcomes of organizational corruption, *Journal of Business Ethics*, 77, 431–449.

Arnulf, J.K. and Gottschalk, P. (2013). Heroic leaders as white-collar criminals: An empirical study, *Journal of Investigative Psychology and Offender Profiling*, 10, 96–113.

Ashforth, B.E., Gioia, D.A., Robinson, S.L. and Trevino, L.K. (2008). Re-reviewing organizational corruption, *Academy of Management Review*, 33 (3), 670–684.

Baird, J.E. and Zelin, R.C. (2009). An examination of the impact of obedience pressure on perceptions of fraudulent acts and the likelihood of committing occupational fraud, *Journal of Forensic Studies in Accounting and Business*, Winter, 1–14.

Barry, B. and Stephens, C.U. (1998). Objections to an objectivist approach to integrity, *Academy of Management Review*, 23 (1), 162–169.

Barton, H. (2004). Cultural reformation: A case for intervention within the police service, *International Journal of Human Resources Development and Management*, 4 (2), 191–199.

Benson, M.L. and Simpson, S.S. (2015). *Understanding white-collar crime—An opportunity perspective*, New York: Routledge.

Bookman, Z. (2008). Convergences and omissions in reporting corporate and white collar crime, *DePaul Business & Commercial Law Journal*, 6, 347–392.

Bradshaw, E.A. (2015). "Obviously, we're all oil industry": The criminogenic structure of the offshore oil industry, *Theoretical Criminology*, 19 (3), 376–395.

Bruinsma, G. and Bernasco, W. (2004). Criminal groups and transnational illegal markets, *Crime, Law and Social Change*, 41 (1), 79–94.

Bucy, P.H., Formby, E.P., Raspanti, M.S. and Rooney, K.E. (2008). Why do they do it?: The motives, mores, and character of white collar criminals, *St. John's Law Review*, 82, 401–571.

Bystrova, E.G. and Gottschalk, P. (2015). Social conflict theory and white-collar criminals: Why does the ruling class punish their own? *Pakistan Journal of Criminology*, 7 (1), 1–15.

Chang, J.J., Lu, H.C. and Chen, M. (2005). Organized crime or individual crime? Endogeneous size of a criminal organization and the optimal law enforcement, *Economic Inquiry*, 43 (3), 661–675.

Chrisman, J.J., Chua, J.H., Kellermanns, F.W. and Chang, E.P.C. (2007). Are family managers agents or stewards? An exploratory study in privately held family firms, *Journal of Business Research*, 60 (10), 1030–1038.

Corcoran, K.E., Pettinicchio, D. and Robbins, B. (2012). Religion and the acceptability of white-collar crime: A cross-national analysis, *Journal of the Scientific Study of Religion*, 51 (3), 542–567.

Dion, M. (2009). Corporate crime and the dysfunction of value networks, *Journal of Financial Crime*, 16 (4), 436–445.

Dodge, M. (2009). *Women and white-collar crime.* Upper Saddle River, NJ: Prentice Hall.

Eberl, P., Geiger, D. and Assländer, M.S. (2015). Repairing trust in an organization after integrity violations: The ambivalence of organizational rule adjustments, *Organization Studies*, 36 (9), 1205–1235.

Eisenhardt, K.M. (1989). Building theories from case study research, *Academy of Management Review*, 14 (4), 532–550.

Fehr, R., Yam, K.C. and Dang, C. (2015). Moralized leadership: The construction and consequences of ethical leader perceptions, *Academy of Management Review*, 40 (2), 182–209.

Felps, W., Mitchell, T.R. and Byington, E. (2006). How, when and why bad apples spoil the barrel: Negative group members and dysfunctional groups, *Research in Organizational Behavior*, 27, 175–222.

Garoupa, N. (2007). Optimal law enforcement and criminal organization, *Journal of Economic Behavior & Organization*, 63, 461–474.

Gibney, P. (2006). The double bind theory: Still crazy-making after all these years, *Psychotherapy in Australia*, 12 (3), 48–55.

Glasø, L. and Einarsen, S. (2008). Emotion regulation in leader-follower relationships, *European Journal of Work and Organizational Psychology*, 17 (4), 482–500.

Glasø, L., Ekerholt, K., Barman, S. and Einarsen, S. (2006). The instrumentality of emotion in leader-subordinate relationships, *International Journal of Work Organisation and Emotion*, 1 (3), 255–276.

Glasø, L., Einarsen, S., Matthiesen, S.B. and Skogstad, A. (2010). The dark side of leaders: A representative study of interpersonal problems among leaders, *Scandinavian Journal of Organizational Psychology*, 2 (2), 3–14.

Galvin, B.M., Lange, D. and Ashforth, B.E. (2015). Narcissistic organizational identification: Seeing oneself as central to the organization's identity, *Academy of Management Review*, 40 (2), 163–181.

Goldstraw-White, J. (2012). *White-collar crime: Accounts of offending behaviour,* London: Palgrave Macmillan.

Gottschalk, P. (2013). Limits to corporate social responsibility: The case of Gjensidige insurance company and Hells Angels motorcycle club, *Corporate Reputation Review*, 16 (3), 177–186.

Gottschalk, P. (2015a). *Fraud examiners in white-collar crime investigations*, Boca Raton, FL: CRC Press, Taylor & Francis.

Gottschalk, P. (2015b). *Investigating financial crime—Characteristics of white-collar criminals*, Hauppauge, NY: Nova Science Publishers.

Gottschalk, P. (2015c). *Internal investigations of economic crime—Corporate case studies and regulatory policy*, Boca Raton, FL: Universal Publishers.

Gross, E. (1978). Organizational crime: A theoretical perspective, *Studies in Symbolic Interaction*, 1, 55–85.

Haines, F. (2014). Corporate fraud as misplaced confidence? Exploring ambiguity in the accuracy of accounts and the materiality of money, *Theoretical Criminology*, 18 (1), 20–37.

Hansen, L.L. (2009). Corporate financial crime: Social diagnosis and treatment, *Journal of Financial Crime*, 16 (1), 28–40.

Hatch, M.J. (1997). *Organizational theory—Modern, symbolic, and postmodern perspectives*, Oxford University Press.

Heath, J. (2008). Business ethics and moral motivation: A criminological perspective, *Journal of Business Ethics*, 83, 595–614.

Hennestad, B.W. (1990). The symbolic impact of double-bind leadership: Double bind and the dynamics of organizational culture, *Journal of Management Studies*, 27 (3), 265–280.

Hill, G.D. and Harris, A.R. (1981). Changes in the gender patterning of crime, 1953–77: Opportunity vs. identity, *Social Science Quarterly*, 62 (4), 658–671.

Hoel, H., Glasø, L., Hetland, J., Cooper, C.L. and Einarsen, S. (2010). Leadership styles as predictors of self-reported and observed workplace bullying, *British Journal of Management*, 21, 453–468.

Hoffmann, J.P. (2002). A contextual analysis of differential association, social control, and strain theories of delinquency, *Social Forces*, 81 (3), 753–785.

Hollow, M. (2014). Money, morals and motives, *Journal of Financial Crime*, 21 (2), 174–190.

Huisman, W. and Erp, J. (2013). Opportunities for environmental crime, *British Journal of Criminology*, 53, 1178–1200.

Hærem, T., Pentland, B.T. and Miller, K.D. (2015). Task complexity: Extending a core concept, *Academy of Management Review*, 40 (3), 446–460.

Ilter, C. (2009). Fraudulent money transfers: A case from Turkey, *Journal of Financial Crime*, 16 (2), 125–136.

Jensen, M.C. and Meckling, W.H. (1976). Theory of the firm: Managerial behavior, agency costs and ownership structures, *Journal of Financial Economics, 3*(4), 305–360.

Judge, T.A., Piccolo, R.F. and Kosalka, T. (2009). The bright and dark sides of leader traits: A review and theoretical extension of the leader trait paradigm, *The Leadership Quarterly*, 20, 855–875.

Kostova, T., Roth, K. and Dacin, M.T. (2008). Institutional theory in the study of multinational corporations: A critique and new directions, *Academy of Management Review*, 33 (4), 994–1006.

Kupatadze, A. (2015). Political corruption in Eurasia: Understanding collusion between states, organized crime and business, *Theoretical Criminology*, 19 (2), 198–215.

Li, S. and Ouyang, M. (2007). A dynamic model to explain the bribery behavior of firms, *International Journal of Management*, 24 (3), 605–618.

Lombardo, R.M. (2002). Black hand: Terror by letter in Chicago. *Journal of Contemporary Criminal Justice*, 18 (4), 394–409.

Lyman, M.D. and Potter, G.W. (2007). *Organized crime*, 4th ed., Upper Saddle River, NJ: Pearson Prentice Hall.

Mathieu, C. (2013). Personality and job satisfaction: The role of narcissism, *Personality and Individual Differences*, 55 (6), 650–654.

Matsueda, R.L. (1988). The current state of differential association theory, *Crime & Delinquency*, 34 (3), 277–306.

Michel, P. (2008). Financial crimes: The constant challenge of seeking effective prevention solutions, *Journal of Financial Crime*, 15 (4), 383–397.

O'Connor, T.R. (2005). Police deviance and ethics. In part of web cited, *MegaLinks in Criminal Justice*. http://faculty.ncwc.edu/toconnor/205/205lect11.htm, retrieved on 19 February 2009.

Pickett, K.H.S. and Pickett, J.M. (2002). *Financial crime investigation and control*. New York: John Wiley & Sons.

Piquero, N.L., Schoepfer, A. and Langton, L. (2010). Completely out of control or the desire to be in complete control? How low self-control and the desire for control relate to corporate offending, *Crime & Delinquency*, 56 (4), 627–647.

Pontell, H.N., Black, W.K. and Geis, G. (2014). Too big to fail, too powerful to jail? On the absence of criminal prosecutions after the 2008 financial meltdown, *Crime, Law and Social Change*, 61 (1), 1–13.

Pratt, T.C. and Cullen, F.T. (2005). Assessing macro-level predictors and theories of crime: A meta-analysis, *Crime and Justice*, 32, 373–450.

Punch, M. (2003). Rotten orchards: "Pestilence," police misconduct and system failure. *Policing and Society*, 13, (2) 171–196.

Puranam, P., Alexy, O. and Reitzig, M. (2014). What's "new" about new forms of organizing? *Academy of Management Review*, 39 (2), 162–180.

Reed, G.E. and Yeager, P.C. (1996). Organizational offending and neoclassical criminology: Challenging the reach of a general theory of crime, *Criminology*, 34 (3), 357–382.

Salter, C.R., Green, M., Ree, M., Carmody-Bubb, M. and Duncan, P.A. (2009). A study of follower's personality, implicit leadership perceptions, and leadership ratings, *Journal of Leadership Studies*, 2 (4), 48–60.

Schoepfer, A. and Piquero, N.L. (2006). Exploring white-collar crime and the American dream: A partial test of institutional anomie theory, *Journal of Criminal Justice*, 34, 227–235.

Scott, W.R. (2008). Approaching adulthood: The maturing of institutional theory, *Theoretical Sociology*, 37, 427–442.

Shadnam, M. and Lawrence, T.B. (2011). Understanding widespread misconduct in organizations: An institutional theory of moral collapse, *Business Ethics Quarterly*, 21 (3), 379–407.

Smith, R. (2009). Understanding entrepreneurial behavior in organized criminals, *Journal of Enterprising Communities: People and Places in the Global Economy*, 3 (3), 256–268.

Steffensmeier, D. and Allan, E. (1996). Gender and crime: Toward a gendered theory of female offending, *Annual Review of Sociology*, 22, 459–487.

Steffensmeier, D., Schwartz, J. and Roche, M. (2013). Gender and twenty-first-century corporate crime: Female involvement and the gender gap in enron-era corporate frauds, *American Sociological Review*, 78 (3), 448–476.

Swart, J. and Kinnie, N. (2003). Sharing knowledge in knowledge-intensive firms, *Human Resource Management Journal*, 13 (2), 60–75.

Tiwana, A. and Keil, M. (2009). Control in internal and outsourced software projects, *Journal of Management Information Systems*, 26 (3), 9–45.

Trahan, A. (2011). Filling in the gaps in culture-based theories of organizational crime, *Journal of Theoretical and Philosophical Criminology*, 3 (1), 89–109.

Valukas, A.R. (2010). *In regard Lehman Brothers Holdings Inc. to United States Bankruptcy Court in Southern District of New York*, Jenner & Block, March 11, 239 pages, http://www.nysb.uscourts.gov/sites/default/files/opinions/188162_61_opinion.pdf.

van Donk, D.P. and Molloy, E. (2008). From organizing as projects, to projects as organizations, *International Journal of Project Management*, 26, 129–137.

Williams, J.W. (2008). The lessons of 'Enron'—Media accounts, corporate crimes, and financial markets, *Theoretical Criminology*, 12 (4), 471–499.

chapter four

Behavioral dimension in convenience theory

The third and final dimension of convenience theory is the behavioral dimension. In this chapter, this dimension is first explained. Thereafter, some aspects of the behavioral dimension are explained in more detail.

Deviant behavior in crime

Most theories of white-collar crime develop along the behavioral dimension. Researchers introduce numerous suggestions to explain white-collar individuals such as Madoff, Rajaratman, and Schilling. Along the behavioral dimension, we find strain theory (Langton and Piquero, 2007), deterrence theory (Comey, 2009; Holtfreter et al., 2008), self-control theory (Holtfreter et al., 2010; Piquero et al., 2010), obedience theory (Baird and Zelin, 2009), fear of falling (Piquero, 2012), negative life events (Engdahl, 2014), slippery slope (Welsh et al., 2014), and the American dream of economic success (Pratt and Cullen, 2005; Schoepfer and Piquero, 2006)—to name just a few. These theories suggest motives for committing white-collar crime, and they make crime a convenient option according to convenience theory. It is convenient for the criminal to be deceitful and breach trust to cause losses to others and gain for oneself (Pickett and Pickett, 2002).

In recent years, neutralization theory seems to increase in importance as a source of explanation. By applying neutralization techniques, white-collar criminals think they are doing nothing wrong. They deny responsibility, injury, and victim. They condemn the condemners. They claim appeal to higher loyalties and normality of action. They claim entitlement, and they argue the case of legal mistake. They find their own mistakes acceptable. They argue a dilemma arose, whereby they made a reasonable tradeoff before committing the act (Siponen and Vance, 2010).

Benson and Simpson (2015: 145) found that white-collar criminals seldom think of injury or victims:

> Many white-collar offenses fail to match this common-sense stereotype because the offenders do not set out intentionally to harm any specific

individual. Rather, the consequences of their illegal acts fall upon impersonal organizations or a
diffuse and unseen mass of people.

White-collar crime is sometimes referred to as victimless crime. However, as evidenced by Gottschalk (2015a,b,c), it is always possible to identify victims of white-collar crime. He found that the most frequent victims are: (1) employers, (2) tax collectors, (3) customers, and (4) banks.

The idea of neutralization techniques (Sykes and Matza, 1957) resulted from work on Sutherland's (1949) differential association theory. According to this theory, people are always aware of their moral obligation to abide by the law, and they are aware that they have the same moral obliga-tion within themselves to avoid illegitimate acts. The theory postulates that criminal behavior learning occurs in association with those who find such criminal behavior favorable and in isolation from those who find it unfavorable (Benson and Simpson, 2015). Crime is relatively convenient when there is no guilt feeling for doing something learned from others.

Evidence of neutralization can be found in autobiographies by white-collar criminals such as Kerik (2015), Bogen (2008), Eriksen (2010), and Fosse and Magnusson (2004). Bernard B. Kerik was the former police com-missioner in New York, who served 3 years in prison. He seems to deny responsibility, to condemn his condemners, and to suggest normality of action.

Bystrova and Gottschalk (2015) phrased the question: Why does the ruling class punish their own? They argue that the elite decide what is right and wrong, and they manage law enforcement. This is in line with social conflict theory. When a member of the elite breaks the law, it is not considered a real crime. The act is not violent, and it is committed by one of their own.

Another important source of explanation is strain theory, ever since Gottfredson and Hirschi (1990) in their classic book on the gen-eral theory of crime wrote about pressure crime. Strain may involve the removal of positively valued stimuli (Johnson and Groff, 2014). Agnew (2005) identified three categories of strain: failure to achieve positive goals, the removal of positive stimuli, and the presentation of negative stimuli. Strain theory posits that each type of strain ultimately leads to deviance for slightly different reasons. All three types tend to increase the likelihood that an individual will experience negative emotions in proportion to the magnitude, duration, and closeness of the stress. Strain characterizes a condition that individuals dislike. The theory argues that structural strain weakens the ability of normative standards to regulate behavior (Pratt and Cullen, 2005). Strain creates the need for a convenient solution to the problem.

Research by Ragatz et al. (2012) is an example of work that explores psychological traits among white-collar offenders. Their research results suggest that white-collar offenders have lower scores on lifestyle criminality, but higher scores on some measures of psychopathology and psychopathic traits compared to nonwhite-collar offenders. Similarly, McKay et al. (2010) examined the psychopathology of the white-collar criminal acting as a corporate leader. They looked at the impact of a leader's behavior on other employees and the organizational culture developed during his or her tenure. Narcissistic behavior is suggested often to be observed among white-collar offenders (Arnulf and Gottschalk, 2013; Galvin et al., 2015; Ouimet, 2009, 2010).

Galvin et al. (2015) suggest narcissistic organizational identification as an explanation for behaviors that exploit the organization for personal benefit. They define narcissistic organizational identification as a form of organizational identification that features the individual's tendency to see his or her identity as core to the definition of the organization. This is in contrast to conventional conceptualizations of organizational identification, where the individual sees the organization as core to the definition of self.

Some theorists believe that authorities can reduce crime by means of deterrents. Crime prevention (the goal of deterrence) assumes that criminals or potential criminals will think carefully before committing a crime if the likelihood of detection and/or the fear of swift and severe punishment are present. According to Comey (2009), deterrence works best when punishment is swift and certain.

Scholars apply self-control theory in two different directions. First, the theory proposes that individuals commit crime because of low self-control. The theory contends that individuals who lack self-control are more likely to engage in problematic behavior—such as criminal behavior—over their life course because of its time-stable nature (Gottfredson and Hirschi, 1990). Second, the desire to control and the general wish to be in control of everything and everybody might be a characteristic of some white-collar criminals, meaning that low self-control can lead to heavy control of others. Desire for control is the general wish to be in control over everyday life events. Desire for control is similar to low self-control in terms of behavioral manifestations and influence on the decision-making power of individuals (Piquero et al., 2010).

Low self-control finds support in anomie theory. Anomie refers to a sense of normlessness, which can occur when there is a strong emphasis on the desirability of material success and individual achievement (Schoepfer and Piquero, 2006). Benson and Simpson (2015) suggest that coupled with the cultural themes of success and endless striving are a cultural uncertainty and confusion about where the line between acceptable and unacceptable business behavior is developing. Sutherland (1983) finds this uncertainty and confusion in social disorganization, where anomie as lack of standards direct the behavior of members of an organization toward deviant behavior.

Anomie theory is also applied to society, where the anomie form of social disorganization is related to change from the earlier system of free competition and free enterprise in pure capitalism, to the developing system of governmental regulation of business and criminalization of certain forms of business conduct as white-collar crime (Sutherland, 1983). For example, it was only two decades ago that corruption was treated as regular marketing expenses in the accounting of Norwegian business enterprises.

Welsh et al. (2014) argue that many recent scandals result from a slippery slope in which a series of small infractions gradually increase over time. Committing small indiscretions over time may gradually lead people to complete larger unethical acts that they otherwise would have judged to be impermissible.

The slippery slope theory thus suggests an incremental progression toward serious white-collar crime. The sliding individual experiences no resistance or reaction, while at the same time starts to gain benefits. An offender first moves and subsequently removes the borderline between right and wrong from his or her mind.

White-collar crime tends to occur when individuals are extremely ambitious on behalf of the organization and on behalf of themselves. Ambitions have to be linked to opportunities to enable financial crime. Convenience theory suggests that the link between ambition and opportunity is at its optimal point when individuals are in their forties. Successful professionals tend to reach the peak of their career in terms of top positions in their late forties. Hence, it is no surprise that the average age of convicted white-collar criminals in Norway is 44 years when they commit financial crime and 49 years when they go to prison (Gottschalk, 2015c). In Germany, they are 47 years old when they go to prison (Blickle et al., 2006), and in the Netherlands white-collar criminals are 42 years old when they are prosecuted (Onna et al., 2014).

A number of situational factors may influence the tendency toward crime. Criminogenic tendency, for example, is dependent on the job situation for the individual. If the individual feels his or her own power base threatened, then corporate crime may revitalize the power base. If the individual feels that he may lose his job, occupational crime can help compensate for future financial loss. If the individual feels badly treated, occupational crime may be an option to cause damage to his employer. In these kinds of situations, criminal behavior might be explained by hygiene factors as suggested by Herzberg, rather than satisfiers such as self-realization as suggested by both Herzberg and Maslow.

Convenience theory argues that it is a convenient option to commit financial crime. It is a planned behavior (Ajzen, 2014). White-collar criminals are comfortable with their own choice of illegal actions. Comfort is the opposite of discomfort. In comfort theory, comfort is characterized by relief, ease, and transcendence. If the criminal is in a comfortable state of contentment, the person experiences comfort in the ease sense, for example, how one might feel after having issues that are causing anxiety addressed (Carrington and Catasus, 2007).

Labeling self-identity of criminals

Labeling theory argues that self-identity and behavior of individuals may be determined or influenced by the terms used to describe or classify them. It is associated with the concepts of self-fulfilling prophecy and stereotyping. Labeling theory holds that deviance is not inherent in an act, but instead focuses on the tendency of majorities to label minorities negatively of those seen as deviant from standard cultural norms. The theory states that the label of deviant, and the stigma that comes with such a label, is more a product of society than it is of the individual committing the deviant act. What people in one society may consider deviant, or at one point in history considered deviant, another society may not consider deviant at all. Thus, deviance is not a quality of the act the person commits, but rather the consequence of the application by others of rules and sanctions to an alleged offender (Mingus and Burchfield, 2012).

Furthermore, labeling theory suggests that once a person receives a deviant label, the person may be denied equal opportunities because of this stigma, and thus will have a greater propensity to repeat the deviant behavior. Furthermore, labeling theory holds that those fettered with an obdurate, stigmatizing label often find it easier to act in accordance with that label than to shed the deviant label. The effects of a labeled situation, then, are external, with constraints imposed on the deviant by society (Mingus and Burchfield, 2012).

Labeling can lead to adoption of a deviant status caused by self-labeling. Self-labeling is a person's social identity which may classify one, in one's own eyes and others' eyes, as normal or deviant, and as a success or a failure (Hayes, 2010). Once a white-collar offender receives the label of a criminal, he may or may not accept this label. He may accept this interpretation of his behavior, but not see it as an aspect of himself that carries over into other areas of his life.

One of the most important meanings in labeling theory is the meaning that people give to themselves. They act toward themselves according to the meanings they have for themselves. Each person's self-image is primarily a result of social interactions with others.

A distinction can be made between primary and secondary deviance, where labeling is causing secondary deviance. While primary deviance refers to behavior an individual committed before public labeling, secondary deviant acts are those that result from the change in self-concept brought about by the labeling process. Secondary deviance occurs through labeling in three ways. First, one's self-concept experiences cause alteration. Second, one's range of conventional opportunities seems limited. Finally, one moves into a deviant subculture.

A subculture is the lower, subordinate, or deviant status of a social group. Labeled subculture groups are distinguished by their class, ethnicity, language, age, generation, and situation. These cultural and socio-structural variables make subcultures relatively homogeneous. Subcultures bear specific and similar cultural identities to qualify as such (Nwalozie, 2015).

Regarding altering one's self-concept, people who violate the law and experience arrest by the police may change their perceptions of and attitudes toward themselves. When tried in court they may alter their self-perceptions and come to think of themselves as criminals or deviants. Even if one's self-concept does not change because of labeling, a second possible effect of labeling is a reduction of opportunities for and harm to the social relationships of individuals labeled by the criminal justice system. Thus, labeling can segregate people from conventional realms even in the absence of physical obstacles such as incarceration. In addition, labeling can push people into antisocial subcultures where they learn criminal motives and skills from peers. Each path reinforces the others, leading to greater involvement in crime and deviance for the labeled individual.

Labeling theory assumes that deviance is not a property of behavior but rather the result of how others regard that behavior. Thus, labeling theory is often referred to as the social reaction perspective. According to the theory, without societal reaction, deviance would most likely remain infrequent and unorganized. Labeling theory in our context focuses its attention on the process of criminalization. Once an individual has engaged in deviance, he or she can be labeled and segregated from society. This process creates outsiders. The criminal label tends to override other labels, so that people think of the person primarily as a criminal. As society begins to view these people as deviant and respond accordingly, the individuals can internalize their labels and react to society's response by continuing to engage in deviance now expected of them.

Labeling theory connects to attribution theory, when individuals search for explanations that lie within the self. This is internal attribution such as, "It's my fault." Attribution theory generally explains how people respond to novel, unexpected, and negative events. One possible response is to blame oneself. However, many criminals have a tendency to attribute causes of crime to everyone else but themselves, "It's somebody else's fault." Attribution theory is about identifying causality predicated on internal and external circumstances (Eberly et al., 2011: 731):

> Identifying the locus of causality has been at the core of attribution theory since its inception and has generated an extensive research stream in the field of organizational behavior. But the question emerges whether the "internal" and "external" categories capture the entire conceptual space of this phenomenon.

Based on this argument, Eberly et al. (2011) suggest there is a third category in addition to internal explanation and external explanation, which they label "relational explanation," "It's the situation's fault." Exploring these three categories of attributes helps seek causal explanations on how persons react in criminal situations.

Attribution theory is a part of social psychology, which studies how humans spontaneously attribute reasons, guilt, and responsibility in situations that arise. The fundamental attribution error is a term used to designate overemphasis on person factors rather than situational factors in order to explain behavior.

When an explanation is sought in the relationship, interdependence theory proposes a variety of situations with different degrees of interdependence, which may be described through characteristics such as the extent to which relationship partners need to rely on each other for information, have covarying versus conflicting interests, and participate in each other's tasks. The more interdependent individuals are, the more their actions affect not only their own outcomes, but also the outcomes of others. However, in a crime perspective, an offender is always a person and never a relationship.

Slippery slope decline

Slippery slope means that a person, a group, or the whole organization slides over time from legal to illegal activities. Arjoon (2008: 78) explains slippery slope theory in the following way:

> As commonsense experience tells us, it is the small infractions that can lead to the larger ones. An organization that overlooks the small infractions of its employees creates a culture of acceptance that may lead to its own demise. This phenomenon is captured by the metaphor of the slippery slope. Many

unethical acts occur without the conscience aware-
ness of the person who engaged in the misconduct.
Specifically, unethical behavior is most likely to follow the path of a slippery slope, defined as a grad-
ual decline in which no one event makes one aware
that he or she is acting unethically. The majority of
unethical behaviors are unintentional and ordinary,
thus affecting everyone and providing support for
unethical behavior when people unconsciously
lower the bar over time through small changes in
their ethical behavior.

Arjoon (2008: 78) argues that sliding and moral collapse might be
explained by a phenomenon related to compromises over time:

It explains how over a period of time mild job frus-
trations develop into a pathological, materialistic
attitude and behavior that leads to devastating consequences. This phenomenon is also known by the
metaphors "the thin edge of the wedge" and "the
camel's nose" (once a camel has managed to place
its nose within a tent, the rest of the camel inevi-
tably follows). The CoC reflects a framework that
demonstrates the potential for radical deterioration
of sociomoral inhibitions and a perceived sense of
permissibility for deviant conduct. In other words,
if something relatively harmless is allowed or
accepted, it may lead to a downward trend that ends
with the unthinkable.

Welsh et al. (2014) argue that many recent scandals can be described
as resulting from a slippery slope in which a series of small infractions
gradually increase over time. Committing small indiscretions over time
may gradually lead people to complete larger unethical acts that they otherwise would have judged to be impermissible.

The slippery slope theory is in contrast to individual theories such
as the standard economic model of rational choice theory as described
in the next chapter. Moral behavior is shaped by psychological and
organizational processes, where individuals are motivated to view
themselves in a positive manner that corresponds with their moral values. Individuals tend to rationalize minor unethical acts so that they
may derive some benefit without being forced to negatively update their
self-concept. For example, a minor transgression such as taking a pen
home from the office may seem permissible, whereas taking money out

of the company cash drawer may more clearly be thought of as stealing (Welsh et al., 2014).

Self-control and desire for control

Those with low self-control are, given the opportunity, more likely to offend than those possessing high self-control. This is the essence of self-control theory (Hansen, 2009). Personality traits such as impulsivity may predict delinquency and other risk-taking behaviors. Individuals with low self-control tend to have a present orientation, as opposed to those oriented toward the future. They tend to be unable to perceive negative, long-term consequences that may outweigh the positive, short-term benefits of the behavior. As criminal acts immediately may gratify an individual's desire, individuals with low self-control will more likely engage in those acts. In addition to impulsivity, risk-taking, and short-sightedness, characteristics include insensitivity and preference for task accomplishment. Gottfredson and Hirschi (1990) also mention preference for physical activity, quick temperedness, and preference for simple tasks.

Those with high desire for control are, given the opportunity, more likely to offend than those possessing low desire for control. Desire for control is defined as the wish to be in control over everyday life events. In our organizational context, desire for control is concerned with desire for control of corporate offending (Piquero et al., 2010). The desire to control and the general wish to be in control of everything and everybody might be a characteristic of some white-collar criminals. Those high in desire for control may be decisive, assertive, and strongly dislike unpleasant situations or failures. They try to avoid negative situations by manipulating events to ensure desired outcomes. They tend to attribute success to their own hard work, while they blame failures on others. Similar to individuals with low self-control, individuals with high desire for control tend to engage in risk-taking behaviors, though only when the task is important to them.

The main distinction between the two concepts of self-control and desire for control is how the future is viewed. Those with low self-control tend not to consider the future and have a present-day orientation. Those with high desire for control tend to be oriented toward the future and responsive to how their acts will impact the situation in the long run. Desire for control is similar to low self-control in terms of behavioral manifestations and influence on the decision-making process. Desire for control appears to be better equipped for explaining corporate criminality, whereas low self-control appears to be better equipped for explaining more traditional offending (Piquero et al., 2010).

Control balance theory measures the potential for individuals to commit corporate crime. Control balance theory utilizes a ratio of control

exercised relative to degree of control experienced. Control balances sur-
pluses, rather than deficits, lead to white collar and corporate deviance
(Hansen, 2009).

Strain for success and status

Classic and general strain theory suggests that strain can and does predict
crime at lower socio-economic levels. The theory implies a causal path
between low social class status and crime. However, the basic focus on the
stresses associated with being poor is incompatible with studies of white-
collar crime. There is indeed a phenomenon of wanting more wealth and
being able to acquire it at all levels of society. Those with wealth can feel
equally strained by the desire to gain even more money as those with less
to begin with.

Thus, strain need not be specifically tied to economic status because it
is a reaction to any perceived negative aspect of an individual's, a group's,
or an organization's environment. Complex, large-scale corporate-type
offenses, such as antitrust and securities violations, tend to be committed
by business executives with a high socio-economic status.

Agnew (2005) identified three categories of strain: failure to achieve
positively valued goals, the removal of positively valued stimuli, and the
presentation of negative or noxious stimuli. Strain theory posits that each
type of strain ultimately leads to deviance for slightly different reasons.
All three types tend to increase the likelihood that an individual will
experience negative emotions in proportion to the magnitude, duration,
and closeness of the stress. Strains most likely to result in crime are those
seen as unjust and high in magnitude, associated with low social control, being close in threat and consequence, and creating some incentive
to engage in criminal behavior.

Strains are defined as events and conditions that are disliked by individuals. Strains lead to negative emotions and thereby create pressure for
corrective action. Crime is one possible action, which might be perceived
as a means to escape from or reduce strains (Froggio and Agnew, 2007).
The strain of pursuing goals within diverse opportunity structures may
lead to adaptations such as crime, delinquency, and other deviant behavior (Hoffmann, 2002). Delinquency results when individuals are unable to
achieve their goals through legitimate channels (Agnew, 2012).

Sources of strain include failure to achieve inspiration, aspiration, and
fair and just outcome. Individuals who suffer failure in inspiration, aspiration, and receiving fair outcome, which increases their reflected appraisal,
would commit financial crime because they want to reclaim their power
of advantage.

In an empirical study by Langton and Piquero (2007), they found
that strain theory was useful for predicting a select group of white-collar

offenses. Using data from convicted white-collar offenders, they examined the ability of strain theory to explain white-collar offenses. First, they found that strain was positively and significantly related to financial motivations for offending. Next, they found that individuals reporting higher levels of strain were more likely to engage in more complex types of financial crime. Third, strain relates to negative emotions. Finally, strain among white-collar offenders was negatively related to business-type motivations for offending.

Strain among white-collar criminals can be measured in terms of events such as (Langton and Piquero, 2007):

1. Number of legal marriages, where two or more legal marriages are assumed to imply more strain.
2. Neighborhood, where lower class or lower middle class are assumed to imply more strain.
3. Academic performance, where failure to achieve positively valued goals is assumed to imply more strain.
4. Total assets, where less wealth is assumed to imply more strain.
5. Total liabilities, where more debt is assumed to imply more strain.
6. Employment history, where failure to achieve positively valued goals is assumed to imply more strain.

Levels of white-collar crime can be measured in terms of offense types, which form a hierarchical pattern in terms of their organizational complexity and the harm they inflicted (Langton and Piquero, 2007):

1. Low-level white-collar crime such as embezzlement, tax offenses, and credit fraud.
2. Mid-level white-collar crime such as mail fraud, bribery, and false claims.
3. Complex large-scale corporate crime such as antitrust and securities violations.

By means of logistic regression, Langton and Piquero (2007) attempted to predict crime level by strain factors. They proposed that more strain would lead to higher level of white-collar crime. Overall, however, they found no significant support for this explanation.

Criminal personality disorders

Perri (2013) studied white-collar criminals in terms of their psychological traits. He found that the prototypical high-socioeconomic-status offenders, such as today's chief executive officers and chief financial officers, can be explained by the application of psychological trait theory. There is a negative synergy that develops when criminal thinking traits combine with the psychological traits of narcissism and psychopathy to create risk factors for white-collar offending. Psychological trait theory may be especially applicable to those who hold some of the highest positions in corporate organizations, who influence corporate culture, and who, at times, are considered visionaries in their respective industries. They may turn out as false prophets.

Lack of self-control is often linked to narcissism and psychopathy. Narcissism and psychopathy increase when there is a lack of self-control, and lack of self-control is often found among chief executives. Narcissism is a visible risk factor for white-collar crime. Narcissists have several typical characteristics (Perri, 2013: 334):

> Narcissists typically display a pervasive pattern of grandiosity, entitlement, exploitative eagerness in the pursuit of goals, a need for admiration, a lack of empathy for others, and a belief that one is superior, unique, coupled with inflated views of their own accomplishments and/or abilities.

Perri (2013) writes that not all psychopaths are in prison, some of them are in the board room. Psychopathy is about irresponsible leadership and increased tendency of white-collar crime. Psychopathy is characterized by manipulation and unsocial behavior. Unsocial behavior refers to avoidance of actions undertaken to benefit others, including donating, sharing, comforting, and helping (Fehr et al., 2015).

The recent approach to studying white-collar crime incorporates the offender's personality disorder(s) as a risk factor in the decision to commit crime, even though there are legitimate debates on how important personality disorders may be, and which specific traits are common among offenders. White-collar criminals tend to harbor antisocial personality disorders and do not necessarily suffer from a temporary moral lapse when committing crime.

McGurrin et al. (2013) argue that white-collar crime research is under-represented in the criminological and criminal justice literature relative to traditional street crime. Less than half of all U.S. doctoral programs offer a white-collar crime course, much less require it. Whether one examines the criminalization of white-collar offenses, the allocation of resources for its enforcement, the prosecution of white-collar crime, the sentencing of white-collar offenders, or the representation of white-collar crime in the research literature, the results are almost uniformly the same: white-collar crime is not treated as seriously as traditional street crime. An explanation for this under-representation is that white-collar crime is considered less serious among higher and more influential levels in society, where these criminals can be found. Even with personality disorders is less attention paid to possible consequences in terms of misconduct and crime.

Walters and Geyer (2004) studied criminal thinking and identity in white-collar offenders depending on whether they had a prior history of crime. Results show that white-collar offenders with no prior history registered lower levels of criminal thinking, criminal identification, and deviance than white-collar offenders previously arrested. The study included both white-collar inmates as well as non-white-collar inmates by survey instruments. Significant group differences were noted on the Psychological Inventory of Criminal Thinking Styles Self-Assertion/Deception Scale, Social Identity as a Criminal Centrality subscale, Social Identity as a Criminal In-Group ties subscale, and Lifestyle Criminality Screening Form-Revised.

Ragatz et al. (2012) extended Walters and Geyer's (2004) work by exploring psychopathic characteristics and psychopathology of white-collar offenders compared with non-white-collar offenders. The study included demographics, psychopathic traits, and psychopathology among white-collar criminals. They attempted to develop a psychological profile of criminal offenders, and how this profile differs from non-white-collar offenders on criminal thinking and lifestyle criminality. Results demonstrated white-collar offenders had lower scores on lifestyle criminality but scored higher on some measures of psychopathology and psychopathic traits compared with non-white-collar offenders. White-collar offenders were found to be more outgoing, calculating, and controlling in social interactions. They tend to be low in agreeableness and high in narcissism. This can reflect high egocentricity, which means that offenders are more likely to appear self-centered and invested in their own needs when interacting with others.

Personality disorders are often classified into main categories and subcategories. One common classification is the three categories' approach of dramatic, eccentric, and anxious. While such classification might seem stigmatizing, it helps explain criminals and their behaviors. However, it is important to be aware of potential shortcomings, including overlap between categories, which often makes it difficult to decide what the primary category is for an offender.

A study in the United States concluded that two main characteristics of white-collar criminals are irresponsibility and antisocial behavior as compared to other white-collar individuals. Collins and Schmidt (1993) examined a personality-based integrity test and homogenous bio data scales as reflected in their ability to discriminate white-collar criminals from other white-collar employees. A bio data scale is a systematic method of scaling life history experiences. The sample included 365 prison inmates incarcerated in 23 federal correctional institutions for white-collar offenses, and 344 individuals employed in upper-level positions of authority. The various measures were administered to prisoners at the prison sites and to employees at their workplaces. Results show that non-offenders scored significantly higher on performance than offenders. Individuals with high scores on the performance scale are described as dependable, reliable, responsible, and motivated to high performance on the job, and rule abiding and conscientious in their work behavior. Furthermore, results show that non-offenders scored significantly higher on socialization than offenders. Individuals who score high on this scale are predicted to be dependable, honest, conscientious, rule abiding, and are not inclined to be opportunistic or manipulative.

The third measure was responsibility, which shares some common characteristics with socialization. The responsibility scale measures the degree to which the individual is conscientious, responsible, dependable, and has a commitment to social, civic, or moral values. Persons who score low on this scale often show antisocial behavior, and, in the workplace, higher scores predict responsibility and attention to duty. Results show that offenders scored significantly lower on the responsibility scale than nonoffenders. The fourth and final measure was tolerance, where nonoffenders had a significantly higher score. Persons scoring high on the tolerance scale are tolerant and trusting, whereas low scorers tend to be suspicious, judgmental toward others, and do not believe they can depend on others. The common theme running through these four scales applied by Collins and Schmidt (1993) is conscientiousness and positive attitudes toward responsible and prosocial behaviors and activities, suggesting that the discriminating factor between offenders and nonoffenders might be conscientiousness. Prosocial behavior refers to voluntary action undertaken to benefit others, including donating, sharing, comforting, and helping (Fehr et al., 2015).

Study in Germany

A study by Blickle et al. (2006) in Germany concluded that two main characteristics of white-collar criminals are hedonism and narcissism as compared to other white-collar individuals. They found that: (1) the greater the degree of hedonism is present in a business person, the greater is the tendency to commit economic offenses; (2) the more diagnostic features of a narcissistic personality disorder an individual in a high-ranking white-collar position exhibits, the higher is the probability that this person will commit a white-collar crime; and (3) the lower the behavioral self-control of a person in a high-ranking white-collar position is in business, the greater is the probability that this person will commit a white-collar crime.

The study by Blickle et al. (2006) examined the following hypotheses in their research:

Hypothesis 1. The greater the degree of hedonism present in a businessperson, the greater the tendency to commit economic offenses.

Hypothesis 2. The more diagnostic features of a narcissistic personality disorder an individual in a high-ranking white-collar position exhibits, the higher the probability that this person will commit a white-collar crime.

Hypothesis 3. The lower the behavioral self-control of a person in a high-ranking white-collar position in business, the greater the probability that this person will commit a white-collar crime.

Hypothesis 4. The higher the rating of conscientiousness that a person in a high-ranking white-collar position gives him or herself, the lower the probability that this person will commit a white-collar crime.

The first hypothesis concerns hedonism. People for whom material things and enjoyment generally possess a high value are called hedonists. Living in a culture in which a very high value is placed on material success and individual wealth can serve as one cause of strong hedonism. With this in mind, the first hypothesis is that, everything else being equal, the greater the degree of hedonism present in a businessperson, the greater the tendency to commit economic offenses.

The second hypothesis concerns narcissism. The essential features are a pattern of grandiosity, a need for admiration, and a lack of empathy.

The third hypothesis concerns self-control. It is argued that criminals lack self-control. Generally, criminals tend to engage in criminal and similar acts such as school misconduct when younger, substance abuse, physical aggression, wastefulness, absenteeism and tardiness, reckless driving, antisocial problem behavior, job quitting, or promiscuous sex.

The fourth hypothesis concerns conscientiousness. This is a concept with attributes like striving for competence, order, fulfillment of duties, achievement, self-discipline, and deliberate action.

Blickle et al. (2006) tested these hypotheses empirically by comparing results from a survey of white-collar criminal prison inmates with managers working in various companies. Their empirical test was thus a comparison of offenders with nonoffenders. Their empirical results indicate support for Hypotheses 1, 2, and 3.

Hypothesis 4 was not supported. Blickle et al. (2006) discuss the lack of support for the last hypothesis by arguing that some kind of conscientiousness might well be needed for individuals committing white-collar crime. Accordingly, no statistically significant difference was found between offenders and nonoffenders.

McKay et al. (2010) examined the psychopathology of the white-collar criminal acting as a corporate leader. They looked at the impact of a leader's behavior on other employees and the organizational culture developed during his or her reign. They proposed the presented 12-step process to explain how an organization can move from a legally operating organization to one in which unethical behavior is ignored and wrongdoing promoted.

There are a number of explanatory approaches to white-collar crime in business from scientific fields such as economics, sociology, psychiatry, and psychology, as documented in this book. In economics, the rational choice approach implies that if the rationally expected utility of the action clearly outweighs the expected disadvantages resulting from the action thus leaving some net material advantage, then every person will commit the offense in question. One of the many suppositions of this theory is that people generally strive for enjoyment and the fulfillment of wishes for material goods (Blickle et al., 2006). Sociological theories of white-collar crime postulate that managers who commit economic offenses live in a social setting, that is, a culture, in which a very high value is placed on material success and individual wealth. Both economic theories and sociological theories are of the opinion that strong striving for wealth and enjoyment in some way contributes to economic crimes committed by managers (Blickle et al., 2006).

Psychiatrists view the behavior of white-collar criminals in terms of narcissistic fantasies of omnipresence. White-collar criminals display little guilt and identify themselves with the ideal of achieving success at any price. The essential features of such individuals are a pervasive pattern of grandiosity, a need for admiration, and a lack of empathy (Blickle et al., 2006).

In psychology, people for whom material things and enjoyment generally possess a high value are called hedonists. Living in a culture in which a very high value is placed on material success and individual wealth can serve as one cause of strong hedonism (Blickle et al., 2006).

Stanton Wheeler's (1992) research into white-collar crime motivation illustrates how psychological factors can work together with situational factors. He asks why persons who are already extremely wealthy take the chance to involve themselves in white-collar crime, when they earn little from the crime compared to what they already possess. One answer is that they fear falling off the financial cliff and losing their wealth and status. Therefore, they work constantly to remain successful, preferably more successful than others, while not having the time to relax and enjoy wealth because of the fear of failure. It is this struggle for financial success and maintenance of that success that are important.

Categories of personality disorder

In line with the state-of-the-art conceptualization of personality disorders, we represented the categorical perspective that personality disorders are qualitatively distinct clinical syndromes. According to the Diagnostic and Statistical Manual of Mental Disorders, Section III from the American Psychiatric Association in 2013, important areas of personality dysfunction are the following six (features selected and cited from Section II):

1. *Schizotypal personality disorder.* The essential feature of the schizotypal personality disorder is a pervasive pattern of social and interpersonal deficits marked by acute discomfort with close relationships as well as by cognitive or perceptual distortions and eccentricities of behavior. Individuals with schizotypal disorder often appear odd. Individuals with schizotypal personality disorder often have ideas of reference, that is, incorrect interpretations of casual incidents and external events as having a particular and unusual meaning specifically for the person. These individuals may be superstitious or preoccupied with paranormal phenomena that are outside the norms of their subculture. They may feel that they have special powers to sense events before they happen or to read others' thoughts. They may believe that they have magical control over others, which can be implemented directly or indirectly through compliance with magical rituals. Their speech may include unusual or idiosyncratic phrasing and construction.

2. *Antisocial personality disorder.* This is a pattern of disregard for, and violation of, the rights of others. Individuals with antisocial personality disorder fail to conform to social norms with respect to lawful behavior. They may repeatedly perform acts that are grounds for arrest (whether they are arrested or not), such as destroying property, harassing others, stealing, or pursuing illegal occupations. Persons with this disorder disregard the wishes, rights, or feelings of others. They are frequently deceitful and manipulative in order to gain personal profit or pleasure. They may repeatedly lie, use an alias, con others, or malinger. A pattern of impulsivity may be manifested by a failure to plan ahead. Decisions are made on the spur of the moment, without forethought and without consideration for the consequences to self or others. Individuals with antisocial personality disorder tend to be irritable and aggressive and may repeatedly get into physical fights or commit acts of physical assault. These individuals also display a reckless disregard for the safety of themselves or others.

3. *Borderline personality disorder.* This is a pattern of instability in interpersonal relationships, self-image, and affects, and marked impulsivity. Individuals with borderline personality disorder make frantic efforts to avoid real or imagined abandonment. The perception of impending separation or rejection, or the loss of external structure,

can lead to profound changes in self-image, affect, cognition, and behavior. These individuals are very sensitive to environmental circumstances. They experience intense abandonment fears and inappropriate anger even when faced with a realistic time-limited separation or when there are unavoidable changes in plans. They may believe that this "abandonment" implies they are "bad." These abandonment fears are related to an intolerance of being alone and a need to have other people with them. Individuals with borderline personality disorder have a pattern of unstable and intense relationships. They may idealize potential caregivers or lovers at the first or second meeting, demand to spend a lot of time together, and share the most intimate details early in a relationship.

4. *Narcissistic personality disorder.* This is a pattern of grandiosity, need for admiration, and lack of empathy. Individuals with this disorder have a grandiose sense of self. They routinely overestimate their abilities and inflate their accomplishments, often appearing boastful and pretentious. They may blithely assume that others attribute the same value to their efforts and may be surprised when the praise they expect and feel they deserve is not forthcoming. Often implicit in the inflated judgments of their own accomplishments is an underestimation (devaluation) of the contributions of others. Individuals with narcissistic personality disorder are often preoccupied with fantasies of unlimited success, power, brilliance, beauty, or ideal love. They may ruminate about "long overdue" admiration and privilege and compare themselves favorably with famous or privileged people. Individuals with narcissistic personality disorder believe that they are superior, special, or unique and expect others to recognize them as such.

5. *Avoidant personality disorder.* The essential feature of this disorder is a pervasive pattern of social inhibition, feelings of inadequacy, and hypersensitivity to negative evaluation. Individuals with avoidant personality disorder avoid work activities that involve significant interpersonal contact because of fears of criticism, disapproval, or rejection. Offers of job promotions may be declined because the new responsibilities might result in criticism from co-workers. These individuals avoid making new friends unless they are certain they will be liked and accepted without criticism. Until they pass stringent tests proving the contrary, other people are assumed to be critical and disapproving. Individuals with this disorder will not join in group activities unless there are repeated and generous offers of support and nurturance. Interpersonal intimacy is often difficult for these individuals, although they are able to establish intimate relationships when there is assurance of uncritical acceptance. They may act with restraint, have difficulty talking about themselves, and

withhold intimate feelings for fear of being exposed, ridiculed, or shamed.

6. *Obsessive-compulsive personality disorder.* This is a pattern of preoccupation with orderliness, perfectionism, and mental and interpersonal control, at the expense of flexibility, openness, and efficiency. Individuals with obsessive-compulsive personality disorder attempt to maintain a sense of control through painstaking attention to rules, trivial details, procedures, lists, schedules, or form to the extent that the major point of the activity is lost. They are excessively careful and prone to repetition, paying extraordinary attention to detail and repeatedly checking for possible mistakes. They are oblivious to the fact that other people tend to become very annoyed at the delays and inconveniences that result from this behavior. Time is poorly allocated, and the most important tasks are left to the last moment. The perfectionism and self-imposed high standards of performance cause significant dysfunction and distress in these individuals. They may become so involved in making every detail of a project absolutely perfect that the project is never finished.

Some white-collar criminals have a cognitive bias including optimism, illusory superiority, and illusion of control, which can thereby lead to neglect of probability of negative events. Optimism bias entails believing that favorable outcomes are more probable than they actually are, and that unfavorable outcomes are less probable than they actually are. Illusory superiority means that the individual believes to be above-average in most circumstances.

As discussed in the empirical study of criminal CEOs, mindsets are automatic cognitive pattern recognition responses that develop after repeated exposure to tasks. Most mindsets are not readily accessible to conscious reflection, and since they are not in themselves related to legal or ethical issues, they will also exert their influence on behavior in illegal circumstances. Increased pressure on accountability for CEOs has paradoxically reduced the possibility of monitoring their behavior, creating greater discretion, more secrecy, and an even greater emphasis on profitability. In adverse times, the CEO mindsets that develop accordingly may become liabilities, predisposing CEOs to seize opportunities for personal maximization of gains rather than gains for other stakeholders.

Crime deterrence mechanisms

Some theorists believe that crime can be reduced through the use of deterrents. Crime prevention (the goal of deterrence) is based on the assumption that criminals or potential criminals will think carefully before committing a crime if the likelihood of getting caught and/or the fear of swift and severe punishment are present. Crime prevention can be defined as any intervention intended to block or reduce the likelihood of the occurrence of a criminal act at a given location or the onset of criminal behavior within an individual.

Based on such a belief, *general deterrence theory* holds that crime can be thwarted by the threat of punishment, while *special deterrence theory* holds that penalties for criminal acts should be sufficiently severe that convicted criminals will never repeat their acts (Lyman and Potter, 2007). Deterrence theory postulates that people commit such crimes on the basis of rational calculations about perceived personal benefits, and that the threat of legal sanctions will deter people owing to fear of punishment (Yusuf and Babalola, 2009). Laws are designed to deter bribery, corruption, and other forms of financial crime (Yeoh, 2011).

According to Comey (2009) and as mentioned earlier in this book, deterrence works best when punishment is swift and certain. White-collar sentencing in the United States in the years since Sarbanes-Oxley, however, has been anything but fast. This is the case in other countries as well. For example, in Norway, white-collar crime investigations typically take more than a year before the suspected white-collar criminal is brought on trial.

Deterrence theory seems more appropriate for occupational crime than for corporate crime (Robson, 2010: 121):

> Both courts and scholars have readily accepted deterrence as a justification for organizational criminal sanctioning. However, from the beginning legal scholars appeared to be uncomfortable with retribution as a goal of organizational criminal liability. Without consciousness and self-awareness, business organizations lacked the capacity to be morally blameworthy.

Deterrence theory argues that more severe punishment will deter potential criminals from committing crime (Lyman and Potter, 2007: 62):

> Special deterrence theory holds that penalties for criminal acts should be sufficiently severe that convicted criminals will never repeat their acts. For example, if a person arrested on a first-time marijuana possession charge is sentenced to spend 60 days in a boot camp designed for first-time offenders, the punishment is to convince him or her that the price for possessing marijuana is not worth the pleasure of using it.

Given the broad range of potential sentences provided after this act, within which judges essentially have complete discretion, the sentence can range from mere months in prison to decades. Moreover, unlike the average aspiring criminal actor, white-collar offenders usually know that they will have access to a lenient plea bargaining system. They are also often well aware of instances in which a court has departed downward from a guidelines sentence that touched the conscience of the court (Comey, 2009).

There is, of course, the alternative argument that deterrence is at its height when potential punishments are severe but unpredictable. Comey (2009) argues that such punishments may be imposed relatively randomly against some perpetrators but not others, and would theoretically provide a greater deterrent effect than a predictable but lower sentence—the probability of sentencing might be lower, but the risk would be much higher. An adherent to this view would see the Sarbanes-Oxley system, with all its disparities and broad-ranging discretion, as a step in the right direction.

Deterrence theory can be traced back to Jeremy Bentham (1748–1832) and Cesare Beccaria (1738–1794). They argued that individuals weigh up costs and benefits when deciding whether to commit a crime, and individuals choose crime when it pays. If an individual believes that the risk of getting caught is high, especially if there is a certainty of sanctions, and severe penalties that will be applied should one be caught (severity of sanctions), then deterrence theory posits that individuals will not commit crime (Siponen and Vance, 2010).

Informal sanctions and shame are included in sanctions today. Examples of informal sanctions are disapproval of friends or peers for a given action, personal media exposure of a negative kind, family breakup, and loss of position in the local society. Shame refers to a feeling of guilt or embarrassment that arises should others know of one's socially undesirable actions. Shame adversely affects an individual's self-esteem. In this perspective, deterrence comes from social bonding theory in the sense that a person would rely on the deterrence that would come from their environment such as relatives. Social bonding theory states that if an individual has a bond with people around them that are all law-abiding, then the person is less likely to commit crime.

The deterrence doctrine hypothesizes that the perceived threat of swift, certain, and severe sanctions will inhibit criminal activity. Schoepfer et al. (2007) asked the question whether perceptions of punishment vary between white-collar and street crime in the population. Using robbery and fraud as two exemplars, the findings indicate that while public perceptions of sanction certainty and severity suggested that street criminals were more likely to be caught and be sentenced to more severe sanctions than white-collar criminals, respondents' perceptions of which type of crime should be more severely punished indicated that robbery and fraud were considered equally serious types of crime. In a study by Holtfreter et al. (2008), respondents reported that violent criminals should be punished more severely than white-collar criminals.

Neutralization techniques

Criminals apply techniques in order to make them feel as though they have not done any wrong. These techniques represent neutralization techniques, whereby the feeling of guilt decreases and possibly disappears. Sykes and Matza (1957) proposed neutralization theory in its original formulation to explain how the desire to conform coexists with deviance.

Neutralization theory encompasses all these techniques, whereby offenders neutralize their feelings of guilt. In their original formulation of neutralization theory, Sykes and Matza (1957) proposed five techniques of neutralization: denial of responsibility, denial of injury, denial of the victim, condemnation of the condemners, and appeal to higher loyalties. These techniques found application in a number of later research studies (e.g., Benson and Simpson, 2015; Bock and Kenhove, 2011; Gottschalk and Smith, 2015; Heath, 2008; Moore and McMullan, 2009; Siponen and Vance, 2010):

1. *Denial of responsibility.* It is the belief by an individual that the person is not blameworthy because responsibility for his or her criminal behavior lies elsewhere. The offender here claims that one or more of the conditions of responsible agency were not present. The person committing the deviant act defines himself or herself as lacking responsibility for his or her actions. In this technique, the person rationalizes that the action in question is beyond his or her control. The offender views himself or herself as a billiard ball, helplessly propelled through different situations. Offenders will propose that they were victims of circumstances or others forced them into situations beyond their control. Corporate leaders can avoid taking on responsibility by claiming that laws regulating practices in many industries are enormously complex and difficult to interpret. They can avoid responsibility for their actions by maintaining ignorance about the risks that they are imposing on others. They can avoid knowing what their subordinates are doing.

2. *Denial of injury.* The offender seeks to minimize or deny the harm done. Denial of injury involves justifying an action by explaining that harm was minimal. The offender does not consider this misbehavior as serious because no party apparently suffers directly as a result of the action. Offenders insist that their actions did not cause any harm or damage. There is no relationship between wrongfulness and possible harm. Denying that actions are injurious is relatively easy for

white-collar criminals because they seldom witness the harm they cause firsthand.

3. *Denial of victim.* The offender may acknowledge the injury, but claims that the victim is unworthy of concern. Any blame for illegal actions are unjustified because the violated party deserves whatever injury it receives. Offenders believe that victims deserved whatever action offenders committed. In some types of securities offenses, such as insider trading, it may be difficult to identify victims in the traditional sense at all. Offenders blame their victims for their own suffering.

4. *Condemnation of the condemners.* The offender tries to accuse his or her critics of questionable motives for criticizing him. According to this technique, the offender neutralizes his or her actions by blaming those who are the target of the action. The offender deflects moral condemnation onto the ridiculing parties by pointing out that they engage in similar disapproved behavior. Offenders maintain that those who condemn their offenses are doing so purely out of spite, or are shifting the blame away from themselves unfairly. If the law itself is not legitimate or necessary and if those who enforce it are not competent or trustworthy, then offenders' moral obligation to obey the law is seriously undermined. Offenders express denial of the legitimacy of those who enforce the law. Some criminals condemn their condemners by developing and presenting conspiracy theories. A conspiracy theory is an explanatory hypothesis that accuses two or more persons, a group, or an organization of having caused or covered up, through secret planning and deliberate action, the investigation, prosecution, and conviction of the white-collar criminal.

5. *Appeal to higher loyalties.* Violating the law is a necessary component of the pursuit of broader, more important goals. The offender denies the act was motivated by self-interest, claiming that it was instead done out of obedience to some moral obligation. Those who feel they are in a dilemma that the offenders must resolve at the cost of violating a law or policy employ this technique. In the context of an organization, an employee may appeal to organizational values or hierarchies. For example, an employee could argue that he or she has to violate a policy in order to get his or her work done. Offenders suggest that their offenses were for the greater good, with long-term consequences that will justify their actions. Employees who experience requests to do something illegal may recognize that their behavior is wrong but argue to themselves that being loyal to their employer or organization is more important. Offenders can also make a distinction between morality and the technical requirements of the law and claim that it is more important to do what they consider the right thing than the legal thing.

After Sykes and Matza (1957) proposed their five techniques of neutralization, researchers later added five more neutralization techniques (Gottschalk and Smith, 2011; Moore and McMullan, 2009; Siponen and Vance, 2010):

6. *Normality of action.* The offender argues that everyone else is doing it, thus he or she has done nothing wrong. It is simply quite normal what the offender did. The criminal has recognized that it is so common to have no respect for the law that the person claims no wrongdoing on his or her part. The offender can argue that it is consensus in the population to ignore the law at this point. Rather than abnormal, the action is normal, meaning conforming to common standards.

7. *Claim to entitlement.* The offender claims he or she was in his or her right to do what he or she did, perhaps because of a very stressful situation or because of some misdeed perpetrated by the victim. This is defense of necessity, which people base on the justification that if the offender views the rule breaking as necessary, one should feel no guilt when committing the action. The entitlement to the action can follow from position and responsibility.

8. *Legal mistake.* The offender argues that the law is wrong, and what he or she did, others should indeed be considered quite acceptable. Therefore, one may violate the law because the law is unreasonable. There is something wrong with the law, since the offender perceives his own act as sensible and correct. It may seem that the law is there to enable law enforcement on a general basis, while it is wrong to apply the law to this specific situation.

9. *Acceptable mistake.* The offender argues that what he or she did is acceptable given the situation and given his or her position. The person feels he or she has been doing so much good for the organization that others should excuse them for their wrongdoing. He or she feels that that their crime is a relatively minor matter when compared to the good they have done and thus others should ignore the matter. This is in line with the metaphor of the ledger, which uses the idea of compensating bad acts with good acts. That is, an individual believes that he or she has previously performed a number of good acts and has accrued a surplus of good will and as the result of all good deeds can afford to commit some bad actions. Executives in corporate environments neutralize their actions through the metaphor of the ledger by rationalizing that their overall past good behavior justifies occasional rule breaking.

10. *Dilemma tradeoff.* The offender argues that a dilemma arose whereby he or she made a reasonable tradeoff before committing the act. Tradeoff between many interests therefore resulted in the offense.

Dilemma represents a state of mind where the difference between right and wrong is not obvious. For example, the offender might have carried out the offense to prevent a more serious offense from happening.

After having studied 369 white-collar criminals in Norway, we suggest two more neutralization techniques:

11. *Victim of crime.* The criminal is convinced that rather than being the offender, he or she is a victim of the crime. The situation and other actors turned the person involuntarily into a criminal. The offender is a victim of the crime, and the offender perceives being a victim of poor treatment after disclosure and arrest. The offender continues to be a victim of the criminal justice system through investigation, prosecution, sentence, and imprisonment. The offender may be a victim because of conspiracy created by others to hurt him or her. Rather than taking on responsibility for the crime, and rather than neutralizing by denial of responsibility, the offender has a completely opposite view of the incident, where the offender suffered injury and became a victim of crime.
12. *Role in society.* Because of the person's prominent role in society, the offender is convinced that other rules and procedures apply to the person's case. The role might have connections to political responsibility, responsibility for employees, and personal attention to society as a whole. The offender may have supported local sports clubs and activities for children. The offender may have donated sums of money to universities and other institutions. The role in society is different from claim to entitlement, since the role includes and requires actions that others may define as crime.

Justifications are socially constructed accounts that individuals who engage in criminal acts adopt to legitimate their behavior. They are beliefs that counteract negative interpretations by articulating why the acts are justifiable or excusable exceptions to the norms (Aguilera and Vadera, 2008).

The idea of neutralization techniques resulted from work on Sutherland's (1949) differential association theory. According to this theory, people are always aware of their moral obligation to abide by the law, and they are aware that they have the same moral obligation within themselves to avoid illegitimate acts. Thus, when persons commit illegitimate acts, they must employ some sort of mechanism to silence the urge to follow these moral obligations. Implicitly, neutralization theory thus rejects suggestions that groups containing delinquents have set up their own permanent moral code, which completely replaces moral obligations.

Differential association is a theory proposing that through inter-action with others, individuals learn the values, attitudes, techniques, and motives for criminal behavior. When criminal behavior is learned, the learning includes techniques of committing the crime, motives and drives for the crime, and rationalizations for the crime. It is the rational-ization for the crime, which implies that offenders know it is wrong what they are doing, but they apply neutralization techniques to justify their behavior.

Personal neutralization of misconduct and crime is not limited to white-collar criminals. However, it seems that such criminals apply these techniques extensively both before and after committing offenses (Benson and Simpson, 2015; Gottschalk and Smith, 2015; Piquero et al., 2005). The role that the criminal or potential criminal occupies makes him or her adopt these techniques.

Stadler and Benson (2012: 494) argue that the feeling of innocence is indeed a characteristic of many white-collar criminals:

> Indeed, a distinguishing feature of the psychologi-cal makeup of white-collar offenders is thought to be their ability to neutralize the moral bind of the law and rationalize their criminal behavior.

Stadler and Benson (2012) base their argument on an empirical study that they conducted among prison inmates. Almost without exception, white-collar inmates denied responsibility for crime. Other inmates felt to a much larger extent responsibility for crime. That the feeling of inno-cence is a characteristic of white-collar criminals was also confirmed in a study by Dhami (2007), who interviewed inmates in a prison in the United Kingdom.

Politically exposed persons exemplify this role theory. A politi-cally exposed person (PEP) is an individual who enjoys the trust to attend prominent public functions. Gilligan (2009) argues that as such individuals pose a potential reputation risk to regulated entities, finan-cial institutions must track them. Most of the high-profile media PEP-related coverage in recent years relates to persons such as the former president of the Philippines, Ferdinand Marcos, and former president of Nigeria, Sani Abacha, who others accused of fostering corruption within their countries and transferring millions of dollars of public funds out of their home countries into bank accounts overseas.

Neutralization theory represents an insightful perspective to shed light on deviant and criminal behavior that is justified or rationalized by the person who commits the offense (Harris and Dumas, 2009). If there obviously is nothing wrong with the actions, there is no need for neutralization (Moore and McMullan, 2009).

Kvalnes and Iyer (2011) link neutralization theory to moral dissonance and moral neutralization. Moral neutralization implies rinsing criminal actions of moral content and meaning, preferably in advance of actions. The moral neutralization lowers the threshold for committing the crime and makes potential moral doubts disappear.

Kvalnes and Iyer (2011: 41) state that the conflict between a person's moral values and alternatives for action create dissonance. If a person perceives no dissonance, it means either that the person finds white-collar crime completely unacceptable, or that the person finds white-collar crime completely acceptable. People who are in between these two extremes will have a greater tendency to apply neutralization techniques.

Neutralization theory is conceptualized as a situational approach employed by offenders to get rid of the guilt they anticipate from misconduct and crime. In a study by Topalli et al. (2014), they identified different neutralization groups among juvenile offenders. Their results suggest that offenders develop into high versus low neutralizers.

Profiling risky individuals

Convenience theory as a general theory of white-collar crime is meant to increase our understanding of this phenomenon. It attempts to describe the behavior of white-collar offenders. The purpose of this inquiry into theories is to identify, or more appropriately, profile individuals within an organization who might become a criminal threat to the organization. The theory focuses on, among others, trustworthiness. Three steps are involved. First, evaluate trustworthiness of the individual. Next, evaluate changes in the trustworthiness of the individual. Finally, identify possible discrepancies between perceived trustworthiness and actual trustworthiness.

To make this theory practical, there is a need for concrete, tangible indicators or behavior traits that could suggest a propensity toward white-collar criminality. It might be something along the lines of a desire to get ahead without sufficient ties to an organization, that is, a transitory career path, or organizational structure with diffuse responsibility, and practice in areas overrun by corruption.

Possible indicators can be derived from the various theories to profile potential offenders:

- The level of strain expressed by the individual
- The extent of risk willingness by the individual
- The extent of self-control by the individual

- The extent of obedience by the individual
- The extent of guilt feeling when doing something wrong
- The extent of personal disorders

Measurement of these indicators is dependent on the situation in which the offender can be found. The situation is determined by opportunity to commit white-collar crime. A person with ample opportunities for criminal activities needs to be monitored more closely in terms of risk factors. For example, a chief financial officer (CFO) who is responsible for all financial transactions and accounting systems in the organization may have ample opportunities to create illegal transactions hidden among legal transactions. Similarly, a chief executive officer (CEO) may have ample opportunity to commit corruption by paying bribes to government officials.

If both CEO and CFO are found to be subject to strain and at the same time have no risk aversion, combined with low self-control and personal

Table 4.1 Comparison of law-abiding versus law-violating white-collar individuals

Characteristics	Law-abiding white-collar individuals	Law-violating white-collar individuals
Gender	Male	Male
Age	50–60 years	40–50 years
Work style	Team	Hierarchy
Attitude	Open	Closed
Skill	Relationships	Tasks
Behavior	Pleasant	Charismatic
Management	Empowerment	Control
Attention	Prosperity	Status
Consciousness	High	Low
Self-control	Strong	Weak
Desire for control	Low	High
Communication	Two-way	One-way
Presence	Self-assured	Arrogance
Association	Dependent	Independent
Integrity	High	Low
Accountability	High	Low
Narcissism	Attention	Exploitation
Satisfaction	Satisfied	Dissatisfied
Qualification	Processes	Results
Self-image	Successful	Clever
Leadership	Cooperation	Competition

disorders, it is certainly important for the board to install two kinds of changes:

1. Reduce the opportunities for both CEO and CFO to commit white-collar crime by introducing more bureaucracy in decision making at the top.
2. Increase monitoring of indicators that reflect behavior traits linked to propensity toward white-collar criminality.

The opportunity perspective developed by Benson and Simpson (2015) implies that rather than introducing even more controls and audits, an alternative route is to reduce opportunities for individuals in the danger zones, such as top executives, procurement managers, and chief information officers (CIO).

Law-abiding versus law-violating white-collar people can be compared as listed in Table 4.1. Characteristics in the table are selected from the literature review, and differences were identified based on theoretical studies as well as empirical studies.

References

Agnew, R. (2005). *Pressured into crime—An overview of general strain theory*, Oxford, UK: Oxford University Press.

Agnew, R. (2012). Reflection on "A Revised Strain Theory of Delinquency," *Social Forces*, 91 (1), 33–38.

Aguilera, R.V. and Vadera, A.K. (2008). The dark side of authority: Antecedents, mechanisms, and outcomes of organizational corruption, *Journal of Business Ethics*, 77, 431–449.

Ajzen, I. (2014). The theory of planned behaviour is alive and well, and not ready to retire: A commentary on Sniehotta, Presseau, and Araújo-Soares, *Health Psychology Review*, 9 (2), 131–137.

Arjoon, S. (2008). Slippery when wet: The real risk in business, *Journal of Markets & Morality*, Spring, 11 (1), 77–91.

Arnulf, J.K. and Gottschalk, P. (2013). Heroic leaders as white-collar criminals: An empirical study, *Journal of Investigative Psychology and Offender Profiling*, 10, 96–113.

Baird, J.E. and Zelin, R.C. (2009). An examination of the impact of obedience pressure on perceptions of fraudulent acts and the likelihood of committing occupational fraud, *Journal of Forensic Studies in Accounting and Business*, Winter, 1–14.

Benson, M.L. and Simpson, S.S. (2015). *Understanding white-collar crime—An opportunity perspective*, New York: Routledge.

Blickle, G., Schlegel, A., Fassbender, P. and Klein, U. (2006). Some personality correlates of business white-collar crime, *Applied Psychology: An International Review*, 55 (2), 220–233.

Bock, T.D. and Kenhove, P.V. (2011). Double standards: The role of techniques of neutralization, *Journal of Business Ethics*, 99, 283–296.

Bogen, T. (2008). *Hvor var du, historien om mitt liv (Where were you, the story of my life)*, Oslo, Norway: Schibsted Publishing.

Bystrova, E.G. and Gottschalk, P. (2015). Social conflict theory and white-collar criminals: Why does the ruling class punish their own? *Pakistan Journal of Criminology*, 7 (1), 1–15.

Carrington, T. and Catasus, B. (2007). Auditing stories about discomfort: Becoming comfortable with comfort theory, *European Accounting Review*, 16 (1), 35–58.

Collins, J.M. and Schmidt, F.L. (1993). Personality, integrity, and white collar crime: A construct validity study, *Personnel Psychology*, 46, 295–311.

Comey, J.B. (2009). Go directly to prison: White collar sentencing after the Sarbanes-Oxley act, *Harvard Law Review*, 122, 1728–1749.

Dhami, M.K. (2007). White-collar prisoners' perceptions of audience reaction, *Deviant Behavior*, 28, 57–77.

Eberly, M.B., Holley, E.C., Johnson, M.D. and Mitchell, T.R. (2011). Beyond internal and external: A dyadic theory of relational attributions, *Academy of Management Review*, 36 (4), 731–753.

Engdahl, O. (2014). White-collar crime and first-time adult-onset offending: Explorations in the concept of negative life events as turning points, *International Journal of Law, Crime and Justice*, doi: 10.1016/j.ijlcj.2014.06.001.

Eriksen, T.S. (2010). *Arven etter Ole Christian Bach—Et justismord (The legacy of Ole Christian Bach—A miscarriage of justice)*, Oslo, Norway: Norgesforlaget Publishing.

Fehr, R., Yam, K.C. and Dang, C. (2015). Moralized leadership: The construction and consequences of ethical leader perceptions, *Academy of Management Review*, 40 (2), 182–209.

Fosse, G. and Magnusson, G. (2004). *Mayday Mayday!—Kapteinene først i livbåtene! (Mayday Mayday!—The captains first in the lifeboats)*, Oslo, Norway: Kolofon Publishing.

Froggio, G. and Agnew, R. (2007). The relationship between crime and "objective" versus "subjective" strains, *Journal of Criminal Justice*, 35, 81–87.

Galvin, B.M., Lange, D. and Ashforth, B.E. (2015). Narcissistic organizational identification: Seeing oneself as central to the organization's identity, *Academy of Management Review*, 40 (2), 163–181.

Gilligan, G. (2009). PEEPing at PEPs, *Journal of Financial Crime*, 16 (2), 137–143.

Gottfredson, M.R. and Hirschi, T. (1990). *A general theory of crime*, Stanford, CA: Stanford University Press.

Gottschalk, P. (2015a). *Fraud examiners in white-collar crime investigations*, Boca Raton, FL: CRC Press, Taylor & Francis.

Gottschalk, P. (2015b). *Investigating financial crime—Characteristics of white-collar criminals*, Hauppauge, NY: Nova Science Publishers.

Gottschalk, P. (2015c). *Internal investigations of economic crime—Corporate case studies and regulatory policy*, Boca Raton, FL: Universal Publishers.

Gottschalk, P. and Smith, R. (2015). Gender and white-collar crime: Examining representations of women in media, *Journal of Gender Studies*, 24 (3), 310–325.

Hansen, L.L. (2009). Corporate financial crime: Social diagnosis and treatment, *Journal of Financial Crime*, 16 (1), 28–40.

Harris, L.C. and Dumas, A. (2009). Online consumer misbehaviour: An application of neutralization theory, *Marketing Theory*, 9 (4), 379–402.

Hayes, T.A. (2010). Labeling and the adoption of a deviant status, *Deviant Behavior*, 31, 274–302.

Heath, J. (2008). Business ethics and moral motivation: A criminological perspective, *Journal of Business Ethics*, 83, 595–614.

Hoffmann, J.P. (2002). A contextual analysis of differential association, social control, and strain theories of delinquency, *Social Forces*, 81 (3), 753–785.

Holtfreter, K., Slyke, S.V., Bratton, J. and Gertz, M. (2008). Public perceptions of white-collar crime and punishment, *Journal of Criminal Justice*, 36, 50–60.

Johnson, S.D. and Groff, E.R. (2014). Strengthening theoretical testing in criminology using agent-based modeling, *Journal of Research in Crime and Delinquency*, 51 (4), 509–525.

Kerik, B.B. (2015). *From jailer to jailed—My journey from correction and police commissioner to inmate #84888-054*, New York: Threshold Editions.

Kvalnes, Ø. and Iyer, N.K. (2011). Skal vi danse? Om korrupsjon og moralsk ansvar (Shall we dance? About corruption and moral responsibility), *Praktisk Økonomi og Finans*, 27 (4), 39–46.

Langton, L. and Piquero, N.L. (2007). Can general strain theory explain white-collar crime? A preliminary investigation of the relationship between strain and select white-collar offenses, *Journal of Criminal Justice*, 35, 1–15.

Lyman, M.D. and Potter, G.W. (2007). *Organized crime*, 4th ed., Upper Saddle River, NJ: Pearson Prentice Hall.

McGurrin, D., Jarrell, M., Jahn, A. and Cochrane, B. (2013). White collar crime representation in the criminological literature revisited, 2001–2010, *Western Criminology Review*, 14 (2), 3–19.

McKay, R., Stevens, C. and Fratzi, J. (2010). A 12-step process of white-collar crime, *International Journal of Business Governance and Ethics*, 5 (1), 14–25.

Mingus, W. and Burchfield, K.B. (2012). From prison to integration: Applying modified labeling theory to sex offenders, *Criminal Justice Studies*, 25 (1), 97–109.

Moore, R. and McMullan, E.C. (2009). Neutralizations and rationalizations of digital piracy: A qualitative analysis of university students, *International Journal of Cyber Criminology*, 3 (1), 441–451.

Nwalozie, C.J. (2015). Rethinking subculture and subcultural theory in the study of youth crime—A theoretical discourse, *Journal of Theoretical & Philosophical Criminology*, 7 (1), 1–16.

Onna, J.H.R., Geest, V.R., Huisman, W. and Denkers, J.M. (2014). Criminal trajectories of white-collar offenders, *Journal of Research in Crime and Delinquency*, 51, 759–784.

Ouimet, G. (2009). Psychology of white-collar criminal: In search of personality, *Psychologie Du Travail Et Des Organisations*, 15 (3), 297–320.

Ouimet, G. (2010). Dynamics of narcissistic leadership in organizations, *Journal of Managerial Psychology*, 25 (7), 713–726.

Perri, F.S. (2013). Visionaries or false prophets, *Journal of Contemporary Criminal Justice*, 29 (3), 331–350.

Pickett, K.H.S. and Pickett, J.M. (2002). *Financial crime investigation and control*. New York: John Wiley & Sons.

Piquero, N.L. (2012). The only thing we have to fear is fear itself: Investigating the relationship between fear of falling and white collar crime, *Crime and Delinquency*, 58 (3), 362–379.

Piquero, N.L., Tibbetts, S.G. and Blankenship, M.B. (2005). Examining the role of differential association and techniques of neutralization in explaining corporate crime. *Deviant Behavior*, 26 (2), 159–188.

Piquero, N.L., Schoepfer, A. and Langton, L. (2010). Completely out of control or the desire to be in complete control? How low self-control and the desire for control relate to corporate offending, *Crime & Delinquency*, 56 (4), 627–647.

Pratt, T.C. and Cullen, F.T. (2005). Assessing macro-level predictors and theories of crime: A meta-analysis, *Crime and Justice*, 32, 373–450.

Ragatz, L.L., Fremouw, W. and Baker, E. (2012). The psychological profile of white-collar offenders: Demographics, criminal thinking, psychopathic traits, and psychopathology, *Criminal Justice and Behavior*, 39 (7), 978–997.

Robson, R.A. (2010). Crime and punishment: Rehabilitating retribution as a justification for organizational criminal liability, *American Business Law Journal*, 47 (1), 109–144.

Schoepfer, A. and Piquero, N.L. (2006). Exploring white-collar crime and the American dream: A partial test of institutional anomie theory, *Journal of Criminal Justice*, 34, 227–235.

Schoepfer, A., Carmichael, S. and Piquero, N.L. (2007). Do perceptions of punishment vary between white-collar and street crimes? *Journal of Criminal Justice*, 35, 151–163.

Siponen, M. and Vance, A. (2010). Neutralization: New insights into the problem of employee information security policy violations, *MIS Quarterly*, 34 (3), 487–502.

Stadler, W.A. and Benson, M.L. (2012). Revisiting the guilty mind: The neutralization of white-collar crime, *Criminal Justice Review*, 37 (4), 494–511.

Sutherland, E.H. (1949). *White collar crime*, New York: Holt Rinehart and Winston.

Sutherland, E.H. (1983). *White collar crime—The uncut version*, New Haven, CT: Yale University Press.

Sykes, G. and Matza, D. (1957). Techniques of neutralization: A theory of delinquency, *American Sociological Review*, 22 (6), 664–670.

Topalli, V., Higgins, G.E. and Copes, H. (2014). A causal model of neutralization acceptance and delinquency, *Criminal Justice and Behavior*, 41 (5), 553–573.

Walters, G.D. and Geyer, M.D. (2004). Criminal thinking and identify in male white-collar offenders, *Criminal Justice and Behavior*, 31 (3), 263–281.

Welsh, D.T., Oronez, L.D., Snyder, D.G. and Christian, M.S. (2014). The slippery slope: How small ethical transgressions pave the way for larger future transgressions, *Journal of Applied Psychology*, http://dx.doi.org/10.1037/a0036950.

Wheeler, S., Weisburd, D., Waring, E. and Bode, N. (1988). White-collar crime and criminals, *American Criminal Law Review*, 25, 331–357.

Yeoh, P. (2011). The UK Bribery Act 2010: Contents and implications, *Journal of Financial Crime*, 19 (1), 37–53.

Yusuf, T.O. and Babalola, A.R. (2009). Control of insurance fraud in Nigeria: An exploratory study, *Journal of Financial Crime*, 16 (4), 418–435.

chapter five

Integrated approach to convenience theory

A model is presented in this chapter to illustrate links between dimensions in convenience theory. Based on the model, a number of research hypotheses are proposed for future empirical research.

Integrating convenience dimensions

The behavioral dimension of crime interacts with the organizational dimension of crime. For example, executives with narcissistic or psychopathic traits (or both in the dark triad) may search for opportunities to commit financial crime in difficult situations, while conforming executives will probably not value opportunities to commit financial crime as attractive options.

The behavioral dimension of crime interacts with the economic dimension of crime as well. For example, the fear of falling (Piquero, 2012) finds causality in situations such as an acute liquidity problem, where executives perceive financial crime as the only way out of the crises. Profit-driven crime is thus not only an issue of making even more money. Rather, it is an issue of survival, and it may be to rescue a sinking ship.

As suggested by Whetten (1989), a theoretical contribution starts by identifying factors (variables, construct, concepts) that are parts of the explanation of the phenomenon. The phenomenon of white-collar crime finds explanation in the concepts of economics, organization, and behavior. This is the what-part of our theory.

Whetten (1989) then suggests the how-part, which is how these concepts are related to each other. Figure 5.1 illustrates six integrated relationships between the economic, organizational, and behavioral dimensions. The figure presents a model of white-collar crime occurrence, which is explained by convenience theory. The model is in line with Alvesson and Sandberg (2011) who define theory as a statement of relations among concepts within a boundary set of assumptions and constraints.

Convenience theory represents the theoretical glue that welds the model together:

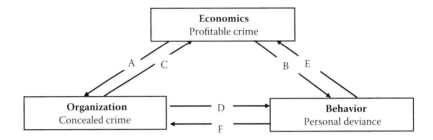

Figure 5.1 A conceptual model of white-collar crime occurrence based on convenience theory.

A. The need and desire for profit and success is satisfied by financial crime that is conveniently carried out and disguised among seemingly legal activities in the organization. Rational economic behavior implies individuals who consider self-interest in terms of incentives and potential costs, where detection and imprisonment are unlikely but possible costs (Welsh et al., 2014). Economic motivation can be found in a self-centered search for satisfaction and avoidance of pain (Chang et al., 2005; Gottfredson and Hirschi, 1990; Hirschi and Gottfredson, 1987). Profit-driven crime in an organizational context has a superficial appearance of legitimacy (Benson and Simpson, 2015) and is easily hidden among other financial transactions (Füss and Hecker, 2008). Because the economic model implies that crime is a rational choice, crime rates will drop when the likelihood of detection rises and when punishment becomes more severe (Pratt and Cullen, 2005). Impulses may play a role in distorting rational preferences and utility functions for white-collar criminals (Kamerdze et al., 2014). Crime is often the easiest and simplest way to goal achievement (Agnew, 2014).

B. The need and desire for profit and success make it attractive to the individual to commit financial crime that implies convenient deviant behavior. Profit-oriented offenses can be caused by both threats and opportunities. The motive in situations of threats might be to protect the interests of the company and secure survival of the enterprise (Blickle et al., 2006) or to enable down payments of personal debt (Brightman, 2009). The motive in situations of opportunities might be expansion into more profitable markets or satisfaction of personal greed, where greed is desires and perceived needs that will always grow (Bucy et al., 2008; Goldstraw-White, 2012; Hamilton and Mickethwait, 2006). The criminal can use illegal profits to seek respect and self-realization at the top level of Maslow's pyramid of personal needs.

C. The profession and position in the organization enables white-collar crime to conveniently satisfy need and desire for profit and success. Opportunity to commit financial crime in an organizational context is a distinct characteristic of white-collar crime when compared to other financial crime offenders (Bucy et al., 2008; Michel, 2008). Executives and others in the elite have an opportunity to involve themselves in economic crime without any substantial risk of detection and punishment (Aguilera and Vadera, 2008; Haines, 2014). Opportunity manifests itself by legal access, different location, and appearance of legitimacy (Benson and Simpson, 2015; Pickett and Pickett, 2002). In a principal-agent perspective, there is an opportunity for the white-collar individual as an agent to carry out the regular job at the same time as crime is committed because the principal is unable to monitor what the agent is doing, what knowledge the agent applies, and what risk the agent is willing to take (Chrisman et al., 2007; Li and Ouyang, 2007; Williams, 2008). Deviant organizational structure and culture can make it easier to commit financial crime and reduce the likelihood of detection and reaction (Dion, 2008; Pontell et al., 2014; Puranam et al., 2014).

D. The profession and position in the organization enables white-collar crime by convenient deviant behavior that is not noticed, questioned, or challenged. The position occupied by the individual in relation to the organization makes it easier to practice and defend deviant behavior (Sutherland, 1949). Social capital accumulated by the individual in terms of actual and potential resources, which are accessible because of profession and position, creates a larger space for individual behavior and actions that others can hardly observe. Many initiatives by trusted persons in the elite are unknown and unfamiliar to others in the organization. Therefore, white-collar criminals do not expect consequences for themselves (Adler and Kwon, 2002). Degrees of freedom grow as individuals climb up the career ladder to the top (Heath, 2008). Degrees of freedom are particularly many when corporate crime is committed to benefit the enterprise (Bookman, 2008; Hansen, 2009; Reed and Yeager, 1996; Trahan, 2011; Valukas, 2010). Degrees of freedom are also ample when several individuals at the top of the organization participate and join forces in crime (Ashforth et al., 2008), and when the organization generally is characterized by an unethical and destructive business culture (O'Connor, 2005; Punch, 2003).

E. The acceptance and neutralization of personal deviant behavior make it convenient to commit financial crime to satisfy need and desire for profit and success. The privileged individual may feel entitled to carry out illegal acts, for example, because the acts are means to reach a higher goal. The white-collar criminal belongs to the elite that make the laws; therefore he or she may feel free to violate the laws (Bystrova and Gottschalk, 2015). The offender notices no damage and no victim. The offender does not feel sorry for banks or tax authorities. By means of neutralization techniques, the offender reduces and eliminates any guilt feelings ahead of and after criminal acts (Sutherland, 1949; Sykes and Matza, 1957). Denial of injury and denial of victim is possible because white-collar crime is nonpersonal and without violence (Benson and Simpson, 2015).

F. The acceptance and neutralization of personal deviant behavior in terms of financial crime is conveniently absorbed in the organizational context. Even if unethical behavior is noticed and suspicion develops, most internal observers will be more concerned about their own job security than blowing the whistle in situations where they are not quite sure. Criminal behavior by privileged individuals might be caused by stress that is perceived by others as well (Agnew, 2014; Gottfredson and Hirschi, 1990; Johnson and Groff, 2014; Langton and Piquero, 2007; Pratt and Cullen, 2005). A privileged person may over time slide on a slippery slope from legal to illegal actions without really noticing or being conscious about it (Arjoon, 2008; Welsh et al., 2014). Punishment appears less likely and less deterrent because crime occurs in professional life in an organizational context (Benson and Simpson, 2015; Comey, 2009; Gottfredson and Hirschi, 1990). Executives with an excessive desire to control others in the organization may be able to expand their own degrees of freedom by making controlled employees more passive (Piquero et al., 2010). Organizations lacking norms and common values will not notice or react to criminal behavior (Schoepfer and Piquero, 2006).

The integrated explanation of white-collar crime as a convenient activity when faced with threats or opportunities represents a model of the road of potentially least resistance. Even though future costs in terms of police investigation, media attention, prosecution, and jail sentence may become substantial and hurt badly both financially and personally, such costs are unlikely to occur because the likelihood of detection is very low. White-collar crime is a response to an occurrence or a situation (Langton and Piquero, 2007). There are few or no obstacles that can stop potential offenders from choosing the criminal road of least resistance. This is particularly the case for heroic white-collar criminals as described by Arnulf and Gottschalk (2013), where there neither is a glass ceiling nor any resistance to heroes' actions within and on behalf of the organization.

Motivation for white-collar crime ranges from greed to panic. A sales executive, who is afraid of losing his job, may in panic offer a potential customer a bribe to increase sales and thereby keep his job. A founder and entrepreneur in panic may manipulate accounting figures for tax evasion to save his empire and continue as a seemingly successful businessman. For persons in similar situations, economic crime emerges as a convenient, accessible, and acceptable course of action.

White-collar criminals on the other side of the scale, at the greed end of the scale, can never get enough. They will look for opportunities to enrich themselves all the time, to emerge as seemingly successful, and to become even more visible in their materialistic environments. They identify shortcuts, relations, and transactions that can be explored for additional profits.

In between panic and greed we find white-collar criminals who may feel forced by others to participate in economic crime, who obey orders from their bosses, or who simply follow what seems to be practice in the enterprise, the business, or the profession (Langton and Piquero, 2007). If those in the middle of the scale are detected, they do not expect to be treated like criminals. They become surprised if the criminal justice system treats them as regular criminals (Kerik, 2015).

The term convenience that we apply here to push our knowledge of white-collar crime can also be found in other fields of criminology. For example, Petrossian and Clarke (2013) studied convenience ports for unloading of illegal goods. They found that oceans close to ports of convenience experienced much more overfishing than oceans further away.

In another field of criminology, McGloin and Stickle (2011) applied the term convenience when they phrased the question, influence or convenience? They studied chronic criminals and found that chronic criminals tend to find it convenient to participate in crime by others.

Criminology reminds us of the meaning of the term convenience when we think of crime in convenience stores. These stores are typically located close to people's homes with a limited selection and high prices. Convenience in terms of closeness and long opening hours comes at the expense of limited selection and higher prices. People shop in these stores because they are convenient. Often, there are no lines in front of the cashier (White and Katz, 2013). In comparison, shopping malls are far away, have limited opening hours, and customers often experience long queues in front of the cashiers.

In our perspective of white-collar crime, advantages often include access, simplicity, and immediate results. Alternatives to crime often require patience, time, and resources with an outcome that is not at all certain. The perceived costs of crime are low, partly because detection of white-collar crime is very rare.

According to convenience theory, an increase in expected future costs of crime can reduce the extent of crime. If detection becomes more likely, and the consequence of criminal behavior becomes more severe, then the extent of crime—such as corruption—is expected to decrease. Ethical guidelines and corporate compliance seem to cover window dressing, but these policies do probably have little or no impact on criminal behavior. There is a need for an increase in the subjective detection probability, which is the likelihood of detection perceived by a potential criminal. Employment of detectives in private and public enterprises may represent a starting point where potential white-collar offenders can feel uneasy about future deviant behavior.

Research hypotheses for convenience

Sutton and Staw (1995) argue that hypotheses represent no theory. Hypotheses can be found on the road from theoretical study to empirical study, where the researcher tests whether theoretical assumptions about reality can be documented in practice. Weick (1995) comments on Sutton and Staw by arguing that hypotheses often represent an important part of theorizing work. Colquitt and Zapata-Pelan (2007) found some research claiming that theory in the sciences implies that assumptions about reality have been tested in the form of hypotheses. This is in line with Eisenhardt (1989), who argues that theory development should include data of actual circumstances.

Earlier in this book, theory was defined without inclusion of hypotheses. However, some hypotheses will be sketched out in the following to enable a bridge from theoretical study to empirical study. A research hypothesis normally contains a claim of relationship between variables, and the claim is usually concerned with causal relationships, where cause and effect is theoretically established among variables. For example, a causal relationship can be established between the extent of opportunity to commit white-collar crime and the actual extent of white-collar crime. Another example might be a causal relationship between the extent of financial threats to the enterprise and the likelihood of white-collar crime by the enterprise. Facts from empirical study are the result of observation, experience, and experiment. Hypotheses link assumptions about practice to facts about practice.

In this chapter, the terms model and theory are not used interchangeably. A theory is a set of statements that are arrived at through a process of abstractions, while a model is a purposeful and simplified representation of reality. The generalized statements in theory can explain a number of models of a specific phenomenon. While theory can explain a model, hypotheses can verify or falsify a theory. Convenience theory explains the model of white-collar crime occurrence, while research hypotheses enable testing of convenience theory.

The integrated model for convenience theory enables formulation of hypotheses for relationships within each dimension as well as hypotheses for relationships between dimensions as indicated by arrows A to F.

All hypotheses should be concerned with convenience in the sense that increasing convenience of white-collar crime will lead to increased extent of white-collar crime in a given situation.

In convenience theory, the term opportunity can be applied in two dimensions with different meanings. An opportunity in the economic dimension represents the availability of something valuable. It is the opposite of a threat, where opportunity can be found in a situation that is attractive to explore and exploit. For example, it is attractive to establish a subsidiary abroad or increase domestic sales, and it is attractive to buy a larger house or get rid of a mortgage. An opportunity in the organizational dimension represents the availability of techniques to commit financial crime. For example, executives have access to corruption options, which in turn can lead to the establishment of a subsidiary abroad. Department heads have access to embezzlement options, which in turn can enable purchase of a larger house. Opportunity is thus found in convenience theory as both crime opportunity and gain opportunity. Opportunity is a favorable or advantageous circumstance or combination of circumstances. Synonyms for opportunity include occasion, opening, and chance. Occasion suggests the proper time for an action or purpose. In the following, occasion is applied as a synonym for gain opportunity.

Convenience theory applies the word convenience both as an absolute and as a relative measure. As an absolute measure, convenience is characterized by savings in efforts and resources to complete a task at the present time, where potential costs in the future are considered. As a relative measure, convenience is characterized by the resource drain at white-collar crime relative to resource consumption for alternative actions to reach the same future state of affairs.

In formulating research hypotheses, the economic dimension is conceptualized in terms of desire for profits, where desire for profits is a combination of individual desire (occupational crime) and organizational desire (corporate crime). The organizational dimension is conceptualized in terms of opportunity to commit white-collar crime, where opportunity is a combination of easiness (access to resources) and lack of detection (access to concealment). The behavioral dimension is conceptualized in terms of willingness to commit white-collar crime, where willingness is a combination of neutralization (acceptance of own actions) and normlessness (lack of self-control).

Convenience theory suggests an effect from the economic dimension on the organizational dimension. Increased desire for profits is expected to influence the extent of organizational opportunity to commit white-collar crime. Financial crime becomes more possible to carry out and hide among legal activities in the organization when the desire for profits based on threats and chances increases. Threats can be met and chances exploited when profits are achieved, where profits serve the self-centered search for satisfaction and avoidance of pain (Chang et al., 2005; Gottfredson and Hirschi, 1990; Hirschi and Gottfredson, 1987). A stronger desire for more profits will influence ways that can be found in the organization to commit white-collar crime (Benson and Simpson, 2015). Financial crime becomes more easily hidden among other transactions (Füss and Hecker, 2008), and criminal action is performed to reduce the likelihood of detection (Pratt and Cullen, 2005). It is a rational choice influenced by impulses (Kamerdze et al., 2014; Welsh et al., 2014), where crime becomes the easiest and simplest way to goal achievement (Agnew, 2014). This reasoning leads to the following first hypothesis.

> Hypothesis A: Increased desire for profits to cover perceived needs increases organizational opportunity for white-collar crime.

Convenience theory suggests an effect from the economic dimension on the behavioral dimension. Increased desire for profits is expected to influence the extent of willingness to commit white-collar crime. Desire for profits and success make it attractive for individuals to commit crime. A stronger motive in situations of both threats (Blickle et al., 2006; Brightman, 2009) and chances (Bucy et al., 2008; Goldstraw-White, 2012; Hamilton and Mickethwait, 2006) can lead to both corporate and occupational crime, where the criminal can use illegal profits to seek respect and self-realization. An increased desire for profits may lead a potential offender faster down the slippery slope (Arjoon, 2008), may reduce the potential offender's ability of self-control (Hansen, 2009), may lead to increased struggle for control (Piquero et al., 2010), may lead to more severe strain for success and status (Agnew, 2005), may open up for more substantial personality disorders, may cause ignorance toward crime deterrence mechanisms (Yusuf and Babalola, 2009), and may strengthen the potential offender's ability to apply neutralization techniques (Gottschalk and Smith, 2015; Sykes and Matza, 1957). This reasoning leads to the following second hypothesis.

> Hypothesis B: Increased desire for profits to cover perceived needs increases willingness to commit white-collar crime.

Convenience theory suggests an effect from the organizational dimension on the economical dimension. The link implies that profession and position in the organization enable white-collar crime (Bucy et al., 2008; Michel, 2008), which make crime more attractive to meet threats and exploit chances of profits. When executives and others in the elite have opportunities to involve themselves in economic crime without any substantial risk of detection and punishment (Aguilera and Vadera, 2008; Haines, 2014), then financial gain becomes relatively more attractive. There may be little effort involved in gaining substantial profits. When two reasons for not accessing illegal profits are removed—that is, lack of opportunity and likelihood of detection—then illegal profits become more attractive. A hurdle is reduced and possibly removed to gain profits for personal or organizational needs. The extent of opportunity is present in terms of legal access, different location, and appearance of legitimacy (Benson and Simpson, 2015; Pickett and Pickett, 2002). In a principal-agent perspective, the principal is unable to monitor what the agent as a potential offender is doing (Chrisman et al., 2007; Li and Ouyang, 2007; Williams, 2008). In addition, deviant organizational structure and culture can increase opportunities and reduce the probability of detection and reaction (Dion, 2008; Pontell et al., 2014; Puranam et al., 2014). If the white-collar criminal suffers from narcissistic organizational identification, where the person's own self is perceived as the core organizational identity, then it is the organization rather than the person that seems to be in need of profit. Narcissistic identification is characterized by the domination of individual identity over organizational identity (Galvin et al., 2015). This reasoning leads to the following third hypothesis.

> Hypothesis C: Increased organizational opportunity for white-collar crime increases desire for profits to cover perceived needs.

Convenience theory suggests an effect from the organizational dimension on the behavioral dimension. Conditions in the organization are such that the potential offender can commit financial crime without being perceived as a deviant person or suspicious person. When nobody notices or reacts to deviant behavior, misconduct, and crime, then the criminal may perceive himself or herself as quite normal and not deviant at all. The position occupied by the individual in relation to the organization makes it easy to defend and get acceptance for deviant behavior (Sutherland, 1949). When a potential offender expects no personal consequences ever from misconduct and crime (Adler and Kwon, 2002), then the individual's willingness is higher than if there would be concern about consequences. Increased degrees of freedom in the organizational dimension (Bookman, 2008; Hansen, 2009; Heath, 2008; Reed and Yeager, 1996; Trahan, 2011) make an individual believe that he or she can get away with almost everything. For example, when Valukas (2010) investigated the collapse of Lehman Brothers, he concluded that executive misconduct was indeed within acceptable business practices and therefore no crime. Executives got away with it, also because several individuals at the top of the organization participated and joined forces in the irregular business practices

(Ashforth et al., 2008), and because the bank organization generally was characterized by a risk-willing, unethical, and destructive business culture (O'Connor, 2005; Punch, 2003). This reasoning leads to the following fourth hypothesis.

> Hypothesis D: Increased organizational opportunity for white-collar crime increases willingness to commit financial crime.

Convenience theory suggests an effect from the behavioral dimension on the economical dimension. Acceptance and neutralization of personal deviant behavior make it easier and more attractive for the white-collar offender to commit crime. Willingness reduces the potential offender's personal barrier toward crime. The desire for profits increases as personal obstacles are removed. As a member of the privileged elite, he or she may feel free to violate the law (Bystrova and Gottschalk, 2015). While illegal profits may not be particularly attractive, there are no personal barriers to commit white-collar crime. The offender notices no damage and no victim (Sykes and Matza, 1957), and differential association theory may explain the acceptance of crime (Sutherland, 1949). When all obstacles are removed (Benson and Simpson, 2015), then illegal profits become more attractive to pursue. This reasoning leads to the following fifth hypothesis.

> Hypothesis E: Increased willingness to commit white-collar crime increases desire for profits to cover perceived needs.

Convenience theory suggests an effect from the behavioral dimension on the organizational dimension. Deviant and criminal behavior is absorbed in an organizational context where it is not noticed. The potential offender's willingness influences the extent to which the individual explores and exploits resources to commit crime. When an offender is willing to commit white-collar crime, then the person will develop organizational opportunities to enable crime to occur successfully. One reason for willingness might be stress (Agnew, 2014; Gottfredson and Hirschi, 1990; Johnson and Groff, 2014; Langton and Piquero, 2007; Pratt and Cullen, 2005), another reason might be sliding on the slippery slope (Arjoon, 2008; Welsh et al., 2014), and a third reason might be a belief in lack of punishment (Benson and Simpson, 2015; Comey, 2009; Gottfredson and Hirschi, 1990). Executives with an excessive desire to control others in the organization may succeed in creating extended opportunities for white-collar crime in the organizational setting (Piquero et al., 2010). The willing offender may get involved in breaking down norms and common values before introducing criminal behavior (Schoepfer and Piquero, 2006). This reasoning leads to the following sixth hypothesis.

> Hypothesis F: Increased willingness to commit white-collar crime increases organizational opportunity for crime.

The above six hypotheses cover relationships in the model for convenience theory. In addition, hypotheses can be formulated to cover the contents within each dimension of convenience theory. Here are some potential hypotheses for the economical dimension related to convenience.

> Hypothesis G: Increased need and desire for profit and success make financial crime more convenient.
> Hypothesis H: Increased need and desire for pleasure and recreation make financial crime more convenient.
> Hypothesis I: More acute need for profit makes financial crime more convenient.
> Hypothesis J: More difficult options for legal satisfaction of need and desire for profit and success make illegal satisfaction more convenient.

Here are some potential hypotheses for the organizational dimension related to convenience.

> Hypothesis K: Increased opportunity for financial crime in the organizational setting makes white-collar crime more convenient.
> Hypothesis L: Improved organizational position for the potential offender makes white-collar crime more convenient.
> Hypothesis M: Improved organizational situation for financial crime makes white-collar crime more convenient.
> Hypothesis N: More synergy between preferred deviant behavior and organizational opportunity make white-collar crime more convenient.

Here are some potential hypotheses for the behavioral dimension related to convenience.

> Hypothesis O: Stronger acceptance of own deviant behavior makes white-collar crime more convenient.

> Hypothesis P: More personal stress makes white-collar crime more convenient.
>
> Hypothesis Q: Stronger identification of offender with organization makes white-collar crime more convenient.
>
> Hypothesis R: Stronger neutralization of deviant behavior makes white-collar crime more convenient.

Empirical testing of these hypotheses is no simple task for research. One option is to study a group of convicted white-collar criminals and compare this group with a group of noncriminal white-collar persons in business positions. Blickle et al. (2006) identified two such groups in Germany, and they found several significant differences between the two groups. First, the convicts were more dominated by hedonism in the sense of enjoying material wealth. Second, convicts had more narcissistic traits in their personalities in the sense of grandiose perceptions of themselves. Finally, convicts reported lower self-control than white-collar persons still in business positions.

Another option for empirical testing is to conduct a cross-sectional survey where each of the three dimensions in convenience theory is measured. Depending on the direction of each hypothesis from one dimension to the next, elements from survey responses can be introduced in multiple item scales to measure each particular variable.

Theorizing white-collar crime and criminals

Whetten (1989) suggests that a theory has to explain the underlying psychological, economic, or social dynamics that justify the selection of factors and the proposed causal relationships. This rationale constitutes the theory's assumptions—the theoretical glue that welds the model together. In the proposed theory, causal relationships exist both within each dimension as well as between the three dimensions.

The integrated explanation of white-collar crime as a convenient option when facing challenges portrays the path of least resistance. Offenders are responding to an event or a situation (Langton and Piquero, 2007). There are no safeguards to stop them from choosing the path of least resistance. Especially heroic white-collar criminals as described by Arnulf and Gottschalk (2013) are uninterrupted and no glass ceiling exists.

The motivation for white-collar crime can range from greed to panic. Someone afraid of losing his job may panic and bribe a customer to get a large order for his firm to save his job. An entrepreneur and founder may panic to save his lifework and commit tax evasion to save his firm and to continue to be successful in his business venture. Crime represents a convenient option to cope with problems, as failure is not an option. People on the other end of the scale, driven by greed, will be looking for opportunities to commit white-collar crime independent of real need as long as they find a suitable target. Between these two extremes, we find people who find themselves coerced by others, obeying orders from superiors, or just following normal business practices of their profession (Langton and Piquero, 2007). If detected, they do not expect others to scrutinize them. Those revealed express surprise by being prosecuted like "regular criminals" (Kerik, 2015).

Convenience is a term also found in crime studies. For example, Petrossian and Clarke (2014) studied ports of convenience for illegal commercial fishing. They found that countries in close proximity to the 10 ports of convenience were more vulnerable to illegal fishing than those that were farther away. McGloin and Stickle (2011) phrased the question, Influence or Convenience? They were studying peer influence versus co-offending for chronic offenders, and found that it is convenient for chronic offenders to involve themselves in co-offending.

Costs of convenience can be illustrated by the convenience store. A convenience store usually charges significantly higher prices than conventional grocery stores or supermarkets. Nevertheless, customers choose to buy there anyway because of closer location, longer opening hours, and shorter cashier lines (White and Katz, 2013). Similarly, white-collar criminals are willing to commit crime because it is convenient and the calculated costs are low.

The proposition of a new theory, convenience theory, takes into account why, where, who, what, when, and how as suggested by the literature on theory discussed above: (1) why: economic profit; (2) where: in a professional setting; (3) who: privileged individuals; (4) what: nonviolent acts of financial crime; (5) when: threats and opportunities; and (6) how: concealment in legal transactions.

The suggested convenience theory is in need of further theoretical work as well as empirical study. The idea of this theory originated from a sample of several hundred white-collar criminals sentenced to prison in Norway in recent years. Almost all criminals communicate in the media as well as in court documents that crime was a convenient solution to a need, a problem, or a challenge, where no obvious alternative was in sight. Norwegian courts sentenced 369 white-collar criminals to prison from 2009 to 2014. Almost all of them are men (93.6%). Offenders were 44 years old when committing crime, and 49 years old at final sentencing after detection, investigation, prosecution, and appeal. The mean age of white-collar criminals in Germany is 47 years when imprisoned (Blickle et al., 2006) and in the Netherlands 42 years when prosecuted (Onna et al., 2014).

All persons in the Norwegian sample received a prison sentence for white-collar crime. The longest prison sentence is 9 years and the shortest is 26 days, and the mean average is 2.3 years imprisonment. Compared to famous U.S. cases such as Madoff and Schilling, these sentences are quite modest. However, in a Norwegian context these prison sentences are quite substantial and only surpassed by organized crime and murder. When comparing to the sample used by Blickle et al. (2006) of white-collar criminals in Germany, the difference is less visible as the average was 3.9 years imprisonment in Germany in their sample of 76 convicts.

Further theoretical work is needed on the suggested convenience theory to create new theoretical insights that advance our understanding of management, organizations, and criminology. The theory should extend in ways that permit the development of testable knowledge-based claims as indicated by research hypotheses in this book. The current description in this book is primarily a review of the literature on financial crime in organizational settings, and, in particular, a review of theories that have been evoked to explain such crime, for example, agency theory, economic model of self-interest, neutralization theory, differential association theory, strain theory, self-control theory, anomie theory, and slippery slope theory. These subtheories are organized along three core dimensions of white-collar crime in the proposed convenience theory.

Future research should be less summative and more formative in advancing novel claims and propositional arguments that go beyond what can be gleaned from the existing literature. Future research should advance novel arguments that extend prior research into a novel set of predictions and explanations. The current description in this book provides a solid foundation for such an endeavor. It is always a challenge to offer new theory while grounding the underlying ideas in the existing literature.

This book deals with the topic of white-collar crime and considers the role of convenience in explaining its occurrence. It puts forward convenience as a theoretical explanation that underlies existing theories and research on white-collar crime.

It seems convenient for some trusted and privileged individuals to commit financial crime to solve their problems and challenges. In a professional setting, they have opportunities to commit crime (economic dimension), to conceal crime by giving it an appearance of legitimacy (organizational dimension), and to justify the crime (behavioral dimension). Convenience documents itself in the relatively easy opportunity, the relatively easy concealment, and the relatively easy justification of crime. Therefore, convenience seems to be a common denominator for all three dimensions in our explanation of white-collar crime.

Although the role of convenience has been considered in previous research, the notion of convenience in this book is novel in the role of an umbrella term for a general theory of white-collar crime. Therefore, this book makes a novel theoretical contribution.

One important implication of convenience theory is that organizations are often to blame for occurrences of white-collar crime in their businesses. While they tend to present themselves as victims, enterprises and other organizations hit by white-collar crime have made crime possible. The organizational dimension of convenience theory has illustrated how lack of control, excessive degrees of freedom enjoyed by privileged individuals, goal orientation without attention to means, and domination in leader-follower relationships have made white-collar crime an attractive option. Organizations that let privileged and trusted professionals do what they like without transparency or control should not be surprised that they are hit by abuse in terms of white-collar crime. When white-collar crime occurs, victims can be found externally, such as customers, banks, and state revenue services. Since the organization allows crime to occur, then the organization is also an offender toward victims such as customers, banks, and state revenue services. Rather than claiming that they are victims of crime, organizations emerge as offenders since they allow crime to happen.

Future research may be concerned with testing and refining the causal model via empirical study of hypotheses that can lead to modification and extension of convenience theory.

Limits to a general white-collar crime theory

Sutherland (1940, 1949) introduced the term white-collar crime, and Gottfredson and Hirschi (1990) presented a general theory of crime. The term white-collar crime has survived for almost a century and has been subject to much research, making an updated general theory of white-collar crime a necessity and requirement to strengthen future research. Too much struggle has occurred in numerous recent articles to apply the concept of white-collar crime. Reviewers may argue that the sample is not of white-collar crime, while authors say it is.

Of course, three suggestions here—economical, organizational, and behavioral dimensions of such a theory—will not survive for long. The contribution of this section lies more in an initiative, rather than a conclusion. It is an initiative to take a step back to reflect on the concept, rather than determine in specific terms and cases what is or is not white-collar crime.

The purpose is to present a systematic view of the phenomenon of white-collar crime. It can be illustrated as the white-collar crime triangle in Figure 5.2. White-collar crime is (1) based on an opportunity for illegal profit, (2) carried out in the arena of an organization, (3) where the decision of criminal acts is causing deviant behavior.

The systematic view is an argument to explain phenomena of white-collar crime. If the profit is both available and desirable, if the arena is both accessible and secret, and if deviant behavior is both acceptable and defendable, then white-collar crime is likely to occur. The theory represents both the conditions under which crime occurs, as well as the sequence of factors. A decision of deviant behavior is based on availability and desirability of profit that is secretly accessible in a legally perceived organizational setting.

The more well-known fraud triangle of opportunity, pressure, and rationalization (Baird and Zelin, 2009) is implicit in the white-collar crime triangle as illustrated in Figure 5.2. Opportunity can be found in desirable profit in accessible arena, while pressure and rationalization leads to the decision to commit crime. Pressure and rationalization are criteria in decision-making. Pressures can also be found in the organization as well as in its competitive environment (Dodge, 2009).

One problem with only three elements in the triangle is the treatment of risk and risk willingness versus risk aversion. Risk is an element included in motivation as well as opportunity, and indeed also in justification. However, risk deserves an equal place at the level of opportunity, motivation, and rationalization. Here we thus propose an alternative to the crime triangle in terms of a crime star as illustrated in Figure 5.3. As in the triangle, the elements in the star are indeed dependent on each other. For example, opportunity without motivation leads to no crime, and opportunity with too great a risk leads to no crime.

Despite McGurrin et al.'s (2013) finding that few educational criminology programs include white-collar crime, research on white-collar crime is currently growing. There is research on how white-collar criminals are sentenced differently and possibly more mildly (Maddan et al., 2012;

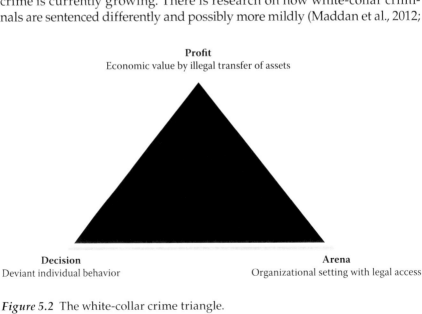

Profit
Economic value by illegal transfer of assets

Decision
Deviant individual behavior

Arena
Organizational setting with legal access

Figure 5.2 The white-collar crime triangle.

Opportunity

Neutralization

Motivation

Risk

Figure 5.3 Crime star for factors affecting the extent of white-collar crime.

Schoepfer et al., 2007; Stadler et al., 2013), on gender gap (Robb, 2006; Simpson et al., 2012; Steffensmeier et al., 2013), occupational versus corporate crime (Bookman, 2008; Heath, 2008; Perri and Brody, 2011), criminal leaders versus criminal followers (Bucy et al., 2008; McKay et al., 2010), criminal profiles (Onna et al., 2014), white-collar defense in court (Weissmann and Block, 2010), and many other interesting perspectives. Such specific perspectives will of course challenge a general theory of white-collar crime.

The white-collar crime triangle covers both offense-based as well as offender-based perspectives. The offense is economic in nature, and it occurs in an organizational setting. The offender makes a decision to commit the crime. It is based on a criminal opportunity with the following five characteristics (Huisman and Erp, 2013) the effort required to carry out the offense, the perceived risks of detection, and the rewards to be gained from the offense, the situational conditions that may encourage criminal action, and the excuse and neutralizations of the offense.

Pratt and Cullen (2005) distinguished between micro-level and macro-level perspectives on crime. Issues of strain, self-control, and other behavioral indicators belong to the individual explanations of crime at the micro-level. Issues of organizational setting, inequality, and availability of illegal profits belong to the people explanations of crime at the macro-level. Thus, our proposed theory covers both micro- and macro-level predictors of crime.

White-collar crime involves some form of social deviance by individuals and represents a breakdown in social order (Heath, 2008). Many scholars emphasize the nonphysical and nonviolent act committed for financial gain as a key characteristic of white-collar crime (Bookman, 2008; Brightman, 2009). While it is included as a characteristic in the proposed general theory here, it is relevant to notice that Perri and Brody (2011) documents that even white-collar criminals may resort to violence including murder to cover up their crime. The origins of elite crime can be explored and then summarized by examining several criminology theories that offer explanations regarding why this type of crime is so prevalent among seemingly respectable individuals.

Maybe future research on a general theory of white-collar crime should focus on theorizing rather than theory. As argued by Weick and cited in Michailova et al. (2014), theory cannot be improved until we improve the theorizing process, and we cannot improve the theorizing process until we describe it more explicitly. Theorizing involves a mixture of observing something, penetrating something, and finding something out, where there is not necessarily a linear process at all. Weick (1995) argued that the process of theorizing consists of activities such as abstracting, generalizing, relating, selecting, explaining, synthesizing, and idealizing. These ongoing products summarize progress, give direction, and serve as place makers.

The activities that make up theorizing—observing, choosing something interesting, formulating the central concept, building the theory, and completing the tentative theory—can happen in a very different order or in no order at all. Observing white-collar criminals is not easy; it will always be in retrospect a story told by newspapers, police, prosecutors, defendants, defense lawyers, witnesses, victims, and court documents. Penetrating the crime is difficult, but penetrating the criminal as an inmate in prison might be easier. Some white-collar inmates may be reluctant to be interviewed, while others would like their story to be told. For those of us who have had the opportunity to interview white-collar inmates, we observe interesting individuals who have the ability to present themselves and their actions in fascinating ways.

Compared to research on members of Hells Angels in organized crime (Gottschalk, 2013) and research on pedophiles who have groomed children on the Internet, research on white-collar criminals is in so many respects different. A white-collar criminal is simply one of us. Maybe that is why Sutherland's (1940, 1949) analysis of white-collar criminality serves as the catalyst for an area of research that continues and grows today.

Michailova et al. (2014) argue that theorizing is inherently personal. It is even argued that there is no theory that is not a fragment carefully prepared of some autobiography, and that all scholarship is self-revelatory. Michailova et al. (2014) suggest that since it is impossible to make sense of a situation without a personal identity, it is important for theorists to decide and declare who they are. Without going too far in this direction, I as the author of this book am certainly willing to testify that I have never committed white-collar crime, that I have observed white-collar crime as a business executive, that I have interviewed and done statistical research on a large sample of convicted white-collar criminals as a professor, and that I have done empirical research on other convicted criminals as well. My background has led me to the belief that people with wealth and power who commit crime against other people's property should be punished just as severely as drug barons and murderers. This is not the case in Norway today, where drug barons and murderers are sentenced to 10 years on average, while white-collar criminals are sentenced to only 2 years on average. Let me add that pedophiles that destroy lives of young children also only get 2 years. Maybe white-collar criminals and offending pedophiles should receive 10 years on average, while drug barons should only be sentenced to 2 years in prison, as long as we don't want the prison population to grow as a whole. This is not in support of deterrence theory, but about relative seriousness of criminal actions as perceived by society. It is just a thought to tell who I am.

In recent years, most published research work on white-collar crime seems to have struggled to define what is and what is not included in the concept. This section represents an initiative to debate and clarify the concept, so that future research will have an easier avenue to follow when developing a sample. Specifically, to identify financial crime as white-collar offense, there has to be an economical dimension, an organizational dimension, as well as a behavioral dimension (Gottschalk, 2015a).

It is the organizational dimension that probably will create most debate, as a computer hacker sitting in his home alone to commit bank fraud is not considered a white-collar criminal. Neither is a fake bank on the Internet white-collar crime, as criminal activities are not hidden in legal activities, and it is not breach of trust. Some will find the organizational requirement too restrictive.

For example, Bookman (2008) avoids the organizational dimension by defining white-collar crime as an illegal act committed by nonphysical means and by concealment, to obtain money or property, to avoid payment or loss of money or property, or to obtain business or personal advantage. The organizational dimension requires that white-collar crime is committed in a setting of legal and organized work, where people relate to each other in a professional environment. However, to open up at the end of this section, it is important to emphasize that the term organization itself can be many things, as long as it can be portrayed as (1) a multi-agent system with (2) identifiable boundaries and (3) system-level goals (purpose) toward which (4) the constituent agent's efforts are expected to make a contribution (Puranam et al., 2014).

In the process undertaken here, if some things have been unduly excluded from the types of cases on which the definition is based, then if the definition is accepted this will subsequently affect things such as which motivations are considered important in white-collar offenders as we analyze them going forward. Including and excluding particular types of crime and theories which seek to explain aspects of what people other than the author may currently consider to be white-collar crime is therefore a key and critical decision making process in this sort of work. Maybe it has not been done with enough care. For example, excluding environment and safety crime needs more explanation. Does environment crime include pollution? If so, that is pretty squarely within current conceptions of profit-driven crime (McGurrin et al., 2013) and would certainly need some further discussion before we excluded it permanently. Occupational health and safety crime are what is meant by the second part, but these are usually financially motivated as well (Tombs and Whyte, 2003), at least in the cost-cutting approach which may involve casual negligence. In fact, McGurrin et al. (2013: 12) in their discussion of white-collar crime argue that if greater attention was paid to "occupational and environmentally related deaths such as air, land, and water pollution, or preventable medical errors and hospital-acquired infectious diseases, as well as occupational diseases contracted on the job, public health would be significantly less relevant than it is today."

The choice at the outset to exclude certain areas from the ambit of white-collar crime is thus probably question-begging to many scholars. It is certainly not a sufficient justification to argue by the inconvenience generated by an overly capacious conceptualization of the object of study. Rather, the justification thus far is that there are indirect financial effects of environment and safety crime.

This book was set out with an ambitious goal, namely to establish an avenue toward a general theory of white-collar crime, thereby resolving long-standing tensions, ambiguities, and disagreements about how such offending behavior is to be conceptualized and explained. Some readers may find that the chapter failed, and that it amounts to a literature review of existing work that focuses variously upon the economical, organizational, and behavioral dimensions of analysis, as represented in the work of others. However, the chapter proposes dimensions drawn from extant studies that can be used in tandem and thereby offer a new theoretical framework for the analysis of white-collar crime.

Contributions from convenience theory

The primary contribution of this book is to put forth convenience as a theoretical explanation that underlies existing theory and research on white-collar crime. While previous research on crime in general and white-collar crime in particular has mentioned the role of convenience, the explicit notion and role of convenience is novel, and thus does allow the current research to make a novel theoretical contribution. Ideas presented here are grounded in the existing literature, while at the same time representing a novel perspective: they answer questions that are not adequately explained by existing literature and provide different answers to "how...?," "why...?," and "when...?" questions. This chapter negotiates this arguably difficult tension—offering new theory while grounding the underlying ideas in the existing literature.

The main theoretical contribution is concerned with the organizational dimension of white-collar crime. White-collar crime only occurs when the individual is in the capacity of a professional and in the position of a trusted and privileged person in an organizational setting. Both the offender-based and the offense-based perspective of white-collar crime stress the importance of an organization. The offender-based perspective stresses the privileged and trusted position of the criminal enjoying authority and economic power in the organization. The offender has legal access and resources available for crime. The offense-based perspective stresses the variety of financial crime opportunities—from fraud via theft and manipulation to corruption—that are available in an organization. In addition, simple concealment options are available to the white-collar criminal, such as transactions with other firms in other countries with different banks and governments.

When Sutherland (1940) coined the term white-collar crime, he focused on crime in relation to business. A business is traditionally interpreted as an enterprise or a firm. We expand business to all kinds of organizations where people make their living. Some are employers, but most are employees. Employers as well as employees commit white-collar crime. The offender commits crime in a professional setting, where the offender conceals and disguises criminal activities in organizational work by seemingly law-abiding behavior. The criminal has power and influence, forms relationships with other persons or professions—both intraorganizationally as well as interorganizationally—that protects from developing a criminal identity, and enjoys trust from others in privileged networks. Both networks and hierarchies are defined as organizations in this context. While a hierarchy is characterized by a boss and subordinates, a network is characterized by a center and peripherals. Politicians and bureaucrats also work in organizations.

In the organizational setting, we find that most individuals struggle for and reach the peak of their careers when they are between 40 and 50 years old. Their ambitions are peaking at that age, both personal ambitions and ambitions on behalf of the business. Ambitions combined with opportunities create a tendency to commit financial crime when other options for success are less convenient.

Sutherland (1940) implicitly focused on crime in relation to business when he applied differential association theory suggesting that a person associating with individuals who have deviant or unlawful mores, values, and norms learns criminal behavior. While not all offenders became white-collar criminals after learning through interaction with other persons in the organization, the organizational environment was perceived by offenders to be suitable for financial crime.

The lack of guilt feeling and the successful application of neutralization techniques can be explained by the organizational context. Since crime is committed within professional activities, the offender may not consider deviant actions as crime. This is especially the case when the offender commits crime to benefit the organization in terms of corporate crime. It is also evident when offenders claim to be followers rather than leaders in crime. As a follower in the hierarchy or the network, the individual may claim to obey orders, as is customary for legal activities as well. Loyalty in the organization extends from legal across the border to illegal activities, without really noticing where the borderline can be found.

Power and influence are characteristics of social relationships among individuals in business, and abuse of legitimate position power can enable white-collar crime. Executives have legitimate power over subordinates, who are to do what they are told. In knowledge organizations (end product is knowledge) and knowledge-intensive organizations (end product is not knowledge), subordinates are normally told what to do, but not necessarily told how to do it. In traditional manufacturing, subordinates are normally also told how to do it. Subordinates are used to obeying orders, and executives are used to giving orders in terms of their decisions. If decisions are made that involve illegal acts, decisions are presented as orders to be followed by subordinates. If subordinates notice the illegitimate nature of orders from above, they will actively have to deny following orders, and thereby risk losing their jobs.

Most business organizations are driven by goals. Strategic goals can include market position, technological position, and alliances. Financial goals can include turnover, profits and return on investments. In public administrations, goals can include response rate, efficiency, effectiveness, and cases solved. The organization identifies means to reach goals. All kinds of legal means are identified and put to work. If goals are not achieved despite tremendous efforts, some organizations lower their ambitions. Other organizations continue their struggle to reach goals and become aware of illegal means. Objectives are so important that crime becomes an option. Even before everything else has been tested, some organizations turn their attention to crime because of convenience.

While white-collar crime is conducted in organizations, it also requires some form of organizing. Within the organization, white-collar crime is organized. It may be organized in terms of statement manipulations, fake invoices, or routines that are purposely changed. Criminal activity can be carried out in a suborganization of the main organization.

In addition to Benson and Simpson's (2015) three characteristics of how white-collar offenses manifest themselves, one more can be added:

1. The offender has legitimate access to the location in which the crime is committed. Location does not have to be a physical place, it can just as well be a virtual place, such as a management information system

where the offender has access and is a regular user. Legitimate access makes crime convenient.

2. The offender is spatially separate from the victim. This opportunity property is present when it comes to banks and other external victims. However, as indicated by Gottschalk's (2015a through c) study, the most frequent group of victims is employers who suffer loss from crime conducted by people associated with the organization. For example, a procurement executive may collaborate with a vendor to submit fake invoices to the company, then approve payment of the invoice, and finally share the profit with the vendor. In this case, the offender is not spatially separate from the victim. The same lack of spatial separation occurs in cases of embezzlement and some other forms of financial crime. Spatial separation makes crime convenient.

3. The offender's actions have a superficial appearance of legitimacy. Illegal actions are organized and carried out in ways that are as similar as possible to legal actions. The criminal dimension of actions is concealed. Superficial appearance of legitimacy makes crime convenient.

4. The offender has a role of power and influence over other individuals. Since most white-collar criminals are leaders rather than followers, and there always is a leader when there is a follower in crime, the offender tends to have legitimate rights to make decisions and give orders that others have to obey. Objecting to orders from superiors or blowing the whistle on superiors may cause harm to subordinates. Power and influence are characteristics of social relationships among individuals in business, and abuse of legitimate position power can enable white-collar crime without causing suspicion or reaction. Power and influence make crime convenient.

A goal-orientation of most organizations, rather than a rule-orientation, makes objectives more important than means to reach goals. It is left to trusted and privileged individuals to decide how they perform their duties. Controls are installed for goal achievements, but not for individual procedures and behaviors.

In summary, there is a need to understand how people work in organizations, how they cooperate, how they make decisions, and what they are striving for in organizations, before the organizational dimension of convenience theory can be further explored.

Theories can provide general insights into a phenomenon such as white-collar crime. Theories can also provide explanations for empirical occurrences of white-collar crime. Thus, convenience theory is useful both ahead of and after experiences have been collected and analyzed. Convenience theory presents an integrated explanation of white-collar crime, while at the same time enabling explanations when new white-collar criminals emerge.

Davis (1971), Alvesson and Sandberg (2011), as well as Hærem et al. (2015) argue that an interesting theory is one that denies certain assumptions of their audience. Convenience theory denies differential association as a significant explanation in the behavioral dimension. Differential association suggests that criminal behavior is learned in association with those who define such criminal behavior favorably and in isolation from those who define it unfavorably. Sutherland (1940, 1949, 1983), who coined the term white-collar crime, argues in all his works that the main explanation for deviant behavior among white-collar criminals is differential association. In line with Davis (1971), one of the reasons convenience theory is interesting is the lack of belief in differential association as a major factor in explaining white-collar crime, which can also be found in empirical studies (Gottschalk, 2015a through c). Convenience theory denies the assumption that differential association is a major factor in the explanation of white-collar criminal behavior.

In revisiting assumptions (Hærem et al., 2015), key justification of white-collar crime is here replaced by convenience. An assumption is something taken for granted. Nobody will deny the existence of opportunity, motivation, risk, and neutralization in the crime star influencing the occurrence of white-collar crime. Convenience theory introduces the assumption that opportunity is found in the organizational dimension, motivation and risk are found in the economical dimension, while neutralization and again risk are found in the behavioral dimension.

Convenience theory addresses an important and interesting topic of misconduct and crime by the elite in society. Convenience theory extends and advances our understanding in significant ways. Convenience theory has clear implications for future research in terms of both theoretical and empirical studies. Convenience theory represents a problematization approach rather than a gap-spotting approach to theory. Problematization tends to create more interesting studies and more relevant research questions as suggested by Sandberg and Alvesson (2011), Alvesson and Sandberg (2011, 2012), and Davis (1971).

Comparison to Sutherland's theory

Sutherland (1983: 240), in the uncut version of his white-collar crime theory, emphasizes that white-collar crime has its genesis in the same general process as other criminal behavior, namely, differential association:

> The hypothesis of differential association is that criminal behavior is learned in association with those who define such criminal behavior favorably and in isolation from those who define it unfavorably, and that a person in an appropriate situation

> engages in such criminal behavior if, and only if,
> the weight of the favorable definitions exceeds the
> weight of the unfavorable definitions.

There are two parts to the above citation. The first part is questionable; the second part can be confirmed in both convenience theory and empirical study of white-collar criminals to follow in the next chapter. It is indeed questionable whether white-collar criminal behavior is learned in association with those who define such criminal behavior favorably and in isolation from those who define it unfavorably.

Convenience theory suggests that a strong profit-orientation, an organizational opportunity, and an acceptable behavior make it attractive to commit white-collar crime. There is not much learning needed to commit crime. Privileged professions have learned in their positions how to reach goals in legal ways, and they have few problems finding out how to do it in illegal ways. For example, a sales executive knows how to promote products through regular marketing, but the individual also knows how to influence potential customers in illegal ways, such as corruption. A CFO knows how to transfer money between company accounts and has no problems finding out how to transfer money from a company account to a personal account. There is no learning involved in different ways of committing financial crime by white-collar criminals.

In a wider sense it might be argued that learning is part of influenced thinking in terms of crime. Differential association is a theory proposing that through interaction with others, individuals learn the values, attitudes, techniques, and motives for criminal behavior. While techniques and motives are questionable as learning requirements for white-collar crime, values and attitudes may have some influence. However, if nobody around you thinks in criminal terms, will you do it? Yes, convenience theory argues, because you may be in a situation where you desperately look for a way out, and you find one that involves breaking the law. Therefore, both convenience theory and the empirical sample in the next chapter do not support the notion by Sutherland (1983) that criminal behavior must be learned from others before crime will occur. There is little or no need for most potential white-collar criminals to learn criminal behavior, including techniques of committing crime, motives and drives for crime, and rationalizations for crime, before their first offense.

The second part of the citation argues that a person in an appropriate situation engages in white-collar crime if, and only if, the weight of the favorable definitions exceeds the weight of the unfavorable definitions. This is in line with rational choice theory, where benefits and costs are compared before crime is committed. Unfavorable definitions include likelihood of detection and consequence by possible detection. This is an important argument in convenience theory, where white-collar crime is expected to increase when the likelihood of detection as well as the consequence by possible detection both decrease.

Sutherland (1983) argues that the government is less critical toward businessmen than toward persons of lower socioeconomic class. Therefore, white-collar offenses are not considered real crime. It follows that offenders do not perceive themselves as real criminals, which makes it easier for them to commit financial crime. This is consistent with convenience theory.

It is also consistent with social conflict theory presented earlier in this book. Sutherland (1983: 251) suggests that the less critical attitude of government toward businessmen is the result of several relationships:

a. Persons in government are, by and large, culturally homogeneous with persons in business, both being in the upper strata of American society.
b. Many persons in government are members of families that have other members in business.
c. Many persons in business are intimate personal friends of persons in government. Almost every important person in government has many close personal friends in business, and almost every important person in business has many close personal friends in government.
d. Many persons in government were previously connected with business firms as executives, attorneys, directors, or in other capacities. In times of war, especially, many persons in government retain their business connections.
e. Many persons in government hope to secure employment in business firms when their government work is terminated. Government work is often a step toward a career in private business. Relations established while in government, as well as inside information acquired at that time, carry over after the person joins a business firm.
f. Business is very powerful in American society and can damage or promote the governmental programs in which the governmental personnel are interested.
g. The program of the government is closely related to the political parties, and for their success in campaigns these political parties depend on contributions of large sums from important businessmen. Thus, the initial cultural homogeneity, the close personal relationships, and the power relationships protect businessmen against critical definitions by government.

An interesting aspect of this list is the mixture of persons and organizations, which can be translated into occupational crime and corporate crime. In the description of social conflict theory earlier in this book, it was discussed why the elite punishes their own. Some reasons were presented that have changed the law enforcement scene since Sutherland (1940, 1983) first introduced his theory almost a century ago.

Sutherland (1983) is mainly focusing on variations in crime by corporations in his book on white-collar crime. He challenges the common psychological and behavioral explanations of white-collar crime (Sutherland, 1983: 258):

> The current tendency is to advocate emotional instability as the psychological characteristic which explains ordinary criminal behavior, and this explanation has been presented particularly by psychiatrists and psychoanalysts. Even these advocates, however, would suggest only a jocular sense that the crimes of the Ford Motor Company are due to the Oedipus complex, or those of the Aluminum Company of America to an inferiority complex, or those of U.S. Steel to frustration and aggression, or those of the DuPont's to traumatic experience, or those of Montgomery Ward to regression to infancy.

Sutherland (1983) dismisses the suggestion frequently made that crime must be explained by the psychological characteristics of the offenders. He argues that as research work on psychological characteristics has continued, the difference between criminals and noncriminals in respect to these characteristics has proved to be insignificant and inconsistent.

Convenience theory is in accordance with Sutherland (1983) in terms of traditional psychological explanations. That is why the third dimension is labeled the behavioral dimension rather than the psychological dimension. The behavioral dimension in convenience theory emphasizes individual labeling, slippery slope, self-control and desire for control, strain and neutralization. Rather than giving criminals some kind of psychological diagnosis, convenience theory presents situations in which individuals in terms of criminals versus noncriminals may react differently. Included in the behavioral dimension are criminal personality disorders, such as a tendency toward narcissism, but this is never presented as a psychiatric diagnosis. Examples mentioned by Sutherland (1983)—such as Oedipus complex, inferiority complex, and traumatic experience—are not considered relevant to convenience theory.

Convenience theory is in disagreement with Sutherland (1983) when he claims that enterprises like Ford Motor Company, Aluminum Company of America, and U.S. Steel are committing crime. Convenience theory argues that there are always individuals in organizations that commit crime. Enron did not commit crime, but Schilling and others within

Enron committed crime. As illustrated in the next chapter, Norwegian organizations did not commit crime, but 405 white-collar criminals committed financial crime that was detected from 2009 to 2015.

In his skepticism against personal characteristics, Sutherland (1983) argues that if personal characteristics play an important part in the causation of white-collar crime, then they should appear especially in the variations among corporations in their frequency of violations of laws. That is exactly the case in convenience theory. Variations among organizations in their frequency of white-collar crime are explained by personal characteristics in the behavioral dimension of convenience theory. Where potential white-collar criminals in a corporation have normal self-control and normal desire for control, when they are not particularly strained, and when they have a hard time neutralizing potential crime, then they will have a tendency to avoid crime. Where potential white-collar criminals in another corporation have low self-control and excessive desire for control, when they are extremely strained, and when they have no problem in neutralizing guilt, then they will have a tendency to commit crime.

Sutherland (1983) opens up for the behavioral dimension as an explanation of white collar crime. He says that personal traits of executives may explain variations among organizations in terms of criminal conduct, although he is not at all certain (Sutherland, 1983: 263):

> It is recognized that some executives of corporations are high-minded, public spirited citizens and others are dishonest, narrowly selfish, and even asinine. It is questionable, however, whether the crime rates of corporations vary on account of these personal variations. In one area two corporations doing the same kind of work and of approximately the same size have exactly the same number of adverse decisions. The chief executive of one of these is a philanthropic, public-spirited citizen, while the chief executive of the other is generally regarded as cantankerous, narrow-minded, and self-seeking.

This statement may seem to be in conflict with Sutherland's (1983) differential association belief, that criminal behavior is learned. If there is no criminal behavior to be learned from the CEO, then there will be fewer tendencies toward crime. Furthermore, the statement is not concerned with the CEO's tendency toward white-collar crime, but rather with crime occurring in an organization where the CEO may be either good or bad.

Sutherland (1983) suggests that if personal traits are to be used as supplements to differential association, they should be traits that are not already included under differential association. This is in conflict with convenience theory of white-collar crime, where differential association is not emphasized at the expense of personal traits.

In conclusion, Sutherland's (1983) definition of white-collar crime and criminals is applied in convenience theory. His explanations, however, are not all applied. For example, his emphasis on differential association and social disorganizations are not included as main explanations of crime frequency. Rather, opportunity structures and situational factors for both the enterprise and the individual are emphasized in convenience theory as main explanations of crime frequency, in addition to behavioral factors.

References

Adler, P.S. and Kwon, S.W. (2002). Social capital: Prospects for a new concept. *Academy of Management Review*, 27 (1), 17–40.

Agnew, R. (2005). *Pressured into crime—An overview of general strain theory*, Oxford, UK: Oxford University Press.

Agnew, R. (2014). Social concern and crime: Moving beyond the assumption of simple self-interest, *Criminology*, 52 (1), 1–32.

Aguilera, R.V. and Vadera, A.K. (2008). The dark side of authority: Antecedents, mechanisms, and outcomes of organizational corruption, *Journal of Business Ethics*, 77, 431–449.

Alvesson, M. and Sandberg, J. (2011). Generating research questions through problematization, *Academy of Management Review*, 36 (2), 247–271.

Alvesson, M. and Sandberg, J. (2012). Has management studies lost its way? Ideas for more imaginative and innovative research, *Journal of Management Studies*, 50 (1), 128–152.

Arjoon, S. (2008). Slippery When wet: The real risk in business, *Journal of Markets & Morality*, Spring, 11 (1), 77–91.

Arnulf, J.K. and Gottschalk, P. (2013). Heroic leaders as white-collar criminals: An empirical study, *Journal of Investigative Psychology and Offender Profiling*, 10, 96–113.

Ashforth, B.E., Gioia, D.A., Robinson, S.L. and Trevino, L.K. (2008). Re-reviewing organizational corruption, *Academy of Management Review*, 33 (3), 670–684.

Baird, J.E. and Zelin, R.C. (2009). An examination of the impact of obedience pressure on perceptions of fraudulent acts and the likelihood of committing occupational fraud, *Journal of Forensic Studies in Accounting and Business*, Winter, 1–14.

Benson, M.L. and Simpson, S.S. (2015). *Understanding white-collar crime—An opportunity perspective*, New York: Routledge.

Blickle, G., Schlegel, A., Fassbender, P. and Klein, U. (2006). Some personality correlates of business white-collar crime, *Applied Psychology: An International Review*, 55 (2), 220–233.

Bookman, Z. (2008). Convergences and omissions in reporting corporate and white collar crime, *DePaul Business & Commercial Law Journal*, 6, 347–392.

Brightman, H.J. (2009). *Today's White-collar crime: Legal, investigative, and theoretical perspectives*, New York: Routledge, Taylor & Francis Group.

Bucy, P.H., Formby, E.P., Raspanti, M.S. and Rooney, K.E. (2008). Why do they do it?: The motives, mores, and character of white collar criminals, *St. John's Law Review*, 82, 401–571.

Bystrova, E.G. and Gottschalk, P. (2015). Social conflict theory and white-collar criminals: Why does the ruling class punish their own? *Pakistan Journal of Criminology*, 7 (1), 1–15.

Chang, J.J., Lu, H.C. and Chen, M. (2005). Organized crime or individual crime? Endogeneous size of a criminal organization and the optimal law enforcement, *Economic Inquiry*, 43 (3), 661–675.

Chrisman, J.J., Chua, J.H., Kellermanns, F.W. and Chang, E.P.C. (2007). Are family managers agents or stewards? An exploratory study in privately held family firms, *Journal of Business Research*, 60 (10), 1030–1038.

Colquitt, J.A. and Zapata-Phelan, C.P. (2007). Trends in theory building and theory testing: A five-decade study of the Academy of Management Journal, *Academy of Management Journal*, 50 (6), 1281–1303.

Comey, J.B. (2009). Go directly to prison: White collar sentencing after the Sarbanes-Oxley act, *Harvard Law Review*, 122, 1728–1749.

Davis, M.S. (1971). That's interesting, *Philosophy of the Social Sciences*, 1, 309–344.

Dion, M. (2008). Ethical leadership and crime prevention in the organizational setting, *Journal of Financial Crime*, 15 (3), 308–319.

Dodge, M. (2009). *Women and white-collar crime*. Upper Saddle River, NJ: Prentice Hall.

Eisenhardt, K.M. (1989). Building theories from case study research, *Academy of Management Review*, 14 (4), 532–550.

Füss, R. and Hecker, A. (2008). Profiling white-collar crime: Evidence from German-speaking countries, *Corporate Ownership & Control*, 5 (4), 149–161.

Galvin, B.M., Lange, D. and Ashforth, B.E. (2015). Narcissistic organizational identification: Seeing oneself as central to the organization's identity, *Academy of Management Review*, 40 (2), 163–181.

Goldstraw-White, J. (2012). *White-collar crime: Accounts of offendig behaviour*, London: Palgrave Macmillan.

Gottfredson, M.R. and Hirschi, T. (1990). *A general theory of crime*, Stanford, CA: Stanford University Press.

Gottschalk, P. (2013). Limits to corporate social responsibility: The case of Gjensidige insurance company and Hells Angels motorcycle club, *Corporate Reputation Review*, 16 (3), 177–186.

Gottschalk, P. (2015a). *Fraud examiners in white-collar crime investigations*, Boca Raton, FL: CRC Press, Taylor & Francis.

Gottschalk, P. (2015b). *Investigating financial crime—Characteristics of white-collar criminals*, Hauppauge, NY: Nova Science Publishers.

Gottschalk, P. (2015c). *Internal investigations of economic crime—Corporate case studies and regulatory policy*, Boca Raton, FL: Universal Publishers.

Gottschalk, P. and Smith, R. (2015). Gender and white-collar crime: Examining representations of women in media, *Journal of Gender Studies*, 24 (3), 310–325.

Haines, F. (2014). Corporate fraud as misplaced confidence? Exploring ambiguity in the accuracy of accounts and the materiality of money, *Theoretical Criminology*, 18 (1), 20–37.

Hamilton, S. and Micklethwait, A. (2006). *Greed and corporate failure: The lessons from recent disasters*, Basingstoke, UK: Palgrave Macmillan.

Hansen, L.L. (2009). Corporate financial crime: Social diagnosis and treatment, *Journal of Financial Crime*, 16 (1), 28–40.

Heath, J. (2008). Business ethics and moral motivation: A criminological perspective, *Journal of Business Ethics*, 83, 595–614.

Hirschi, T. and Gottfredson, M. (1987). Causes of white-collar crime, *Criminology*, 25 (4), 949–974.

Huisman, W. and Erp, J. (2013). Opportunities for environmental crime, *British Journal of Criminology*, 53, 1178–1200.

Hærem, T., Pentland, B.T. and Miller, K.D. (2015). Task complexity: Extending a core concept, *Academy of Management Review*, 40 (3), 446–460.

Johnson, S.D. and Groff, E.R. (2014). Strengthening theoretical testing in criminology using agent-based modeling, *Journal of Research in Crime and Delinquency*, 51 (4), 509–525.

Kamerdze, S., Loughran, T., Paternoster, R. and Sohoni, T. (2014). The role of affect in intended rule breaking: Extending the rational choice perspective, *Journal of Research in Crime and Delinquency*, 51 (5), 620–654.

Kerik, B.B. (2015). *From jailer to jailed—My journey from correction and police commissioner to inmate #84888-054*, New York: Threshold Editions.

Langton, L. and Piquero, N.L. (2007). Can general strain theory explain white-collar crime? A preliminary investigation of the relationship between strain and select white-collar offenses, *Journal of Criminal Justice*, 35, 1–15.

Li, S. and Ouyang, M. (2007). A dynamic model to explain the bribery behavior of firms, *International Journal of Management*, 24 (3), 605–618.

Maddan, S., Hartley, R.D., Walker, J.T. and Miller, J.M. (2012). Sympathy for the devil: An exploration of federal judicial discretion in the processing of white collar offenders, *American Journal of Criminal Justice*, 37, 4–18.

McGloin, J.M. and Stickle, W.P. (2011). Influence or convenience? Disentangling peer influence and co-offending for chronic offenders, *Journal of Research in Crime and Delinquency*, 48 (3), 419–447.

McGurrin, D., Jarrell, M., Jahn, A. and Cochrane, B. (2013). White collar crime representation in the criminological literature revisited, 2001–2010, *Western Criminology Review*, 14 (2), 3–19.

McKay, R., Stevens, C. and Fratzi, J. (2010). A 12-step process of white-collar crime, *International Journal of Business Governance and Ethics*, 5 (1), 14–25.

Michailova, S., Piekkari, R., Plakoyiannaki, E., Ritvala, T., Mihailova, I. and Salmi, A. (2014). Breaking the silence about exiting fieldwork: A relational approach and its implications for theorizing, *Academy of Management Review*, 39 (2), 138–161.

Michel, P. (2008). Financial crimes: The constant challenge of seeking effective prevention solutions, *Journal of Financial Crime*, 15 (4), 383–397.

O'Connor, T.R. (2005). Police deviance and ethics. In part of web cited, MegaLinks in Criminal Justice. http://faculty.ncwc.edu/toconnor/205/205lect11.htm, retrieved on 19 February 2009.

Onna, J.H.R., Geest, V.R., Huisman, W. and Denkers, J.M. (2014). Criminal trajectories of white-collar offenders, *Journal of Research in Crime and Delinquency*, 51, 759–784.

Perri, F.S. and Brody, R.G. (2011). The Sallie Rohrbach story: Lessons for auditors and fraud examiners, *Journal of Financial Crime*, 18 (1), 93–104.

Petrossian, G.A. and Clarke, R.V. (2013). Explaining and controlling illegal commercial fishing, *British Journal of Criminology*, 54, 73–90.

Pickett, K.H.S. and Pickett, J.M. (2002). *Financial crime investigation and control*, New York: John Wiley & Sons.

Piquero, N.L. (2012). The only thing we have to fear is fear itself: Investigating the relationship between fear of falling and white collar crime, *Crime and Delinquency*, 58 (3), 362–379.

Piquero, N.L., Schoepfer, A. and Langton, L. (2010). Completely out of control or the desire to be in complete control? How low self-control and the desire for control relate to corporate offending, *Crime & Delinquency*, 56 (4), 627–647.

Pontell, H.N., Black, W.K. and Geis, G. (2014). Too big to fail, too powerful to jail? On the absence of criminal prosecutions after the 2008 financial meltdown, *Crime, Law and Social Change*, 61 (1), 1–13.

Pratt, T.C. and Cullen, F.T. (2005). Assessing macro-level predictors and theories of crime: A meta-analysis, *Crime and Justice*, 32, 373–450.

Punch, M. (2003). Rotten orchards: "Pestilence," police misconduct and system failure. *Policing and Society*, 13, (2) 171–196.

Puranam, P., Alexy, O. and Reitzig, M. (2014). What's "new" about new forms of organizing? *Academy of Management Review*, 39 (2), 162–180.

Reed, G.E. and Yeager, P.C. (1996). Organizational offending and neoclassical criminology: Challenging the reach of a general theory of crime, *Criminology*, 34 (3), 357–382.

Robb, G. (2006). Women and white-collar crime, *British Journal of Criminology*, 46, 1058–1072.

Sandberg, J. and Alvesson, M. (2011). Ways of constructing research questions: Gap-spotting or problematization, *Organization*, 18 (1), 23–44.

Schoepfer, A. and Piquero, N.L. (2006). Exploring white-collar crime and the American dream: A partial test of institutional anomie theory, *Journal of Criminal Justice*, 34, 227–235.

Schoepfer, A., Carmichael, S. and Piquero, N.L. (2007). Do perceptions of punishment vary between white-collar and street crimes? *Journal of Criminal Justice*, 35, 151–163.

Simpson, S.S., Alper, M. and Benson, M.L. (2012). *Gender and white-collar crime in the 21st century.* Paper presented at the American Society of Criminology, Chicago, IL.

Stadler, W.A., Benson, M.L. and Cullen, F.T. (2013). Revisiting the special sensitivity hypothesis: The prison experience of white-collar inmates, *Justice Quarterly*, iFirst, 1–25.

Steffensmeier, D., Schwartz, J. and Roche, M. (2013). Gender and twenty-first-century corporate crime: Female involvement and the gender gap in Enron-era corporate frauds, *American Sociological Review*, 78 (3), 448–476.

Sutherland, E.H. (1940).White-collar criminality, *American Sociological Review,* 5, 1–12.

Sutherland, E.H. (1949). *White collar crime*, New York: Holt Rinehart and Winston.

Sutherland, E.H. (1983). *White collar crime—The uncut version*, New Haven, CT: Yale University Press.

Sutton, R.I. and Staw, B.M. (1995). What theory is not, *Administrative Science Quarterly*, 40, 371–384.

Sykes, G. and Matza, D. (1957). Techniques of neutralization: A theory of delinquency, *American Sociological Review*, 22 (6), 664–670.

Tombs, S. and Whyte, D. (2003). Scrutinizing the powerful: Crime, contemporary political economy, and critical social research. In S. Tombs and D. Whyte (eds.), *Unmasking the crimes of the powerful*, New York: Lang, pp. 3–48.

Trahan, A. (2011). Filling in the gaps in culture-based theories of organizational crime, *Journal of Theoretical and Philosophical Criminology*, 3 (1), 89–109.

Valukas, A.R. (2010). *In regard Lehman Brothers Holdings Inc. to United States Bankruptcy Court in Southern District of New York*, Jenner & Block, March 11, 239 pages, http://www.nysb.uscourts.gov/sites/default/files/opinions /188162_61_opinion.pdf.

Weick, K.E. (1995). What theory is not, theorizing is, *Administrative Science Quarterly*, 40, 385–390.

Weissmann, A. and Block, J.A. (2010). White-collar defendants and white-collar crimes, *Yale Law Journal*, 116, 286–291.

Welsh, D.T., Oronez, L.D., Snyder, D.G. and Christian, M.S. (2014). The slippery slope: How small ethical transgressions pave the way for larger future transgressions, *Journal of Applied Psychology*, http://dx.doi.org/10.1037/a0036950.

Whetten, D.A. (1989). What constitutes a theoretical contribution? *Academy of Management Review*, 14 (4), 490–495.

White, M.D. and Katz, C.M. (2013). Policing convenience store crime: Lessons from the glendale, arizona smart policing initiative, *Police Quarterly*, 16 (3), 305–322.

Williams, J.W. (2008). The lessons of 'Enron'—Media accounts, corporate crimes, and financial markets, *Theoretical Criminology*, 12 (4), 471–499.

Yusuf, T.O. and Babalola, A.R. (2009). Control of insurance fraud in Nigeria: An exploratory study, *Journal of Financial Crime*, 16 (4), 418–435.

chapter six

Empirical study of white-collar criminals

Convenience theory invites and asks for empirical studies of research hypotheses. Unfortunately, we do not have empirical data for both convicted white-collar criminals and white-collar individuals in position. We only have access to data about convicts. Since 2009, we have registered convicted white-collar criminals in Norway in a separate database. After six years in 2015, there are 405 white-collar criminals registered in the database with information from court documents as well as newspaper reports and media reports in general. Thus on average, every year 68 privileged individuals in Norway have been detected, prosecuted, convicted, and sentenced to prison. There are 5 million inhabitants in Norway.

Sample of criminals in Norway

There are 375 men and 30 women among the 405 white-collar criminals in Norway. The fraction of women is only 7.4 percent.

Average age when crime was committed is 44 years old. The youngest one was 21 years, while the oldest was 73 years. There is close to a normal distribution among offenders, which implies that there are many more criminals in their forties than criminals in other age groups. A total of five offenders committed crimes after they were 70 years old. They were a fish exporter, a chief executive officer, a manager, a chairman of the board, and one retired. The youngest ones were a kebab shopper, an heir, a reality celebrity, a painter, and a self-employed person.

Average age at final conviction in court was 49 years. This implies that it took on average five years from criminal act to court ruling. The youngest convict was 25 years, while the oldest was 77 years. The oldest was Odd Arhur Olsen (born 1933) in the Swaco case. He was the father of Henry Olav Olsen (born 1958). The father produced fictive invoices from his company for corruption payments and thereby contributed to money laundering of 7 million Norwegian kroner, which is the equivalent of $1 million (Gulating, 2009). The son was a warehouse manager at the oil service company Swaco. The father was sentenced to almost 3 years in prison, while the son was sentenced to almost 5 years.

The most severe sentence in terms of prison was 9 years, while the shortest was 4 months. There is no difference between jail and prison in Norway. The average prison sentence was 2 years and 4 months. The 10 longest prison sentences are listed in Table 6.1.

One reason for the long time duration from crime to verdict—on average five years—is time in the criminal justice system. Especially when cases are appealed, and when cases go back and forth, many years tend to elapse in the system. The 405 cases became final in the following courts:

District courts: 227 white-collar criminals (56%)
Courts of appeal: 152 white-collar criminals (38%)
Supreme Court: 26 white-collar criminals (6%)

It took on average 4.5 years for criminals convicted in district courts. It took on average 5.6 years for criminals convicted in courts of appeal, and it took 5.0 years for cases visiting the Norwegian Supreme Court. The latter may seem surprising. Without going into procedural details, the role of the Supreme Court is often to return cases back to courts of appeal because of mistakes.

Most of the criminals worked in privileged positions in the private business sector. Few criminals had positions in the public sector. There were 374 criminals from the private sector and 31 criminals from the public sector. Hence, public sector criminals represent only 7.7 percent of all criminals in the database.

It might be worth speculating in the low female fraction and the low public sector fraction. Gottschalk and Smith (2015) and Gottschalk (2014) explain the low female fraction by the glass ceiling in terms of lack of opportunity and by the biased suspicion of crime toward men rather than women. Gottschalk and Smith (2016) explain the low fraction of public

Table 6.1 White-collar criminals with longest jail sentences

Case	Criminal	Prison	Position
Finance Credit	Trond Kristoffersen	9 years	CEO
Acta	Fred Anton Ingebrigtsen[a]	9 years	Board member
Vannverk	Ivar T. Henriksen	8 years	Vice president
Marine Subsea	Mårten Rød[a]	8 years	Board chairman
Eltek	Alain Angelil[a]	8 years	Founder
Drosjesvindel	Henry Amundsen	8 years	Accountant
Finance Credit	Torgeir Stensrud	7 years	Board chairman
Undervisningsbygg	Frank Murud	7 years	Property manager
TSMarine	Birger Østraat	7 years	Vice president
Doping	Gunnar Jacobsen	6.5 years	Bodybuilder

[a] Appealed.

sector criminals by public service motivation theory, which argues that individuals enter into privileged positions in the public sector for other reasons than profit and financial success.

There might be some interesting statistical relationships between gender, age, prison, court levels and sectors in the database. Men were on average 49 years old when convicted. Women were 47 years old. This represents a marginal difference in terms of gender. A significant difference in terms of gender can be found in prison sentences. Men were sentenced to prison for 2.3 years, while women were sentenced to prison for 1.3 years. Some of this discrepancy might be explained by the amount of money involved in the crime. Women were convicted of financial crime with much less money involved. Women seem to appeal their sentences to higher courts less frequently than men. Female white-collar criminals like males worked mainly in the private sector.

Older white-collar criminals were convicted to longer prison sentences. This might be explained by the amount of money involved in crime, which was higher for older criminals.

There is no statistical link between prison and court level, which means that there is no reason to suggest that more severe cases are appealed to higher court levels. There is, however, a statistical relationship between age and court level, which suggests that older defendants tend to appeal their verdicts more often than younger defendants.

Economical dimension in crime

All 405 white-collar criminals had profit as motive for their crime. The average amount of money involved was 45 million Norwegian kroner (about $7 million). The smallest amount was a few thousand; the largest amount was 1.2 billion Norwegian kroner (about $200 million). The largest amount was found in the collapse of Finance Credit, a collections agency that had borrowed heavily from a number of banks based on misleading financial statements. The chairman, Torgeir Stensrud, was sentenced to 7 years in prison, while the chief executive officer, Trond Kristoffersen, was sentenced to 9 years in prison. The firm Finance Credit's external auditor, John Haukland, was sentenced to 10 months in prison.

It is likely that it was the threat of bankruptcy that caused Stensrud and Kristoffersen to manipulate accounting figures to enable Finance Credit to stay afloat based on millions from banks. Since they were unable to save the firm, which they had built themselves through hard work, the bank fraud was detected as part of the bankruptcy.

The second largest crime amount in the database is 800 million Norwegian kroner (about $130 million). It is the case of Sponsor Service, which was a firm that channeled sponsoring funds from enterprises to top athletes. The case is similar to Finance Credit in that the firm was on the brink of bankruptcy when management started with bank fraud. Management presented sponsoring contracts that were not yet signed to banks, telling banks that the contracts would soon be signed. But they were never signed. Terje Bogen, the CEO, and Mark Sjuve, the CFO, were sentenced to 4.5 years and 1 year, respectively. The external auditors, Jan Korsmo and Erland Stenberg, were sentenced to 3 months and 1 month, respectively.

In the database, distinctions are made between four main categories of financial crime: fraud, theft, manipulation, and corruption. Distribution of criminals among these categories is listed in Table 6.2.

The most frequent crime category is fraud, which can be defined as an intentional perversion of truth for the purpose of inducing another in reliance upon it to part with some valuable thing belonging to him or to surrender legal rights. Fraud is unlawful and intentional making of a misrepresentation, which causes actual prejudice or which is potentially prejudicial to another.

The second most frequent category is manipulation, which can be defined as a means of gaining illegal control or influence over others' activities, means, and results. For example, by manipulating accounting figures the criminal influences activities of the internal revenue service and other tax authorities.

The table shows that the crime amount by fraud was 63 million Norwegian kroner on average (about $10 million). The average imprisonment for fraud was 2.7 years. By theft and corruption, amounts were much lower in comparison, 5 and 6 million, respectively. An example of theft is Kjell Engstrøm who illegally took over the travel agency Troll Travel and thereafter purchased goods and services charged to the travel agency. Engstrøm was sentenced to 10 months in prison for stealing the agency and for procurement of 342,000 kroner on behalf of the agency.

Corruption is the final category defined as the giving, requesting, receiving or accepting of an improper advantage related to position, office, or assignment. The improper advantage does not have to be connected to a specific action or to not-doing this action. It is sufficient if the advantage can be linked to a person's position, office, or assignment. Corruption involves, on average, 6 million Norwegian kroner, as listed in the table.

Table 6.2 Main categories of financial crime

Crime category	Criminals	Fraction	Amount	Prison
Fraud	171	42%	63 mill.	2.7 years
Theft	17	4%	5 mill.	1.1 years
Manipulation	142	35%	48 mill.	2.1 years
Corruption	75	19%	6 mill.	1.9 years
Total	405	100%	45 mill.	2.3 years

The database provides no answer to the question of how many white-collar criminals commit financial crime because of threats versus criminals who did it because of opportunities. The general impression from the sample is, however, that theft and corruption occur in opportunity situations. The main categories of fraud and manipulation may just as frequently occur in threat situations. The overall impression based on personal knowledge of the cases is, however, that most of the 405 convicted criminals carried out financial crime because of opportunities for extraordinary and unjustified profits in a convenient manner. Future costs in terms of detection, prosecution, and prison were quite unlikely to all of them. They experienced an unlucky situation by being detected because the general impression is that the detection rate for white-collar crime is extremely low.

The database does not enable identification of white-collar criminals who explored possibilities because of greed. Many of the judgments in court documented in sentences of several pages provide a clear impression of convenience in the form of simple financial gain, easy organizational manipulation, and no real guilt feeling that led defendants to commit crime. But court documents support no general impression of greed as the dominating motivation for convicted white-collar criminals.

Since the majority of white-collar criminals explored opportunities for financial gain, rather than avoided threats of financial collapse, we can study Maslow's hierarchy of needs in which they find themselves. Income, tax, and net wealth for each criminal is registered in the database in terms of official figures from the internal revenue service in 2009. Few individuals have figures in the database that create an impression of poverty. The average registered income was 451,000 kroner, tax payment was 209,000 kroner, and net taxable assets were 2.8 million kroner. These are quite normal figures for upper-class people as they tend to reduce their own tax burden as much as possible. Thus, most white-collar criminals can be found at the top of Maslow's pyramid where crime is committed to contribute to success, prestige, respect, and self-realization, as well as prosperity.

The economic model of rational self-interest has probably been applied implicitly or explicitly by most of those who committed white-collar crime. On the one hand, the profit was attractive and significant, while at the same time accessible and timely. On the other hand, future costs were unlikely because consequences could not be expected for an individual criminal in the organizational context. Criminals know that it is only randomness and bad luck that can cause them to get caught.

In the database, there are 405 persons who have been detected and convicted in the last six years. The average number per year was 68 white-collar criminals. With a population of 5 million people in Norway, out of which 2 million are working in professional jobs, it can be assumed that 5 percent have the opportunity to commit white-collar crime. This leads to an estimated 100,000 individuals who are potential offenders. The tendency to commit crime—the crimigenity—can be estimated at 2 percent, which implies that 2 out of 100 potential offenders commit financial crime in a given year. This number game results in 2000 white-collar criminals annually in Norway. Only 68 of them are caught. The resultant detection probability is then 3.4 percent. The likelihood of not getting caught is 96.6 percent.

Future costs for white-collar criminals are low since there is only a 3.4 percent of chance of getting caught. The economic model for rational self-interest will thus easily lead to potential criminals committing financial crime in situations of threats and possibilities. The risk is very low. Risk is defined as the joint effect of consequence and likelihood. While the consequence is quite substantial in terms of punishment and loss, the likelihood is so small that when multiplying consequence and likelihood with each other, the resulting figure for risk becomes very low.

As estimated above, 68 detected and prosecuted white-collar criminals annually, and 405 detected and prosecuted from 2009 to 2015, represent an insignificant fraction of all white-collar criminals. Disclosed crime was detected by persons listed in Table 6.3.

Journalists are at the top of the list when it comes to number of disclosures as well as crime amount. Smart journalists in leading financial and national newspapers and other media dug up stories that later were picked up by the police, the prosecution, and eventually the courts. The starting point for journalists was often information revealed to them from whistleblowers. Whistleblowing is a disclosure by organizational members of illegal, immoral, or illegitimate practices under the control of their employers, to persons or organizations that may be able to effect action (Vadera et al., 2009).

Table 6.3 Professionals who detected white-collar criminals

Detective	Criminals	Fraction	Crime amount	Prison
Journalists in the media	101	25%	106 mill.	2.5 years
Victims of crime	52	13%	34 mill.	2.4 years
Bankruptcy lawyers	45	11%	16 mill.	2.6 years
Internal auditors	45	11%	6 mill.	2.1 years
Clerks at tax authority	25	6%	16 mill.	2.6 years
Clerks at bank	18	4%	24 mill.	2.6 years
External auditors	18	4%	6 mill.	1.6 years
Police investigators	9	2%	16 mill.	2.3 years
Clerk at stock exchange	4	1%	1 mill.	1.1 years
Others	88	22%	29 mill.	2.1 years
Total	405	100%	45 mill.	2.3 years

Convenience theory discusses the relationship between principal and agent. The agent carries out tasks for the principal. Although the agent may have different priorities than the principal, the principal will not discover deviance because the agent enjoys freedom to complete tasks. The principal has no way of controlling what the agent is doing. The principal has an opinion about what should be done, but the principal has no way of telling how the agent does it. This is typical for trusted and privileged individuals as agents who commit white-collar crime.

The extent of freedom and the limits to control can be interpreted based on positions held by convicted white-collar criminals. For example, there are 19 attorneys in the database. Most of the attorneys have either embezzled or otherwise abused client funds. Clients of attorneys are, in this context, principals while attorneys are agents. A client has little or no chance of controlling what the attorney is actually doing.

Chief executive officers (CEOs) represent a large group in the database. A total of 36 convicted CEOs are registered in the database. A CEO reports to a collection of individuals called the board, which meets regularly to evaluate what the CEO is doing and what the CEO is intending to do. In most countries, the board consists of individuals whose main job is somewhere else. Board members are typically CEOs in other organizations and take on the extra task of being on the board of another CEO's organization. Board members spend little time with the other organization and express complete confidence in the CEO at that organization. Therefore, both control possibilities and control willingness are very limited.

Even worse is the situation for board members and chairpersons of the board. A chairperson is elected by an assembly that meets only once a year. There are a total of 14 chairpersons in the database who were sentenced to prison for white-collar crime.

Organizational dimension in crime

White-collar criminals are professionals who occupy trusted positions in enterprises and other kinds of organizations in the private and public sector. A professional is a person who earns his or her living from a specified activity. Examples include procurement managers, financial executives, and property developers. Some white-collar criminals are only loosely connected to the organization as, for example, board members and investors. Some white-collar criminals are self-employed in their own small firms. What they all have in common is that they commit financial crime as an activity in their profession and position associated with a private or public business.

In the database, organizational size is registered both in terms of turnover and in terms of employees. The average business where white-collar crime occurred had an annual turnover of 322 million Norwegian kroner (about $50 million) and 288 persons employed. One hundred fourteen businesses had only one single person employed, which was the white-collar criminal.

The largest organization had 8000 employees. It was the global fertilizer manufacturer Yara, where the former CEO and three more executives where sentenced to prison in 2015. They have appealed their verdict and expect to appear in court again in 2016. Prosecutors accused the men of paying around $8 million in bribes to officials in India and Libya—including to the family of former Libyan leader Muammar Gadhafi's oil minister and the family of a financial adviser in India's Ministry of Chemicals and Fertilizers—for the right to establish joint ventures. Former CEO Thorleif Enger got the longest sentence of 3 years. Former legal officer Kendrick Wallace, a U.S. citizen, was sentenced to 2 1/2 years in prison, while former head of upstream activities Tor Holba and former deputy CEO Daniel Clauw, a French citizen, were both given 2-year jail terms (Berglund, 2015).

The second largest enterprise in the database is Din Baker (Your Bakery), a major food group, where the CEO Jørn Bertheussen was sentenced to prison for disloyalty to the company. He got the food group to pay bills issued from his own private firm that he had set up in Sweden. Bertheussen was sentenced to 120 days in prison for embezzling 860,000 kroner (about $140,000). According to figures from the internal revenue service, Bertheussen had an annual income of 1.8 million Norwegian kroner (almost $300,000), which makes it likely that he committed financial crime because of greed combined with opportunity (Asker and Bærum district court, 2012).

The organizational dimension of convenience theory emphasizes that white-collar criminals have extensive freedom without control to carry out transactions of illegal character that are easily disguised among legal transactions. A sign of freedom and independence is the title of the position occupied. Lawyers, CEOs, CFOs and chairpersons have been mentioned already. In their professional capacities, these individuals have considerable power and influence that they can abuse.

Also persons further down the hierarchy have substantial power, influence, independence, and freedom, but in limited areas of the business. For example, a property developer or a chief information officer (CIO) enjoys freedom in selecting suppliers of maintenance services and computer equipment to the organization. In their positions, they can easily select vendors that return personal favors without anyone approving or noticing. Another example is finance executives, who handle company bank accounts and simply can transfer money to unauthorized accounts, such as accounts owned by relatives and friends.

Convenience theory emphasizes that crime committed on behalf of the business makes it particularly evident that there is an organizational connection. When a sales manager bribes a customer, it is mainly to achieve sales that probably otherwise would not take place. When the accounting manager manipulates traffic numbers in deserted areas, it is mainly to enable the shipping company to receive more government subsidies for the line. When the CFO manipulates sales figures, it is mainly to reduce company payments of value added tax to the government.

Out of 405 white-collar criminals, 68 persons (17%) committed financial crime on behalf of the business. The remaining 83 percent did it to enrich themselves. Those who committed corporate crime were, on average, 53 years old, committed crime for 131 million Norwegian kroner (about $20 million), and were connected to organizations with 769 employees on average. Those who committed occupational crime were on average 48 years old, committed crime for $27 million, and were linked to organizations with 104 employees. The tendency is that corporate crime is committed in larger organizations when compared to occupational crime.

Convenience theory stresses that crime dominated by a rotten apple barrel rather than a single rotten apple very clearly illustrates the organizational connection in criminal activities. Based on media coverage and court documents, it was possible to classify 405 white-collar criminals into a barrel with others or into a single offender. The database shows a total of 254 white-collar criminals (63%) belonged to rotten apple barrels, while 151 offenders (37%) were rotten apples. This finding implies that most white-collar criminals worked in an environment where the tendency to financial crime was present among multiple privileged professionals.

This finding is also confirmed when looking at the number of persons prosecuted in each white-collar crime case in court, which is also registered in the database. A white-collar criminal committed crime together with three other offenders.

There are 110 persons in the database who were prosecuted and convicted alone. All remaining 295 persons were prosecuted and convicted with accomplices. The case with the largest number of accomplices was the Tromsdal case involving 15 persons. They worked in different organizations, but they had established a criminal network, which is also an organizational form. Christer Tromsdal has been sentenced for financial crime several times. In June 2015, he was sentenced to 6 years in prison. Anthony Bratli, a surveyor, and Terje Hvidsten, an art dealer, were both at the same time sentenced to 4 1/2 years in prison. At about the same time, Arne Aarsæther, an attorney, was sentenced to 4 months in prison for handling illegal proceeds (Borgarting, 2015).

The second largest collection of criminals can be found in the Unibuss case, where nine persons were convicted and more persons were waiting for their trials in 2015. The Unibuss scandal started in Germany where it was revealed that German bus manufacturer MAN was systematically bribing public transportation companies to make them buy MAN busses. For example, MAN made procurement officials specify the need for busses of exactly 18 meters and 75 centimeters in length. The only bus manufacturer supplying exactly that length was MAN. Corruption also occurred toward executives at Oslo city transportation company Unibuss (Haugan, 2014).

The database has registered white-collar criminals as leaders or followers in crime. Bucy et al. (2008) made distinctions between leaders and followers in white-collar crime. Motives for leaders differ from follower motives. Compared to the view that leaders engage in white-collar crime because of greed and opportunity, followers are nonassertive, weak people who trail behind someone else, even into criminal schemes. Followers may be convinced of the rightness of their cause, and they believe that no harm can come to them because they are following a leader whom they trust or fear. Followers tend to be naïve and unaware of what is really happening, or they are simply taken in by the personal charisma of the leader and are intensely loyal to that person. In an organizational context, the typical leader is the boss and supervisor for the follower.

In the database, there are 255 leaders and 150 followers. Most of the criminals were leaders, among others because all 110 single criminals were classified as leaders. Table 6.4 compares leaders and followers in terms of age, prison, amount, and income. Leaders and followers are on average the same age. Leaders receive a significantly longer prison sentence. Crime amount is somewhat larger for followers. Normally, a larger crime amount leads to a longer prison sentence. This is not the case here. Despite smaller crime amount, leaders receive a more severe prison sentence. Taxable income according to figures from the internal revenue service in 2009 indicates that leaders make more money than followers.

The difference between leaders and followers is statistically significant for length of prison sentence. Differences for age, amount, and income are not significant because the significance indicator is greater than 0.05.

A distinction is made in the database between criminal entrepreneurs, corporate criminals, criminal followers, and female criminals (pink-collar criminals). There were 218 criminal entrepreneurs, 47 corporate criminals, 121 criminal followers, and 19 female criminals (which were not allocated to the other groups).

Table 6.4 Differences between leaders and followers in white-collar crime

Characteristics	Leaders	Followers	Significance
Age of criminal	49 years	49 years	0.651
Prison sentence	2.7 years	1.6 years	0.000
Crime amount	$41 million	$51 million	0.497
Personal income	523,000 kroner	328,000 kroner	0.077

Behavioral dimension in crime

Convenience theory postulates that neutralization of guilt feelings is quite common among white-collar criminals. Although several news reports and court documents confirm neutralization among defendants and convicts, it was not possible to register the extent of neutralization for each individual in the database. However, some white-collar criminals have been so much exposed in the media and elsewhere that it is possible to recognize neutralization techniques in their statements and explanations. Some white-collar criminals have even written books about their own criminal cases where they explicitly express lack of guilt.

An example of frequent media appearance is Christer Tromsdal. He was convicted several times for white-collar crime, and his latest sentence of 6 years in prison is from 2015. Table 6.5 shows neutralization techniques applied by Tromsdal, as they appear in numerous media reports and court documents in the most recent decade. "Yes" means that Tromsdal applies this neutralization technique, while "No" means that there is no sign of this neutralization technique in the many interviews in the media with Tromsdal (Bjørndal and Kleppe, 2013; Dahle, 2011; Hultgren, 2012; Kleppe, 2015; Meldalen, 2015; NTB, 2015; Oslo district court, 2015).

Examples of white-collar criminals who have written books about their own sentences are Bogen (2008), Eriksen (2010), and Fosse and Magnusson (2004) in Norway. A quote from Bogen's (2008: 271) book can illustrate some of his neutralization by denial of responsibility:

> I was never informed or updated of what was recognized, and what was restored, but as CEO I knew of course that we had this practice. In court, it emerged that many of the agreements Økokrim (the prosecutor) claimed I should be judged for, were reversed by the firm's finance department. The accounting executive confirmed then also during her witness statement in court that she had reversed the accounting entries under "agreements at work", without this being conferred with me. She, like the auditor, also confirmed that she had very little direct contact with me in these questions. She dealt with many project managers in the company.

Autobiographies by white-collar criminals can be found in other countries as well. In the United States, former police commissioner in New York, Bernard B. Kerik, published his autobiography, where there is evidence of denial of responsibility, condemnation of condemners, and claim for normality of action (Kerik, 2015).

Table 6.5 Neutralization techniques applied
by white-collar criminal Christer Tromsdal

#	Neutralization technique	Yes/No	Explanation
1	Rejects responsibility for the crime and disclaims leadership role in the action.	Yes	He blames others and says he only tried to help some friends. "It is not my responsibility" (Bjørndal and Kleppe, 2013).
2	Denies injury from the crime and refutes that harm has occurred.	No	There is no sign of this neutralization technique.
3	Dismisses victims of the crime and rejects that anyone has suffered harm.	No	There is no sign of this neutralization technique. However, he seems to consider himself as the main victim of the crime. "I have let myself be used by others" (Bjørndal and Kleppe, 2013).
4	Condemns the condemners and is skeptical of those who criticize his action.	Yes	He feels that he has been a victim of a witch-hunt by Økokrim for more than 10 years, and he condemns investigators and prosecutors at Økokrim. "I choose to call the whole process for a witch hunt" (Hultgren, 2012). "People say it is the crook that cheated all the old people" (Kleppe, 2015).
5	Invokes appeal to higher loyalties as a reason for his action.	Yes	He had to do it for his friends and acquaintances. "I have helped friends and acquaintances" (NTB, 2015).
6	Alleges normality of action and argues that action is quite common.	Yes	"When someone hears the word 'straw man', it sounds scary, but to me it is like an assistant" (Meldalen, 2015).
7	Claims entitlement to action because of the situation.	No	There is no sign of this neutralization technique.
8	Notes legal mistake and considers infringement irrelevant because of error in the law.	Yes	"In my head it is not illegal to do business with others" (Kleppe, 2015).

(Continued)

Table 6.5 (Continued) Neutralization techniques applied
by white-collar criminal Christer Tromsdal

#	Neutralization technique	Yes/No	Explanation
9	Feels entitled to make mistakes and argues action is within acceptable mistake quota.	Yes	Since he once was a police informant, he feels entitled to do business his own way. "I was shot at work for Oslo police" (Dahle, 2011).
10	Presents dilemma tradeoff by weighing various concerns with conclusion of committing the act.	No	There is no sign of this neutralization technique.

A common neutralization technique among white-collar criminals is denial of victim. Offenders claim that nobody is hurt, and that their actions lead to no victimization of anybody. Even scholars have suggested that white-collar offenses represent victimless crime. If there is a victim, then nobody feels sorry for them, it is argued. Nobody feels sorry for banks losing money or tax authorities losing revenues. However, when banks lose money, it causes harm to those who deposit money in the bank. When tax authorities miss revenues, then others in society have to contribute more, or public services have to be reduced.

In the database, the following victim categories are defined: employers, banks, tax authorities, customers, shareholders, and others. Table 6.6 lists these victim categories.

Table 6.6 Victims of white-collar crime

Victim of white-collar crime	Number of white-collar criminals	Fraction of white-collar criminals	Crime amount in NOK
Employers where criminals worked	115	28%	16 million
Tax authorities for government revenues	84	21%	137 million
Customers investing and buying	68	17%	26 million
Banks lending out money	57	14%	156 million
Shareholders by insider trading	30	7%	45 million
Other victims of white-collar crime	51	13%	11 million
Total	405	100%	45 million

The largest group of victims can be found among employers, where the white-collar criminal victimized his or her own organization. The second largest category is internal revenue service's collecting taxes to finance public government and public services. When individuals and businesses commit tax evasion and thereby reduce government income, then the government either has to reduce public services or increase taxes for those who pay their taxes. Customers are the third largest victim category. When customers invest in Ponzi schemes, or when customers pay for goods or services never delivered, then they become victims of financial crime. Banks become victims of white-collar crime when firms manipulate their contract base and accounting report to attract more bank loans to their operations.

The table illustrates that it is indeed possible to identify victims of crime. But contrary to violent crime and other kinds of street crime, the victim tends to be somewhere else, and the victim does not necessarily notice the loss. For example, tax authorities do not automatically notice when someone does not pay required taxes to the internal revenue service.

The table lists damage caused by white-collar crime in terms of million Norwegian kroner. One Norwegian krone is six to seven United States dollars. Banks were hit by the largest average amount of 156 million. Tax authorities come second with 137 million, and shareholders third with 45 million. Although employers are the most frequent victim of white-collar criminals, the loss every time is substantially lower at 16 million.

Strain is a reason for financial crime according to the behavioral dimension of convenience theory. Strain can occur when an enterprise is threatened by bankruptcy. Then it can be tempting to enter into tax evasion and VAT fraud to try to save the company. If the company nevertheless goes bankrupt, then it is usually a simple task for the bankruptcy lawyer or auditor to detect and document financial crime. The previous table for detection showed that 45 white-collar criminals who are registered in the database were detected by bankruptcy lawyers and auditors. Most of them (65%) were convicted of manipulating accounting figures to avoid tax and VAT. Some (35%) had manipulated accounting to cheat on banks.

In addition to neutralization theory and strain theory, self-control theory and slippery slope theory are important subtheories in the behavioral dimension of convenience theory. The database has no information concerning self-control or control of others. We are thus unable to test the suggestion that white-collar criminals have low self-control or need for excessive control of others.

We find some anecdotal evidence for slippery slope in terms of convicts who explained in the media and in the court that they did not notice that they crossed the line and ended up on the wrong side of the law. An example is Robert Hermansen, who was CEO at the national coal mining company on the island of Spitsbergen. He signed long-term agreements with a ship owner for transportation of coal from Spitsbergen to the continent. The agreements were exclusive and quite profitable for the ship owner. On several occasions, the ship owner provided loans privately to Hermansen, who did not pay back the loans, which was probably not expected to happen. Hermansen was sentenced to prison for 2 years (Østerbø, 2013).

The behavioral dimension of convenience theory suggests that offenders are in their forties when they commit white-collar crime. In their forties, ambitions and opportunities are at their maximum in combination. Empirical study confirms this theoretical suggestion in that the average age when crime was committed is 44 years old, and that the normal distribution shows a large fraction of criminals in their forties.

The case of Kerik neutralization

Mayor Rudolph Giuliani appointed Bernard Kerik as the 40th police commissioner of New York City. Prior to his appointment, Kerik was commissioner of the Department of Correction. He served with the New York Police Department on uniformed duty for several years, and he received the Medal of Valor, among many other awards for meritorious and heroic service. His stewardship of NYPD in the aftermath of the September 11, 2001, attacks on the World Trade Center brought him recognition.

Kerik was born in Newark, New Jersey, in 1955. He served in the United States Army from 1974 to 1977 before working various law enforcement jobs in the United States and abroad. He joined the NYPD in 1986.

President George W. Bush appointed Kerik as the interior minister in Iraq following the 2003 invasion. Bush nominated Kerik in 2004 to be head of the Department of Homeland Security (Kerik, 2015: 146):

> I was standing there alone with the president. He looked more relaxed than the last time I'd seen him, at campaign functions before the election. He held out his hand and grabbed mine.
>
> "I'm looking for a secretary of Homeland Security," he said. "You want it?"
>
> The question seemed delivered in slow motion. Although I knew what I was there for and expected exactly this, a flash went through me. I had come a long way from walking a perimeter fence as a military police dog-handler at a nuclear missile base in South Korea in the 1970s. (…)

> I had lived a version of the American dream: a
> high school dropout who with ambition, hard work,
> and a lot of good luck rose to the cusp of one of the
> highest positions in the land.

In the week after President Bush nominated Kerik for secretary of Homeland Security, the New York and national press began investigating his career, accusing him of having connections to organized crime and implying that there was something devious about a stock transaction. The media dissected his past. They found that he had paid just a small fraction of a bill for renovation of an apartment, and that a person connected to organized crime had paid the rest. They found that he employed a nanny who was an illegal immigrant.

Kerik faxed the president at the White House one week after his official nomination (Kerik, 2015: 155):

> Dear Mr. President:
> It is with deep regret that I inform you that I cannot continue forward in the confirmation process for the position of Secretary of the Department of Homeland Security.

Two years later, in 2006, Kerik pleaded guilty to two ethics violations. The following year, a federal grand jury indicted Kerik on charges of conspiracy, tax fraud, and making false statements. In 2009, Kerik pleaded guilty to eight felony tax and false statement charges. He went to prison in 2010. He got out of prison in 2014 and wrote the book that is the case study in this chapter.

Kerik (2015: 197) understood he had committed white-collar crime since he hired Barry Berke and Eric Tirschwell, of Kramer Levin Naftalis & Frankel, LLP; "a prestigious Manhattan law firm specializing in white-collar crime litigation." He spent $2 million in legal fees (Kerik, 2015: 220), what very few other criminals, and certainly no street criminals, can afford. Kerik (2015: 266) does not think white-collar criminals should go to prison, since they only committed nonviolent crime, "If you say, 'Well, guys like that, these white-collar criminals, are scammers and cheats', then all the more reason for society to get something back from them."

The research technique applied is concerned with contents analysis of the book written by Kerik (2015), which we label an autobiography. An autobiography is a written account of the life of a person written by that person. It is a story that the person wrote about himself. We searched for quotes in his book that seem to resemble attitudes recognized by neutralization techniques. We found varying degrees of supportive statements for the various neutralization techniques.

Kerik sets the neutralization stage already in the introduction chapter of his book by statements such as presenting himself as a victim ("The system beats you down in a way that remains" and "It's about how short-sighted, inefficient, and cruel our criminal justice system is"). He stresses his performance for the nation ("I saved my wounded partner in a gun battle" and "seized tons of cocaine and millions of dollars from the Cali cartel"). He does only take on responsibility for the consequences of his actions ("I am accountable and responsible for how my life has turned out").

Throughout the 288-page book, we find the following supporting quotes for the various neutralization techniques:

1. *Denial of responsibility.* "My accountants made mistakes" (p. 11). "I had called my accountant and told him that I wanted to pay the payroll tax" (p. 153). "I let him" pay the renovation bill for me (p. 157).
2. *Denial of injury.* There is no sign of this neutralization technique, while at the same time there is no confirmation of injury in the book.
3. *Denial of victim.* There is no sign of this neutralization technique, while at the same time there is no confirmation of victim in the book.
4. *Condemnation of the condemners.* "Accusing me of having connections to organized crime" and "I thought were downright preposterous" (p. 149). "If this is how the members of the House and Senate want to apply their scrutiny, then more than half of them should step down and go find another job, because they certainly wouldn't make it through the process intact" (p. 151). "Prosecutors too often overcriminalize, overreach, and overpunish" (p. 195). Kerik goes on condemning government prosecutors: "They can distort and exaggerate their justifications to lock up your property, bank accounts, and other assets. They can drain you and your family of everything you've ever worked for; rip you in the court of public opinion; destroy your family's financial future; and do everything in their power to prevent you from being able to pay for your defense" (p. 232). On page 239, Kerik develops a conspiracy theory involving a number of powerful people named in the book, suggesting that they all took part in "continually bashing Giuliani and me in the press." The conspiracy theory centers on him as a republican versus others who were democrats. "Was it general political ill will, or were these men boosting their careers on my conviction?" (p. 240).
5. *Appeal to higher loyalties.* There is no sign of this neutralization technique related to his crime. However, there is a strong message about his loyalty to the nation in serving his country.
6. *Normality of action.* "The indictment criminalized minor ethical issues and accounting errors" (p. 194). "I understand that 'But everybody's doing it' is rarely a winning argument—even if it is in large part true" (p. 201).

7. *Claim to entitlement.* Kerik claims a very stressful work situation for many years.
8. *Legal mistake.* "I was prosecuted criminally for what are essentially civil violations" (p. 12). "Everything I was charged with—tax fraud; false statements—could have been handled ethically or civilly, without criminal charges" (p. 241). "There are tens of thousands of nonviolent, first-time, white-collar offenders and drug offenders in prison today serving draconian sentences, individuals who could have been punished with alternatives to incarceration, such as fines and restitution, home confinement or house arrest, and community service" (p. 243). "I do believe that a fair, objective look reveals my case and prosecution to have been selective and political. I don't feel that it was justice" (p. 270).
9. *Acceptable mistake.* "Feds were taking honest mistakes by me and my accountants and alleging they were crimes" (p. 194).
10. *Dilemma tradeoff.* "This was one of those ethical moments that any person in public office faces repeatedly," about not stopping the extra renovation work paid by others (p. 157).
11. *Victim of crime.* "They would subpoena and harass my friends, family, colleagues, and just about everyone I knew" (p. 156). "Investigators ripped my life to shreds, harassing and intimidating my friends, family, and colleagues" (p. 158).
12. *Role in society.* "I had defended, worked, fought, and nearly died for our country many times in the past thirty years and was now being jailed" (p. 201).

We find support for 10 out of 12 neutralization techniques in Kerik's book. It is interesting to note that we only find support for three out of five of the original neutralization techniques developed by Sykes and Matza (1957). This could mean that Sykes and Matza had mainly had violent street crime in mind when they developed their neutralization theory.

Kerik served mainly in public service. His book illustrates his dedication to work for his country, and the final sentence in his book is "But I still believe in this great country of ours, and I am still searching and fighting for justice" (p. 284).

Kerik is dedicated to public service. A theory relevant to shed light on his dedication is public service motivation theory. This theory seeks to explain why individuals choose public service or private service, given the perceived disparities in pay scale, advancement opportunities, and overall work environment (Kjeldsen and Jacobsen, 2013; Perry et al., 2010). The theory suggests that some individuals work in the public sector based on their values. They have a desire to contribute to the well-being of society in general through their work (Nalbandian and Edwards, 1983).

The concept of public service motivation is a theorized attribute of government employees that provides them with a desire to serve the public (Perry and Wise, 1990).

Kerik's (2015) book indicates a strong public service motivation by these characteristics. Now, after his rise and fall, he makes the case for reform and calls for wholesale change that will make America "smart on crime" and forestall what he calls "the erosion of the very fabric of our nation." While his book details the fall from grace through the criminal justice system, it also offers a perspective on the American penal system as he details life on the inside with the experience of an acclaimed correction commissioner from the outside. He takes readers deep into what he calls the "wasteland," where inmates are warehoused and treated like animals, abused by those with power and authority, and deprived not only of their freedom but also of respect and basic human dignity. He expresses public service motivation by not mainly complaining about his own treatment, but focusing on those around him in prison.

Kerik emphasizes his social concern. A theory relevant to shed light on his dedication is social concern and crime theory suggested by Agnew (2014). Social concern involves an inclination that can lead people to pay more attention to others than to their own interests. It is the opposite of self-interest as motivation for behavior. Most people Kerik presents in his book are his social concern.

This case of Kerik above has studied neutralization theory in terms of neutralization techniques applied by a white-collar criminal. We found evidence of 10 out of 12 neutralization techniques applied by Kerik (2015) in his book. He strongly condemns his condemners, he denies responsibility, he claims normality of action, and he argues that prosecutors charged him criminally for what are essentially civil violations.

Autobiographies and memoirs seem to be a suitable source of secondary material to study neutralization techniques applied by criminals. It would be interesting to see analysis of more autobiographies and memoirs in future research. Based on future research, characteristics of neutralization may find new characteristics to be included in future versions of neutralization theory.

References

Agnew, R. (2014). Social concern and crime: Moving beyond the assumption of simple self-interest, *Criminology*, 52 (1), 1–32.

Asker and Bærum district court (2012). Case 12-066481MED-AHER/2, *Asker og Bærum tingrett*, 30.05.2012.

Berglund, N. (2015). Ex-Yara bosses sentenced to jail, *NewsinEnglish.no*, http://www.newsinenglish.no/2015/07/07/ex-yara-bosses-sentenced-to-jail/, published July 7.

Bjørndal, B. and Kleppe, M.K. (2013). –Mulig jeg har vært dumsnill (I may have been dum nice), daily Norwegian business newspaper *Dagens Næringsliv*, http://www.dn.no/nyheter/politikkSamfunn/2013/10/21/-mulig-jeg-har-vaert-dumsnill, published October 21.

Bogen, T. (2008). *Hvor var du, historien om mitt liv (Where were you, the story of my life)*, Oslo, Norway: Schibsted Publishing.

Borgarting (2015). Court of appeals case number 14-181913AST-BORG/02, *Borgarting lagmannsrett (Borgarting Court of Appeals)*, 08.07.2015.

Bucy, P.H., Formby, E.P., Raspanti, M.S. and Rooney, K.E. (2008). Why do they do it?: The motives, mores, and character of white collar criminals, *St. John's Law Review*, 82, 401–571.

Dahle, D.Y. (2011). Christer Tromsdal var politiagent (Christer Tromsdal was police agent), daily Norwegian newspaper *Aftenposten*, http://www.aften posten.no/nyheter/iriks/Christer-Tromsdal-var-politiagent-6369334.html, publisched October 19.

Eriksen, T.S. (2010). *Arven etter Ole Christian Bach—Et justismord (The legacy of Ole Christian Bach—A miscarriage of justice)*, Oslo, Norway: Norgesforlaget Publishing.

Fosse, G. and Magnusson, G. (2004). *Mayday Mayday!—Kapteinene først i livbåtene! (Mayday Mayday!—The captains first in the lifeboats)*, Oslo, Norway: Kolofon Publishing.

Gottschalk, P. (2014). *Policing white-collar crime: Characteristics of white-collar criminals*, Boca Raton, FL: CRC Press, Taylor & Francis.

Gottschalk, P. and Smith, R. (2015). Gender and white-collar crime: Examining representations of women in media, *Journal of Gender Studies*, 24 (3), 310–325.

Gottschalk, P. and Smith, C. (2016). Detection of white-collar corruption in public procurement in Norway: The role of whistleblowers, *International Journal of Procurement Management* (forthcoming).

Gulating (2009). Case number 08.196041AST-GULA/AVD2, *Gulating court of appeals*, Bergen, Norway, dated September 15.

Haugan, B. (2014). Unibuss-sjefen legger alle kortene på bordet: -Det var så dumt (Unibuss chief puts all cards on the table: -It was so stupid), *E24*, http://e24 .no/lov-og-rett/unibuss-sjefen-legger-alle-kortene-paa-bordet-det-var-saa -dumt/23303411, published June 25.

Hultgren, G. (2012). Seks års fengsel for Christer Tromsdal (Six years prison for Christer Tromsdal), daily Norwegian newspaper *Dagbladet*, http://www .dagbladet.no/2012/11/02/nyheter/christer_tromsdal/krim/24159912/, published November 2.

Kerik, B.B. (2015). *From jailer to jailed—My journey from correction and police commissioner to inmate #84888-054*, New York: Threshold Editions.

Kjeldsen, A.M. and Jacobsen, C.B. (2013). Public service motivation and employment sector: Attraction or socialization? *Journal of Public Administration Research and Theory*, 23 (4), 899–926.

Kleppe, M.K. (2015). Tromsdal: -Der er han skurken som lurte de gamle menneskene (There is the crock who cheated the old people), daily Norwegian business newspaper *Dagens Næringsliv*, http://www.dn.no/nyheter/2015/01/08/1336 /Kriminalitet/tromsdal-der-er-han-skurken-som-lurte-de-gamle-menneskene, published January 8.

Meldalen, S.G. (2015). –Når noen hører ordet "stråmann," høres det skummelt ut (When someone hears the word "straw man," it sounds scary), daily Norwegian newspaper *Dagbladet*, http://www.dagbladet.no/2015/01/08 /nyheter/innenriks/christer_tromsdal/bedrageri/37075845/, published January 8.

Nalbandian, J. and Edwards, J.T. (1983). The professional values of public administrators: A comparison with lawyers, social workers, and business administrators. *Review of Public Personnel Administration*, 4, 114–127.

NTB (2015). Økokrim ber om seks års fengsel for Tromsdal (Økokrim asks for six years prison for Tromsdal), daily Norwegian newspaper *Klassekampen*, http://www.klassekampen.no/article/20150320/NTBO/928007743, published March 20.

Oslo district court (2015). Case number 14-035631MED-OTIR/05, *Oslotingrett*, June 19, 2015.

Østerbø, K. (2013). –Fengselet ble ikke den leirskolen jeg hadde trodd (-Prison did not turn out to be the camp I expected), daily Norwegian newspaper *Aftenposten*, Saturday, March 16, p. 20.

Perry, J.L. and Wise, L.R. (1990). The motivational bases of public service. *Public Administration Review*, 50 (3), 367–373.

Perry, J., Hondeghem, A. and Wise, L. (2010). Revisiting the motivational bases of public service, *Public Administration Review*, 70 (5), 681–690.

Sykes, G. and Matza, D. (1957). Techniques of neutralization: A theory of delinquency, *American Sociological Review*, 22 (6), 664–670.

Vadera, A.K., Aguilera, R.V. and Caza, B.B. (2009). Making sense of whistleblowing's antecedents: Learning from research on identity and ethics programs, *Business Ethics Quarterly*, 19 (4), 553–586.

chapter seven

Statements for testing convenience hypotheses

Convenience theory was introduced earlier in this book. The theory consists of an economical, an organizational, and a behavioral dimension. These dimensions were presented in an integrated model, and research hypotheses were developed to represent relationships between dimensions. Later in this book, a sample of convicted white-collar criminals in Norway was presented to shed some light on convenience in an empirical study. However, the sample was not collected to test convenience hypotheses, but rather to provide some factual insights into white-collar crime in general.

This chapter builds on theory descriptions as well as sample findings presented earlier to explore how research hypotheses developed for convenience theory might be empirically tested in future research.

In addition to statements for testing convenience hypotheses, this chapter also presents some cases to illustrate white-collar crime convenience: the case of fraudulent attorneys, the case of two sides in corruption, and the case of Yara corruption in Libya.

Desire in the economical dimension

The economical dimension of convenience theory suggests that the desire for profits is caused by perceived needs. There are both organizational needs and individual needs that are desirably covered by financial profits, and there are situations of both threats and chances for profits.

To measure the strength of the desire for profits, a scale can be developed from "weak" to "strong" or from "low" to "high" desire. Items to measure the extent of desire for profits to cover perceived needs can include the following statements, where the first set of statements measure corporate desire (statements 1 to 6), while the second set of statements measure personal desire (statements 7 to 12).

1. Desire for coporate profits to cover perceived needs to avoid business bankruptcy.
2. Desire for corporate profits to cover perceived needs to avoid other threats.

3. Desire for corporate profits to cover perceived needs to handle market structures and forces.
4. Desire for corporate profits to reach operational goals.
5. Desire for corporate profits to reach financial goals.
6. Desire for corporate profits to reach strategic goals.
7. Desire for personal profits to avoid personal bankruptcy.
8. Desire for personal profits to solve other personal problems.
9. Desire for corporate profits to earn a personal bonus.
10. Desire for personal profits to improve personal standard of living.
11. Desire for personal profits to improve personal self-respect.
12. Desire for personal profits to improve personal reputation.

The economical dimension of convenience theory suggests that it is convenient to satisfy the desire for profits by white-collar crime. Again, there are both corporate needs and personal needs that are desirably covered by financial profits, and there are situations of both threats and possibilities for profits.

To measure the extent of convenience in satisfying desires for profits by economic crime, a scale can be developed from "very" convenient to "not at all" convenient, or from "low" to "high" convenience. Items to measure the extent of convenience to satisfy desire for profits to cover perceived needs can include the following statements, where the first set of statements measure corporate desire (statements 1 to 6), while the second set of statements measure personal desire (statements 7 to 12).

1. Convenience of economic crime to satisfy desire for corporate profits to cover perceived needs to avoid business bankruptcy.
2. Convenience of economic crime to satisfy desire for corporate profits to cover perceived needs to avoid other threats.
3. Convenience of economic crime to satisfy desire for corporate profits to handle market structures and forces.
4. Convenience of economic crime to satisfy desire for corporate profits to reach operational goals.
5. Convenience of economic crime to satisfy desire for corporate profits to reach financial goals.
6. Convenience of economic crime to satisfy desire for corporate profits to reach strategic goals.
7. Convenience of economic crime to satisfy desire for personal profits to avoid personal bankruptcy.
8. Convenience of economic crime to satisfy desire for personal profits to solve other personal problems.
9. Convenience of economic crime to satisfy desire for corporate profits to earn a personal bonus.

10. Convenience of economic crime to satisfy desire for personal profits to improve personal standard of living.
11. Convenience of economic crime to satisfy desire for personal profits to improve personal self-respect.
12. Convenience of economic crime to satisfy desire for personal profits to improve personal reputation.

While the first set of statements measure the extent of desire, the second set of statements measure convenience. It can be expected that the two sets will be empirically linked in terms of increased desire making white-collar crime more convenient.

Opportunity in the organizational dimension

The organizational dimension of convenience theory suggests that the profession and privileged position of the potential offender provides an opportunity to commit crime and makes crime a convenient action.

To measure the extent of opportunity to commit white-collar crime, a scale can be developed from "strongly agree" to "strongly disagree." Here are some possible statements to measure the extent of convenient opportunity for white-collar crime in the organization.

1. Economic crime can easily be committed in the organization by trusted people.
2. Trusted people have access to resources to commit economic crime.
3. Economic crime can be committed within the confines of positions of trust.
4. There is a presence of a favorable combination of circumstances in the organization that renders economic crime a possible course of action.
5. Economic crime is never detected in the organization.
6. Detected economic crime in the organization has no consequence in terms of punishment for the offender.
7. Executives have large degrees of freedom in their work to commit white-collar crime.
8. Executives have large degrees of freedom to hide and conceal white-collar crime.
9. Executives enjoy complete trust from all stakeholders despite deviant behavior.
10. There is no control of privileged persons in the organization despite deviant behavior.
11. Economic crime can be committed with a superficial appearance of legitimacy.
12. The corporate culture stimulates violations of the law.
13. There is no way the activities of trusted professionals can be controlled.

14. Economic crime can be concealed in legal organizational activities.
15. Top management is never suspected of any misconduct or wrongdoing.

Willingness in the behavioral dimension

The behavioral dimension of convenience theory suggests that members of the elite are willing to commit white-collar crime. To measure the extent of willingness to commit white-collar crime, a scale can be developed from willingness "to a large extent" to willingness "to a small extent." Here are some possible statements to measure the extent of convenient willingness to commit white-collar crime.

1. Executives in the organization feel no guilt when they deviate from the law.
2. Executives are successful in defending and explaining their own misconduct.
3. Executives feel entitled to break the law when necessary to achieve corporate goals.
4. Executives have low self-control.
5. Executives have a strong need to control others.
6. Executives tend to slide down the slippery slope from legal to illegal activities without really noticing.
7. Executives are very ambitious on behalf of the organization.
8. Executives are very ambitious on behalf of themselves.
9. Executives are very stressed in their work.
10. Executives are successful in applying neutralization techniques.

Research model for convenience theory

A conceptual model for convenience theory was presented earlier in this book. Now it is time to present a research model, where the tendency toward white-collar crime is defined as the dependent variable. The research model suggests that criminogenity—the tendency to commit crime and the actual occurrence of white-collar crime—is determined by the desire for profits, the opportunity for crime, and the willingness for crime, as illustrated in Figure 7.1.

Based on the research model, a new set of hypotheses can be formulated:

Hypothesis 1: Increased desire for profits increases the occurrence of white-collar crime.
Hypothesis 2: Increased opportunity for crime increases the occurrence of white-collar crime.
Hypothesis 3: Increased willingness for crime increases the occurrence of white-collar crime.

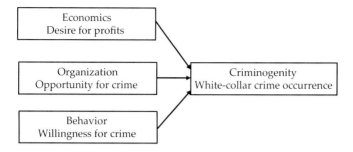

Figure 7.1 A research model of white-collar crime occurrence based on convenience theory.

The dependent variable criminogenity has to be represented by statements to measure the extent of expected white-collar crime occurrence.

The case of fraudulent attorneys

A lawyer trust account is a business checking account or its equivalent, established by the law firm to hold client funds. Funds deposited into a trust account are neither the lawyer's property nor the law firm's property. Depending on the jurisdiction, a law firm must adhere to standards of separating client funds from lawyer funds, and separating funds from different clients. Client funds are not allowed to be commingled with a law firm's business funds. In most jurisdictions, client funds must be deposited into a separate attorneys' trust account in a bank and designated as such. Trust account funds may not be utilized by the law firm until they eventually are earned. Trust account funds that are to be transferred externally at a later point in time may not be touched or temporarily abused by the law firm. A client account is an account of practice kept at a bank or similar institution for holding client client money. A lawyer can only handle trust account money based on instruction from or agreement with the client.

Lawyers or attorneys are trained in general legal principles and procedures, and in the substantive and procedural aspects of the law and are supposed to have the ability to analyze and provide solutions to legal problems. Lawyers are knowledge workers. They are professionals who have gained knowledge through formal education and through learning on the job. Many lawyers work in law firms. A law firm is a business entity formed by one or more lawyers to engage in the practice of law. Law firms apply legal knowledge to clients' unique problems to provide solutions.

In the database of 405 white-collar criminals, there are 19 lawyers (4.7%) sentenced to prison for white-collar crime. They were convicted of abuse of clients' trust accounts held by their law firms. The average age of convicted lawyers is 52 years old, and the average prison sentence is 2 years.

The economical dimension of convenience theory suggests that the desire for profits is caused by perceived needs. Convicted fraudulent lawyers in Norway were not concerned with organizational desire for profits on behalf of the law firm. They were concerned with individual desire for profits. Their motives were mainly a desire for personl profits to solve other personal problems (8), a desire for personal profits to improve personal standard of living (10), and a desire for personal profits to improve personal reputation (12).

The organizational dimension of convenience theory suggests that the position and privileged position of the potential offender provides an opportunity to commit crime and makes crime a convenient option. In terms of a principal-agent perspective, the client is a principal, while the attorney is an agent. The client as principal has no way of controlling what the attorney is doing. Economic crime can easily be committed in the law firm by the lawyer as a trusted person (1), the lawyer has access to resources to commit economic crime (2), economic crime by the lawyer is committed within the confines of a position of trust (3), there is a presence of favorable circumstances (4), as removal of funds from one client can be replaced by funds from another client, and economic crime is never detected within the law firm (5) but rather when the law firm gets into trouble with tax authorities or is unable to transfer client funds as requested.

The behavioral dimension of convenience theory suggests that members of the elite—such as lawyers—are willing to commit white-collar crime. Lawyers feel no guilt as they are only "borrowing" client money (1 and 2). They had low self-control (4), and they were sliding down the slippery slope from legal to illegal activities without really noticing (6), and with a belief that they would return the money to client fund accounts.

Among the 19 convicted lawyers in Norway, Rolf Eckbo (born 1953) received the longest prison sentence of 5 years. He committed fraud in a trust where he was a legal advisor as well as a board member. The sum of money involved in his fraud was 10 million Norwegian kroner ($1.4 million). The trust was established by his grandfather who had prevented his children and grandchildren from inheriting substantial assets. The second longest prison sentence was passed to lawyer Christian Frick (born 1953). The sum of money involved in his fraud was 35 million Norwegian kroner ($5 million). He was prosecuted by the Norwegian serious fraud office (Økokrim) for fraud, misleading explanations in court, as well as tax evasion and theft of client money. Økokrim's investigation into Frick's activities, which included Liechtenstein as a tax haven, lasted for more than three years. Frick appealed his case from the district court via the court of appeals to the Supreme Court in Norway. Frick as a lawyer argued his privileged status, including his right to protect documents with confidential information based on the client-attorney privilege. Frick received a prison sentence of 3 1/2 years.

Attorney Odd Arild Drevland was sentenced to 2 1/2 years in prison because of fraud in client funds mismanagement amounting to 2 million Norwegian kroner ($300,000). His case received massive media attention in 2015 because he was married to the mayor of the second largest city in Norway. His wife, Trude Drevland, was mayor in Bergen city. She got involved in a scandal of corruption the same year by being accused of having misused her position as mayor in connection with a cruiseship christening (Elster and Magnus, 2015).

It seems safe for law firms to abuse client fund accounts, since clients have no access to transactions in their accounts. Those 19 lawyers who were detected, prosecuted, and sentenced to prison were detected for the following reasons. First, 7 fraudulent lawyers were detected when they were unable to perform financial transactions as requested by their clients, and their clients became victims of their lawyers' misconduct. Second, 6 fraudulent lawyers were detected by journalists when the media was disclosing criminal activities by other criminals, and it emerged that lawyers were involved as well. Third, 3 fraudulent lawyers were detected by external auditors. Fourth, 1 fraudulent lawyer was reported to the police by relatives. Fifth, 1 fraudulent lawyer was detected by the police when they were investigating a financial crime case. Finally, 1 fraudulent lawyer reported himself to the police when he was hospitalized in a psychiatric clinic.

The case of two sides in corruption

Most financial crime is characterized by being one-sided misconduct. Corruption is different by being two-sided: someone is bribing and someone is being bribed. Convenience theory can be applied to explain both briber and bribed in a corruption relationship. Some court cases only cover the briber, other court cases cover the bribed, while yet other court cases cover both briber and bribed. In our sample of 405 convicted white-collar criminals, there are 75 offenders (19%) who were sentenced for corruption.

Financial crime is classified into four categories (Gottschalk, 2015): fraud, theft, manipulation, and corruption. Corruption can be defined as the giving, offering, promising, requesting, receiving, taking, agreeing to taking, or accepting of an improper advantage in terms of money or other consideration related to position, office, or assignment (Boles, 2014). The improper advantage does not have to be connected to a specific action or to not doing an action. It is sufficient if the advantage can be linked to a person's position, office, or assignment. An individual or group is guilty of corruption if they accept money or money's worth for doing something that they are under a duty to do anyway or that they are under a duty not to do, or to exercise a legitimate discretion for improper reason (Ksenia, 2008). Corruption is to destroy or pervert the integrity of fidelity of a person in his discharge of duty, it is to induce to act dishonestly or unfaithfully, it is to make venal, and it is to bribe.

Seventy-five corrupt white-collar criminals in Norway were sentenced to prison in 25 court cases, which means that three persons on average were involved in each case. Three cases involved only briber(s), and eight cases involved only bribed white-collar criminals. The remaining 14 court cases involved both bribing and bribed persons:

1. Two construction firm brothers were convicted of bribing a city official for obtaining a building permit in a restricted area.
2. Two police officers were convicted of receiving a bribe from a business executive to take the executive temporarily out of jail officially for interrogation so that he could visit his office.
3. A purchasing manager in an oil company was bribed by two vendor representatives.
4. Nine different suppliers of maintenance services to public school buildings were convicted of bribing a city official in charge of school buildings.
5. Two purchasing managers were convicted of corruption for receiving a bribe from a vendor.
6. A vendor bribed three employees in the customer organization.
7. Five family members running a maintenance service firm bribed another family member in charge of building maintenance in the city administration.
8. A billionaire bought a yacht and also bought himself a boat license to maneuver the boat from a corrupt ship inspector.
9. A vendor bribed a United Nations UNICEF official.
10. A vendor bribed an oil company executive.
11. A planning official received a bribe from a winter area developer of mountain cabins.
12. A planning official received a bribe for a property developer.
13. Four executives in the city's public transportation services were bribed by two private bus service providers.
14. Three public road construction officials were bribed by one supplier of road construction services.

Convenience can be explored on both sides of the corruption transaction as well as in the relationship between bribing person(s) and bribed person(s). For the bribed person, corruption is always a monetary benefit to cover personal needs and desires in the economic dimension, such as a desire to avoid financial problems (7 and 8), and a desire to improve standard of living (10), self-respect (11), and reputation (12). For the bribing person, corruption is always a monetary benefit to cover corporate desires in the economic dimension. While corruption is occupational crime on the bribed side, it is corporate crime on the bribing side. People in the organization offer bribes to external people to improve business performance, such as avoidance of bankruptcy (1), and desire for more corporate profits (2, 3, 4, 5, and 6).

In the organizational dimension of convenience theory, we find that briber and bribed are again in different situations. The bribed person must avoid detection by receiving the bribe outside the location and attention sphere of the employer. The bribing person uses company money illegally by hiding the illegal transfer among legal transactions. While the bribed person must mainly be concerned with detection by keeping the illegally received funds far away from regular business operations, the bribing person must mainly be concerned with hiding illegal transactions. The bribing person commits economic crime with a superficial appearance of legitimacy (10), and economic crime can be concealed in legal organizational activities (13). The bribed person finds corruption convenient in the organizational setting when the corporate culture stimulates violations of the law (11), and there is no way the activities of trusted professionals can be controlled (12).

In the behavioral dimension of convenience theory, bribing executives feel entitled to break the law when necessary to achieve corporate goals (3), and they are very ambitious on behalf of both the organization (7) and on behalf of themselves (8). They tend to slide down the slippery slope from legal to illegal activities without really noticing (6). The bribed person has typically low self-control (4), and feels no guilt or wrongdoing since it is the bribing organization that voluntarily offers the benefit. The bribing organization is not perceived as a victim, since bribers belong to top management of the bribing organization.

Corruption is difficult to detect since both sides of the transaction have an interest in never disclosing their crime. Detection in our sample of 14 cases occurred in the following manner:

1. A property developer was unwilling to pay bribes to the city official and reported the crime to the police.
2. The wife of the bribing executive reported the crime to the police.
3. A whistle-blower reported that a colleague had received a bribe.
4. The bribed city official bought an extremely expensive property by paying cash, and the bank reported it to the authorities.
5. A fired executive threatened his former employer to disclose corruption if the firm did not accept his demands. The firm decided to report the case to the police.
6. An auditor discovered that money was missing.

7. Tax authorities discovered in a routine control of accounts that income statements in one of the construction firms did not match financial transactions.
8. Investigative journalists discovered that the billionaire had no real boat license.
9. An internal audit in UNICEF discovered the corruption.
10. An internal audit in the oil company discovered the corruption.
11. An internal audit in the bank discovered the corruption.
12. An employee blew the whistle on the planning official in the city.
13. An employee blew the whistle on executives in the public transportation organization.
14. A union leader in the organization blew the whistle on corrupt executives.

Case number 13 on the list is concerned with four executives in the city's public transportation services who were bribed by two private bus service providers. An employee blew the whistle on executives in the public transportation organization. Two corruption activities occurred at the same time in the public transportation unit independent of each other. One corruption activity was carried out by the German bus provider MAN. German bus manufacturer MAN bribed executives at Norwegian bus operator Unibuss at the planning stage. The Germans influenced the specification drafting by making Norwegians specify a certain bus length in their procurement requirements. It was specified that Unibuss needed busses that were 18 meters and 75 centimeters long. The only bus manufacturer that produced buses of this particular length was MAN. None of the competing bus manufacturers were able to bid on this kind of bus length request. When Unibuss procurement executives from Norway visited MAN sales executives in Germany, they received envelopes with Euros in cash during social events. Some years later, a Unibuss employee was on vacation in Munich in Germany where he read a local newspaper. He read that MAN sales executives were prosecuted in Germany for corruption scandals. In the newspaper article, several countries were mentioned, including Norway. When the Unibuss employee returned home from vacation, he went to his superior that he trusted, and told him about the news report.

The other corruption activity was local in Norway, where a supplier of bus operations bribed executives. A sales executive at bus operator VestBuss bribed executives at Unibuss to get operating contracts with the public transportation company. Detection of corruption between VestBuss and Unibuss occurred as a result of the investigation into the first corruption incident between MAN and Unibuss. A third briber was also detected. It was Komplettbygg, which provided maintenance services to Unibuss.

While MAN executives where sentenced to prison in Germany, the following six corrupt individuals were sentenced to prison in Norway (Oslo district court, 2014):

- Technical executive Nils Aksel Ellingsen (61) was sentenced to 5 years and 6 months in prison for receiving bribes from sales executive Dag Hagerup at MAN.
- Procurement executive Erik Ernst Andersson (69) was sentenced to 5 years in prison for receiving bribes from sales executive Dag Hagerup at MAN.
- Managing director Helge Leite (61) at Unibuss was sentenced to 3 years and 6 months in prison for receiving bribes from sales executive Tor Gaarder at Komplettbygg.
- Construction site manager Knut Øverbø (52) was sentenced to 9 months in prison for receiving bribes from sales executive Tor Gaarder at Komplettbygg.
- Sales executive Dag Hagerup (67) at MAN in Norway was sentenced to 5 years in prison for bribing technical executive Nils Aksel Ellingsen and procurement Erik Ernst Andersson at Unibuss.
- Sales executive Tor Gaarder (59) at Komplettbygg was sentenced to 4 years in prison for bribing managing director Helge Leite and construction manager Knut Øverbø at Unibuss.

Court cases against executives at VestBuss were expected to start in Oslo district court in 2016.

The economic dimension for managing director Helge Leite at Unibuss was to expand his house in Oslo paid for by Komplettbygg and VestBuss. The organizational dimension was his top position at Unibuss where he was treated privately by vendors. The behavioral dimension was that he found himself underpaid by the city and thought he deserved some more compensation. He considered the risk of detection almost non-existent.

The case of Yara corruption in Libya

Many business enterprises want to become international and global actors in their markets. Companies want to expand into other countries and regions of the world. Major Norwegian business organizations are no exceptions. Leading Norwegian companies want to expand their business into the European Union, the United States, and Canada, as well as other markets and economies that are similar to their home environment in Norway. Some of the companies also want to expand their activities into other regions of the world where corruption is a common marketing tool to establish and do business locally. While corruption is illegal in Western countries because of foreign corrupt practices acts, global businesses find no other way than corruption to establish and do business in countries where the regime as well as the society at large are corrupt.

Transparency International publishes their corruption perception index. The least corruption is perceived in Denmark, New Zealand, Finland, Sweden, and Norway. The most corruption is perceived in Somalia, North Korea, Sudan, and Afghanistan. Norwegian global businesses have established themselves in a number of corrupt nations. Corruption is a convenient action to succeed in these countries. The amount of money involved is small compared to benefits achieved, the local organization is able to hide illegal transactions by concealment among legal transactions, and wrongdoing is perceived as quite normal. The economic, organizational, as well as behavioral dimensions of convenience theory all seem to be in favor of corruption. Rather than spending time in endless meetings and submitting an endless sequence of proposals and applications, it is convenient to bribe some key public officials to succeed in local business.

An example is the Norwegian fertilizer manufacturer Yara, where the former CEO and three more executives where sentenced to prison in 2015 in district courts. They have appealed their verdict and expect to appear in court again in 2016. Prosecutors accused the men of paying around $8 million in bribes to officials in India and Libya—including to the family of former Libyan leader Muammar Gadhafi's oil minister and the family of a financial adviser in India's Ministry of Chemicals and Fertilizers— for the right to establish joint ventures. Former CEO Thorleif Enger got the longest sentence of 3 years. Former legal officer Kendrick Wallace, a U.S. citizen, was sentenced to 2 1/2 years in prison, while former head of upstream activities Tor Holba and former deputy CEO Daniel Clauw, a French citizen, were both given 2-year jail terms (Berglund, 2015).

This corruption case probably never would have been detected if the Gadhafi regime had continued. But because of armed rebellion and NATO bombing in Libya, the Gadhafi regime collapsed. U.S. authorities went into Libya with its coalition partners, and the FBI discovered that many public officials had been bribed by multinational companies. The FBI found Norwegian company Yara among the bribing companies. At the same time, investigative journalists at the newspaper *Dagens Næringsliv* (similar to the *Wall Street Journal*) received information from an internal whistleblower at Yara that the company had being paying bribes abroad.

Desire and convenience in the economical dimension of convenience theory can be found in the desire for corporate profits to reach strategic goals (6). It may also be the case that those involved could expect a personal bonus if successful in establishing business in Libya (9).

Convenient opportunity in the organizational dimension of convenience theory we may find in several statements: executives have large degrees of freedom in their work (7), executives enjoy complete trust from all stakeholders (8), there is no control of privileged persons in the organization (9), corruption can be committed with a superficial appearance of legitimacy in the form of paying consultants (10), there was no way the activities of trusted professionals could be controlled (11), and top management was never suspected of any miscounduct or wrongdoing (12).

Convenient willingness in the behavioral dimension of convenience theory can be found in several statements: executives think they are successful in defending and explaining their misconduct (2), executives feel entitled to break the law when necessary to achieve corporate goals (3), some executives had low self-control (4), executives were very ambitious on behalf of Yara, and some were also ambitious on behalf of themselves (8).

A combination of many factors—such as strong goal orientation toward ambitious goals, long distance from headquarters to corruption arena, and no monitoring of executive activities—made corruption a convenient option for Yara to explore and exploit business opportunities in distant markets.

In the Yara corruption investigation in Norway, both a private investigation and a police investigation were carried out. Several suspects and witnesses were interviewed by both private investigators and police investigators. One of them was Tom Østlyngen, who was a witness based on his previous role as project manager for the Libya project. He testified in court in February 2015, where he commented on the different interviews. He found interviews by Økokrim—the national police unit for fraud and other kinds of financial crime—quite acceptable. Interviews by private investigators from the law firm Wiersholm, however, were not found acceptable (Dugstad and Ånestad, 2015: 14):

> Økokrim has with respect a more case-oriented approach to asking people than Wiersholm has, as I experienced it, says Østlyngen.

We return to the issue of private investigations of financial crime suspicions later in this book.

The former CEO at Yara, Thorleif Enger, was twice warned about possible corruption in connection with Yara investments in Libya. There were also suspicions of corruption in India. As evidenced in many corruption cases, it turns out that foreign heads of state and their families help themselves by virtue of their position of power to receive bribes from Norwegian and other foreign companies. Yara had indeed paid money to the Gadhafi clan in Libya. In late 2008, the new CEO at Yara decided to ignore suspicions of corruption when he learned about them. But almost three years later, the fertilizer company changed its mind, as the uprising against Gadhafi in Libya was a fact, and after Norwegian daily business newspaper *Dagens Næringsliv* (DN) started to question Yara executives about their foreign operations (Dugstad et al., 2011). Yara hired private investigators from the law firm Wiersholm, who recommended that Yara to go to the police (Dugstad and Ånestad, 2015).

Attorney Jan Fougner at the law firm Wiersholm was hired as a financial crime specialist by Yara to investigate the suspicions. Thorleif Enger had by that time resigned as CEO at Yara, and Jørgen Ole Haslestad, who had been on the board at Yara for several years, took over in 2008. Haslestad had experience from the corruption scandals at German multinational company Siemens, where he was one of the top executives (Dugstad and Ånestad, 2012).

Yara chief Haslestad claims his predecessor did not inform him about corruption suspicions (Dugstad et al., 2011: 4):

> *Haslestad:* The last thing I asked Enger about when I took over his office was, "Is there anything I should know?"
>> "No," was the answer he gave.
> *DN Reporter:* Should he have told you this?
> *Haslestad:* Yes, he should. I think it would have been natural that he had given notice.
> *DN Reporter:* Did Enger pass on the message to the board about what Holba had told?
> *Haslestad:* I was never informed of this when I was on the board.

However, neither Haslestad nor Enger reacted when they first heard about the corruption case in Libya. More than 2 1/2 years, almost 3 years, passed after Haslestad himself first learned about it from Holba, before Haslestad initiated an investigation. His initiative came after the Norwegian daily business newspaper *Dagens Næringsliv* had started to dig into rumors of money claims from intermediaries in Libya (Dugstad et al., 2011).

Executive vice president Holba was repeatedly exposed to people who felt entitled to money in connection with negotiations, but he argued that money demands he received from Libya in the summer of 2008 were unique (Dugstad et al., 2011: 6):

> This is a very special case where a mediator came on with a pecuniary claim after so many years of negotiations in Libya.

According to a report from the U.S. Securities and Exchange Commission (SEC), which also investigated Siemens where Haslestad had been one of the top leaders, transporting cash across borders was a method that was used to hide bribes. According to the report, it was from the business area headed by Haslestad at Siemens that bribes were paid 89 times in a total of $130 million in the period from March 2001 to September 2007. Haslestad headed the business area from September 2001 until he left Siemens in 2008. When confronted by journalists in *Dagens Næringsliv*, he said that he had never personally been criticized for anything that happened in the Siemens Group for which he was responsible (Dugstad and Ånestad, 2015).

Haslestad was a witness in the corruption court case in 2015. Four Yara executives were prosecuted in Oslo district court in 2015: Thorleif Enger, Tor Holba, Kendrick Wallace, and Daniel Clauw (Dugstad and Ånestad, 2015).

The Wall Street Journal reported the indictments in 2014 under the heading "Four Former Yara Executives Indicted for Corruption" (Hovland, 2014):

> Four former Yara International ASA executives denied allegations of corruption after police in Norway indicted them for agreeing to pay over $8 million in bribes in India and Libya. The partly state-owned chemical company this week accepted Norway's biggest-ever corporate fine after it admitted to paying bribes.
>
> "The indictment regards very serious acts of corruption, and the police believe we can prove that these people were involved. But it's up to the courts to make a decision on their guilt," said public prosecutor Marianne Djupesland on Friday.
>
> Norway's police unit on economic crime indicted the four Yara executives on charges of bribery in Libya and three of them also on charges of bribery in India seven years ago. Yara, 36% owned by the Norwegian government, is among the world's biggest fertilizer producers.
>
> Among the indicted were former chief executive Thorleif Enger, former executive Tor Holba, former chief operating officer and deputy chief executive Daniel Clauw, a French national, and former chief legal officer Kendrick Taylor Wallace, a U.S. national.
>
> "Mr. Enger is completely uncomprehending towards this indictment," his defense lawyer, Ellen Holager Andenæs, told *The Wall Street Journal*. "I sincerely do hope that people realize that these are allegations and nothing else."

FBI special agent Leslie A. Nelson was following the trial in Oslo district court from a back row seat in the courtroom. She was paying special attention to former legal executive at Yara, Ken Wallace, who is a U.S. citizen. She took part in interviews with Wallace and was interested in hearing what he had to say in court. In the United States, there is no law that forbids double punishment. Nelson confirmed that they theoretically could prosecute Wallace in the United States, even if he was prosecuted in Norway. She said to Norwegian newspaper *Dagens Næringsliv* that the FBI at this stage only support Norwegian Økokrim and does not consider prosecution (Dugstad and Ånestad, 2015).

It is quite obvious from media reports over the years that top management at Yara were reluctant to disclose corruption to Norwegian police in anticipation that some of them might be investigated and prosecuted in court. CEO Jørgen Ole Haslestad left the chief executive position and Yara in 2015. He was never prosecuted.

References

Berglund, N. (2015). Ex-Yara bosses sentenced to jail, *NewsinEnglish.no*, http://www.newsinenglish.no/2015/07/07/ex-yara-bosses-sentenced-to-jail/, published July 7.

Boles, J. (2014). The two faces of bribery: International corruption pathways meet conflicting legislative regimes, *Michigan Journal of International Law*, 35 (4), 673–713.

Dugstad, L., Solberg, R.M. and Vanvik, H. (2011). Frykter bevis går tapt (Fears that evidence will get lost), daily Norwegian business newspaper *Dagens Næringsliv*, Saturday, April 16, pp. 4–7.

Dugstad, L. and Ånestad, M. (2012). Holdt styret uvitende i to år (Kept the board in the dark for two years), daily Norwegian business newspaper *Dagens Næringsliv*, Thursday, May 24, pp. 4–5.

Dugstad, L. and Ånestad, M. (2015). Han er en hedersmann (He is a solid person), daily Norwegian business newspaper *Dagens Næringsliv*, Wednesday, February 18, p. 14.

Elster, K. and Magnus, P.C. (2015). Det er for få slike saker (There are too few cases like this), Norwegian Public Broadcasting Corporation *NRK* Hordaland, http://www.nrk.no/hordaland/_-det-er-for-fa-slike-saker-1.12560947, published September 18.

Gottschalk, P. (2015). *Internal Investigations of Economic Crime—Corporate Case Studies and Regulatory Policy*, Boca Raton, FL: Universal Publishers.

Hovland, K.M. (2014). Four former Yara executives indicted for corruption, *The Wall Street Journal*, www.wsj.com, published January 17.

Ksenia, G. (2008). Can corruption and economic crime be controlled in developing countries and if so, is it cost-effective? *Journal of Financial Crime*, 15 (2), 223–233.

Oslo district court (2014). Case number 13-195526MED-OTIR/08, *Oslo tingrett*, December 3, 2014.

chapter eight

Corporate social responsibility

White-collar crime is committed in an organizational setting. The organization enables crime to occur and to be hidden in legal transactions. While organizations tend to claim that they are victims of white-collar crime, they do in fact represent enablers of financial crime. Therefore, organizations carry responsibility for crime and crime prevention. Crime prevention and detection is part of corporate citizenship, where the organization should avoid causing costs to society in terms of prosecution and punishment of white-collar criminals. When organizations allow white-collar crime to happen, then harm is caused to society. This is the opposite of corporate social responsibility, where the organization is expected to contribute benefits to society.

The individual profession and position in the organization makes it possible for the white-collar criminal to commit financial crime. Convenience theory and empirical study of white-collar criminals shows that it is in the organizational context that white-collar crime is possible and is committed. Organizations should therefore be held responsible for crime occurring among their trusted and privileged executives.

Both public and private businesses have responsibility for preventing others from being victimized by their own white-collar criminals. Empirical study indicates that customers, banks, tax collectors, and others are victims of white-collar crime committed in other organizations. Although there are always individuals who carry out the actual crime, nevertheless it is the business that opened up possibilities for carrying out crime. By showing confidence and trust, and by providing privileges, power, and influence, with little or no control installed, the business opens up for financial crime.

Empirical study shows that employers are the single largest group among white-collar crime victims. Embezzlement, fraud, and other forms of financial crime makes it possible for trusted employees to enrich themselves at the expense of the business. The business itself is hurt. At the same time, the business itself is to blame. The business has enabled—and not prevented—white-collar crime to occur.

When employers become crime victims

Leif Marius Schatvet (born 1963) was a chief financial officer (CFO) at Aschehoug publishing house in Oslo, where he embezzled a total of

9 million Norwegian kroner (about $1.4 million). The publishing house was part owner of a bookstore chain from which Aschehoug decided to remove itself. Schatvet was asked to close the relationship with the chain. A number of financial transactions occurred between the publishing house and the bookstore chain that were all handled by Schatvet and controlled by nobody else. He discovered an opportunity to transfer some of the money to his own bank account, which he did. After having transferred 9 million, he was in the process of transferring one more million to his private bank account, when he entered a wrong account number for his own bank account. The typing mistake was reported by the bank to one of his subordinates in the accounting department, who blew the whistle on the CFO to the CEO. The CEO hired professional services firm KPMG to do an internal investigation by fraud examiners. Schatvet said in court that he was short of money because of an expensive divorce and purchase of a winter cabin in the mountains (Hegnar, 2014).

Are Blomhoff (born 1952) was a priest and the CEO at diaconal institution Betanien Foundation. The foundation runs nursing homes, kindergartens, and other social institutions in Norway. In addition, it is in charge of a nursing home for retired Norwegians in Spain. Blomhoff frequently visited the nursing home in Spain and bought himself an apartment in the neighborhood. He opened a bank account for himself in a local Spanish bank and started to transfer some Betanien money to his private bank account in Spain. The embezzled money paid for his housing expenses as well as wild parties, where he paid local prostitutes to join his parties. Two junior employees at Betanien tried to blow the whistle on Blomhoff, but nobody on the board of directors believed their accusations of wrongdoing on the part of the priest and chief executive. Therefore, Blomhoff's embezzlement could continue for many years. Finally, someone on the board of directors believed the whistleblowers, and the board hired fraud examiners from BDO to investigate the matter. BDO investigators found evidence of several million Norwegian kroner embezzled by Blomhoff, and he was later sentenced to 3 years in prison by a district court (Drammen tingrett, 2015).

Bente Selvaag (born 1952) was assistant manager at BNP Paribas, where she was in charge of collection cases after the financial crisis in the banking sector in Norway. Some of the collected money was not transferred to the bank, but rather to interim accounts and onward to her personal accounts. She was able to continue her embezzlement activity for 9 years before she was randomly detected. Then the total embezzled amount was 13 million Norwegian kroner ($2 million). Her position made it possible to embezzle, since the bank had introduced no control system for her function in the bank (Kleppe, 2011).

Jørn Bertheussen (born 1952) was chief executive officer at the grocery and bakery chain Din Baker. He charged expenses to company accounts at Fokus Bank and Voss Bank by means of invoices and payment requirements issued by two Swedish companies, Finshyttan Fastighet and Herrgården Finshyttan. Bertheussen owned both of them. According to internal revenue service figures for 2009, Bertheussen had an annual income of 1.8 million Norwegian kroner (about $300,000), which is quite an acceptable wage in Norway. His position in the company allowed him to embezzle because the owners had introduced no control mechanism related to CEO activities. The board at Din Baker hired private investigators from PwC to examine fraud. Bertheussen was sentenced to 4 months in prison by a district court in Norway (Asker og Bærum tingrett, 2012).

Lars Brorson (born 1973) was chief financial officer at Hadeland and Ringerike Broadband. He was hired into this position, although someone in the parent company had heard of his previous convictions and jail sentences because of fraud. Brorson had complete control of financial transactions between sister companies and to and from the parent company. He approved transactions both in the transferring and in the receiving units because there were so many different legal entities in the group. His fraud was revealed when it was detected that he was involved in financial crime outside his regular job as well. Brorson was sentenced to 4 years and 6 months in prison by a district court in Norway. At the same time, PwC (2014a,b) were hired by the board at Hadeland and Ringerike Broadband to identify and present how fraud had occurred.

Aschehoug, Betanien, BNP Paribas, Din Baker, and Hadeland and Ringerike Broadband are only five examples of business organizations that have made it possible for trusted individuals to commit white-collar crime to enrich themselves. In the database of 405 convicted white-collar criminals in Norway, 115 persons (28%) were able to victimize their own organizations by financial crime.

One hundred and fifteen persons caused damage to their employers because their employers had enabled them to commit financial crime. At the same time, damage was caused to society because criminals had to be prosecuted and kept in correctional institutions while serving their prison sentences. Should companies be held responsible for damage caused to society? If these companies had installed controls, reduced degrees of freedom, and relied less on trust then fewer potential white-collar criminals would commit financial crime. This is according to convenience theory, which argues that the tendency to criminality is reduced when opportunities decline and detection likelihood increases.

When others become crime victims

Among 405 white-collar criminals, 115 of them caused financial losses to their own organization, while 300 criminals caused financial damage to external parties. Eighty-four criminals caused economic losses to the society at large, since the internal revenue service did not get tax payments as required. Sixty-four offenders caused financial losses to customers, 57 offenders caused losses to banks, and 30 criminal shareholders caused financial damage to other shareholders, while the remaining 51 offenders caused financial losses to a variety of victims.

When tax authorities such as the internal revenue service are victimized, then society at large becomes a victim. Financial revenue to the state is dedicated to two main objectives. First, there is authority and government such as police, military, and other functions equipped with power on behalf of the state. Next, there is service provision to inhabitants such as medical care, hospitals, and roads. When tax revenues decline, then the state can either increase taxes for taxpayers who pay, or the state can reduce its administration and service. In a taxi fraud case in Norway, the accounting firm of Henry Amundsen produced accounting figures for hundreds of taxi owners who did not have to pay taxes because of misrepresentation of financial results. Amundsen was sentenced to 8 years in prison. Art painter Odd Nerdrum sold his paintings abroad, but did not report his income to Norwegian tax authorities. He was sentenced to 2 years and 8 months in prison. Morten Stang Sausage Factory did not report sales of kebab food. Several members of the Stang family were sentenced to prison (Borgarting, 2009).

When customers are victimized, then innocent individuals and firms are financially hurt. One example is attorneys, who abuse client funds. Some clients place their money in attorney accounts, for example as security deposit, as transfer for payments, or as receipt of payments. Attorney Odd Arild Drevland was convicted of client fraud and sentenced to prison for 2 years and 6 months. Another example is container firm Uniteam run by father and son Harald (born 1942) and Tommy Engh (born 1985). They were sentenced in a court of appeals to 3 1/2 years, and 3 years, respectively, for fraud against the Norwegian Army. Fraud occurred because father and son stated incorrect material costs to their customer (Næss and Ravn, 2013).

When banks are affected, owners and depositors as well as borrowers are hurt. A bank becomes less profitable when bank fraud occurs, and bank owners (shareholders) lose money. Depositors can be hurt because the bank may put down the deposit rate. Borrowers can be hurt because the bank may set up the lending rate. A bank is in the business of connecting people with too much money (depositors) with people who have too little money (borrowers). When borrowers commit bank fraud and thus do not pay back their loans, then all stakeholders in the bank suffer financial loss. When Finance Credit in Norway went bankrupt, then a number of banks lost a total of 1 billion Norwegian kroner ($160 million). Bankruptcy arose long after the firm Finance Credit was broke. Torger Stensrud, chairperson of the board, and Trond Kristoffersen, chief executive, had for years presented misleading economic statements to banks, making banks fund more and more of debts that did not exist. Stensrud and Kristoffersen were sentenced to 7 and 9 years in prison, respectively (Riisnæs, 2014).

The last group of victims is shareholders. Some shareholders were able to sell shares at extremely high prices, or they were able to buy shares at extremely low prices, because they had information that other shareholders did not possess. It is not illegal to have exclusive information, which represents an information asymmetry among shareholders. What is illegal is exclusive information from a particular source. The particular source is internal people in the organization that is owned by the shareholders. If internal people leak stock-price sensitive information to selective people who act in the stock market on the information, both those who leak and those who trade commit financial crime. It is called insider trading, which is illegal in most countries. Insider trading is organizationally anchored when someone on the inside knows something that is profitable for themselves and also profitable for people on the outside. The Acta case is an example of insider trading in Norway (Stavanger tingrett, 2012).

There are considerable differences between these four groups of victims. Tax authorities such as the internal revenue service has in no way been involved, and the service has no way of telling whether tax evasion has occurred. The only way they can find out is to actively retrieve and search documents from tax payers to control tax payers' statements. Tax authorities do not know whether accounting statements have been manipulated until they eventually discover misconduct by their own investigations. Similarly, tax authorities have no information about an art painter selling his paintings abroad, unless they are actively investigating the finances of the artist. Tax authorities are not involved in any way unless they start auditing and other forms of investigations.

The second group of victims is customers. They have some opportunity to know what is going on, since they have involved themselves with someone who turned out to be a criminal. Customers have the possibility of checking the correctness of invoices and other information from the supplier. However, a client in a law firm has often little or no insights into internal operations in the firm.

The third group of victims is banks. They are involved, and they may be to blame when they become victims of bank fraud. Banks are actively involved in paying out money to borrowers. When the borrowers present fake documents and manipulated statements, it is the responsibility of banks to avoid payments based on such misleading information. If banks do pay in such situations, then their risk assessment and background checks of potential borrowers have failed. Norwegian banks trusted blindly Stensrud and Kristoffersen at Finance Credit for many years, without installing proper controls. It was an investigating journalist who revealed that Finance Credit was in reality bankrupt several years before. Similarly, banks trusted blindly the CEO at Sponsor Service, Terje Bogen, who claimed that sponsoring contracts for top athletes would all be signed in the near future. Banks lost 400 million Norwegian kroner because of their trust in Bogen. In these cases of bank fraud, there is organizational failure not only on the part of the fraudsters, but also on the part of the banks. Because banks have improper controls with potential fraudsters, society is frequently required to punish offenders when they are detected. Therefore, banks do not only lose money. They also cause expenses for society in courts and prisons.

Other shareholders are not responsible for being cheated by insider trading. They had no inside information. If they had possessed inside information, it is not obvious that they would have acted on the information. A company owned by shareholders is like a zero-sum game when the value of the company at a given point in time is constant. When someone is able to acquire a share of the company similar to the share owned by someone else, but at a lower price, then the same value is obtained at lower cost.

Gjensidige Insurance and Hells Angels

The empirical sample in this book is concerned with financial crime in general and with white-collar crime in particular. Thus far in this chapter, we have discussed the extent to which businesses may themselves be responsible for crime occurrences, although they initially are perceived as victims of crime. It is a matter of corporate social responsibility, where organizations are accountable and responsible to society for their own negative impacts.

In this section we will visit a completely different kind of crime often labeled organized crime. The example is concerned with Norwegian insurance company Gjensidige and their responsibility for combatting crime in society whenever there is a chance for the company to do so. It is a matter of corporate social responsibility as well, where organizations are expected to take responsibility for society and the environment in broad terms. This example is interesting because the insurance company found themselves in a peculiar situation after a claim settlement.

A woman was killed in an explosion that occurred in the city of Drammen in June 1997. In 2003, five men were convicted of blowing up the headquarters of Bandidos. Some of the convicts were members of Hells Angels MC Norway. The buildings in Drammen were insured by Gjensidige Insurance Company. The insurance company tried to recover some of its losses by collecting money from Hells Angels members. Gjensidige took pledge in a club house at Ringsaker outside the city of Hamar, where some of the convicts were part owners. Gjensidige has renewed its majority pledge every five years, so that the pledge would not become obsolete (Gottschalk, 2013). Still, in 2015, however, Gjensidige has this pledge without taking any actions to retrieve the money.

This case study addresses the relevance of corporate social responsibility (CSR) to Gjensidige Insurance Company in the context of their pledge in a clubhouse of the Hells Angels Motorcycle Club (HAMC). HAMC is a criminal matrix organization, where the motorcycle club is a legal organization along the vertical axis, while it organizes criminal activities along the horizontal axis. In terms of CSR, the issue is whether and how Gjensidige might use its majority pledge in contributing to societal welfare, compensating for others' negative impacts, and taking responsibility for society and the environment.

This case study links two different contexts. One is about the insurance business in general as it is exposed to a specific kind of negative event. The negative event leads the insurance company unwillingly into the context of law enforcement as a CSR issue. The other, though more marginal context, is concerned with the extent of symbolic CSR to be found in the conduct of MC clubs to influence their own reputation. The link can be found when a legal enterprise is facing challenges in relation to outlaws and outlaw MCs that portray themselves as socially responsible individuals and organizations.

Gjensidige Insurance Company

Gjensidige has safeguarded assets ever since the first mutual fire insurers were established in the 1820s. The company offers all kinds of insurance and is divided into three main sectors: private, agriculture, and business. It also offers retail banking products through its subsidiary Gjensidige Bank as well as pensions and savings products. In November 2007, Gjensidige applied for a listing on the Oslo Stock Exchange, and made its debut on the exchange in 2009.

The social mission of the company is to safeguard life, health, and assets for its customers. This is the company's corporate social responsibility. Loss prevention is an important part of this work, and the company is involved in many projects. This is how the company presents itself on the Internet (https://www.gjensidige.no/group/social-mission /social-responsibility#Section1):

> *Well prepared with loss prevention.* We are involved in the lives of people and enterprises, **before** and **after** claims. Over the course of many years, we have gathered knowledge about what causes losses and how they can be avoided. We give this knowledge back to our customers,

the authorities and society at large through advice, collaboration projects and participation in social debate.

Responsible and good conduct. Gjensidige plays an important role in society, and we have to manage the responsibility this involves in a good way. We make strict ethical demands of ourselves, our suppliers and our financial investments. We have zero tolerance for corruption and facilitation payments. Our operations cause few greenhouse gas emissions and have little environmental impact on the environment, and we strive to further reduce it. Gjensidige aims to offer a health encouraging working environment.

Climate advice and surveying. There is broad agreement among scientists that human activities cause global warming and climate change. For several years, Gjensidige has contributed to research on the consequences of climate change, and there is much to suggest that water damage in Norwegian homes will become more common in the future.

According to the annual report of 2013, Gjensidige had solid growth in premiums in all market segments, improved quality in the customer portfolios and efficient operations, which formed the basis for a good profit performance in 2013. The letter from the CEO in the annual report read as follows:

> Gjensidige recorded a profit before tax expense of NOK 4.6 billion for 2013, an underwriting result of NOK 2.0 billion and a combined ratio for the whole general insurance operations of 89.2. This is very satisfying. The banking and pension operations in Norway also developed very positively in 2013 and they are making a bigger and bigger contribution to Gjensidige's results.

The basis for profitable growth and development was strengthened in 2013 through the acquisitions of Gouda Travel Insurance, which operates in the three Scandinavian countries, and Solid Försäkringar's motor and home content insurance portfolio in Sweden. The distribution agreement with Nykredit, which was adjusted during this year, strengthens our position in the Danish private market, and new partnership agreements with the Norwegian Trekking Association and the Norwegian Association of Hunters and Anglers provide new opportunities for business in Norway.

Hells Angels MC Norway

A distinction must be made between noncriminalized and criminalized bikers. The latter, outlaw bikers, are typically motorcycle club members referring to themselves as "1 percenters." Among the criminal biker clubs, we find Hells Angels, Outlaws, Bandidos, Pagans, Black Pistons, Mongols, and Coffin Cheaters. The most well-known being HAMC, which is in charge of many criminal business enterprises all over the world.

Lavigne (1996, p. 1) described criminal bikers in this way:

> The darkness of crime lies not in its villainy or horror, but in the souls of those who choose to live their lives in the abyss. A man who toils from youth to old age to violate the line that divides civilization from wilderness, who proclaims he is not of society, but an outsider sworn to break its laws and rules, yet who readily seeks refuge in its lenient legal system, embraces its judicial paternalism and gains substance from its moral weakness; whose very existence as an outlaw is defined by society's being, is but a shadow of the real world, bereft of freedom and doomed to tag along in society's wake.

When reviewing the history of HAMC, it started in 1948 and has since grown to encompass several thousand members worldwide (www.wikipedia.org—search Hells Angels):

> The Hells Angels were originally formed in 1948 in Fontana, California through an amalgamation of former members from different motorcycle clubs, such as The Pissed Off Bastards of Bloomington. The Hells Angels website denies the suggestion that any misfit or malcontent troops are connected with the motorcycle club. However, the website notes that the name was suggested by Arvid Olsen, an associate of the founders, who had served in the Flying Tigers 'Hells Angels' squadron in China during World War II. The name 'Hells Angels' was believed to have been inspired by the common historical use,

in both World War I and World War II, to name squadrons or other fighting groups by a fierce, death-defying name.

Over the years, studies of HAMC have repeatedly shown that running an outlaw club is costly and that the funds required are earned by organized crime (Quinn and Koch, 2003; Rassel and Komarnicki, 2007). In Scandinavia, a war on organized drug crime broke out in the 1990s that involved the Hells Angels (www.wikipedia.org—search Hells Angels):

> A gang war over drugs and turf between Hells Angels and the Bandidos, known as the 'Great Nordic Biker War', raged from 1994 until 1997 and ran across Norway, Sweden, Denmark and even parts of Finland and Estonia. By the end of the war, machine guns, hand grenades, rocket launchers and car bombs had been used as weapons, resulting in 11 murders, 74 attempted murders, and 96 wounded members of the involved motorcycle clubs. This led to fierce response from law enforcement and legislators, primarily in Denmark. A law was passed that banned motorcycle clubs from owning or renting property for their club activities. The law has subsequently been repealed on constitutional grounds.

The historical background for this case study of Gjensidige Insurance Company and Hells Angels motorcycle club is set against an account of one of the bombs that exploded during the 'Great Nordic Biker War' in 1997 (Gottschalk, 2013).

Hells Angels club house

After the bomb exploded in the city of Drammen outside of Oslo in Norway in 1997, police investigations concluded that it had been placed outside the Bandidos clubhouse by members of HAMC Norway. Several HAMC members were tried and given jail sentences. Furthermore, Gjensidige Insurance Company, which had insured the destroyed buildings, had to pay out close to $100 million to the owners of the buildings. Following several court sentences of HAMC members, Gjensidige sought repayment from those members. Although the members did not pay, Gjensidige discovered that they owned shares in a clubhouse outside the city of Hamar and acquired a majority pledge in the club house based on the debts of these members. More than a decade later, in 2015, Gjensidige had still not taken any action to retrieve the money, despite holding this pledge.

Gjensidige argues that their role is to retrieve money lost in insurance payments that arose due to the Drammen bomb. They say that forcing Hells Angels out of the club house does not make sense for three main reasons. Firstly, the value of the club house is less than $1 million, and Gjensidige lost $100 million dollars. Secondly, the efforts and costs involved in throwing Hells Angels members out will probably exceed the benefits for Gjensidige. Thirdly, it is not the responsibility of a business firm to become involved in law enforcement, even if it is a matter of serious organized crime where the firm might make a difference.

The small town of Ringsaker where the club house is located would very much like to be rid of the Hells Angels and view Gjensidige's pledge as a golden opportunity to displace the criminals. All of the politicians in the town have encouraged Gjensidige to deploy their economic and legal force to evict HA members from the club house and then sell it on the open market. Similarly, local police in Ringsaker would also very much appreciate some help from Gjensidige in order to get rid of the club, the members, and the associated criminal activity in drugs, prostitution, and violence.

In an attempt to localize Gjensidige in terms of corporate social responsibility in the Hells Angels case, a maturity model presented later in this book is applied.

Evaluation of CSR

In this case study, the specific context of Gjensidige is concerned with the firm's contribution to fight organized crime as carried out by members of Hells Angels Motorcycle Club in Norway. We evaluate what the firm can do and what the firm is willing to do. Gjensidige is willing to renew its majority ownership in the HA club house. Gjensidige is not willing to expel HA members from the club house and prevent the house from being sold back to the criminally loaded MC club. Gjensidige considers such an action to be the responsibility of the police and other public authorities.

Based on this situation of Gjensidige, the following evaluation can be justified in terms of the extent Gjensidige in the Hells Angels context already has CSR in place:

1. Being accountable: Gjensidige takes on business responsibility to society by controlling the ownership of a club house where a number of organized criminals are living as members of the legal HAMC Norway. The firm applies a business perspective, where it keeps the pledge as long as persons have debts to the firm. Conclusion: Yes, Gjensidige is being accountable.
2. Compensating its own negative impacts: The issue of whether Gjensidige is compensating for its own negative impacts, which is

a matter of business responsibility for society, is not relevant in our context of HAMC. Conclusion: No, Gjensidige is not compensating.

3. Compensating for others' negative impacts: This is an issue of business responsibility for society, where Gjensidige certainly could do more to fight a criminal organization, since the firm has a majority pledge in the club house of HAMC. Conclusion: No, Gjensidige is not compensating.

4. Contributing to societal welfare: Again, here Gjensidige could do much more. Many citizens who live in the neighborhood of the club house dislike it, and the city of Hamar is not at all happy to have a local Hells Angels MC gang in their region. Societal welfare is not only threatened by organized crime but also by international parties held in the club house, where members tend to recruit young local girls for pleasure. Conclusion: No, Gjensidige is not contributing.

5. Operations: The issue of whether Gjensidige is operating their business in an ethically, responsible, and sustainable way in terms of business responsible conduct is not really relevant for the HAMC context, apart from its professional handling of the majority pledge. Conclusion: No, Gjensidige is not operating ideally.

6. Broad responsibility: Gjensidige is not taking responsibility for society and the environment in broad terms. Rather, they argue that their business mission is to insure people to help with loss prevention. But this is how they make money; it has nothing to do with CSR. Conclusion: No, Gjensidige is taking no broad responsibility.

7. Managing by business its relationships with society: Yes, this is exactly what Gjensidige does. The firm considers its relationship with society as a business issue. To relate to society has to do with transactions that can be justified by short-term or long-term profitability. Conclusion: Yes, Gjensidige manages business relationships.

The list above is concerned with the current situation. The next list is based on the desired situation. The following evaluation can be justified in terms of the extent Gjensidige in the Hells Angels context can have CSR in place in the future. The list represents recommendations for how firms ending up in similar situations can behave to successfully manage their corporate social responsibility:

1. Being accountable (business responsibility to society): Yes, is already in place.

2. Compensating for its own negative impacts (business responsibility for society): No, this aspect is not really relevant for organizations that end up in similar situations with outlaw organizations, even though they want to practice CSR.

3. Compensating for others' negative impacts (business responsibility for society): Yes, by reducing the financial muscles of outlaw biker gangs, an insurance firm can compensate for their negative impacts.

4. Contributing to societal welfare (business responsibility for society): No, this is not relevant for the circumstance of law enforcement.

5. Operating their business in an ethically, responsible, and sustainable way (business responsible conduct): No, this is not relevant for the circumstance of law enforcement.

6. Taking responsibility for society and the environment in broad terms: Yes, this is already in place.

7. Managing by business its relationships with society: Yes, this is already in place.

The insurance business is all about helping people and enterprises avoid heavy losses in case of negative events. The business model is simple: everyone pays a little premium every year, and those hit by an accident receive a larger sum. This is a useful contribution to society, but it has nothing to do with corporate social responsibility. CSR goes beyond the business itself (Adeyeye, 2011; Basu and Palazzo, 2008; Mostovicz et al., 2009; Zollo et al., 2009). This we have tried to illustrate with the case of Gjensidige. CSR is about what the insurance business does in addition to insuring people and places.

Thus far in this case study, only CSR for Gjensidige has been discussed. But also organizations such as Hells Angels MC Norway should engage in responsible efforts in support of society, even though some of the members make their living from organized crime. And there are indeed examples of contributions from Hells Angels in Norway. The club has engaged itself in activities for children in general and disabled children in particular. The club has staged events for the public to communicate differences for peaceful coexistence.

Seven criteria were applied to evaluate the extent of corporate social responsibility by Gjensidige Insurance Company as it relates to their majority pledge in a club house occupied by Hells Angels Motor Cycle Club Norway. Two criteria seem irrelevant for the specific context of HAMC: Compensating its own negative impacts and Gjensidige operating its business ethically. Two criteria seem to be met by Gjensidige: Being accountable and managing by business its relationships with society.

Three remaining criteria are not being met by Gjensidige: Compensating for others' negative impacts, contributing to societal welfare, and taking on a broad responsibility for society.

Asset recovery in 2015

Gjensidige had a total claim of 300 million Norwegian kroner against members of Hells Angels MC Norway after the bombing at Bandidos in

1997. In the spring of 2015, the insurance company was able to retrieve and recover 2 million. At the same time, Gjensidige had once again renewed its claim in the club house. The asset recovery is a sign of increased corporate social responsibility by Gjensidige Insurance Company (Rostad and Sletmoen, 2015):

> The bombing of the Bandidos clubhouse in Drammen in 1997 led to serious material damage, and a woman passerby was killed. Seven Hells Angels members were sentenced to heavy penalties after the attack. The insurance company Gjensidige filed a claim of NOK 300 million in damages. Now they have succeeded in collecting two million kroner. The money has come in through valuable items such as cars and boats and was recovered in the spring. This has happened through a distraint, says Bjarne Rysstad, chief of public information at Gjensidige.
>
> Rysstad and Gjensidige do not expect to get into all of the 300 million, but will keep trying. Gjensidige has therefore taken pledge in a variety of assets among members of Hells Angels to secure the greatest possible part of the claim. Perhaps the most important item is a lien on 55.5 percent of the club house of the Hells Angels in Ringsaker. Part of the strategy to bring in money is to ensure that the money claim does not become obsolete. A forced sale of the club house is one of the alternatives the insurance company is looking into.
>
> We think long term and look at all the ways how we can recover assets. When it comes to the house, a forced sale is not applicable at present, but this is something that could change, says Rysstad.
>
> Professor Petter Gottschalk on BI has written several books on organized crime. In the book "White-collar crime and corporate responsibility" he has devoted over 100 pages to the bombing in Drammen and the economic aftermath.
>
> For me Hells Angels is a criminal organization, and they admit themselves that they consist of individuals with criminal backgrounds. Therefore, it is positive that Gjensidige has managed to get out parts of the claim. I have long believed that this is

an important part of their social responsibility at Gjensidige, Gottschalk says.

He does not exclude that the payment may be part of a strategy in which HA is trying to move away from the piston as a criminal organization.

As far as I know the case, I am surprised over the payment. It poses many questions, and one can speculate on whether this is a deliberate strategy of HA. They have long been working to improve their reputation, and this could be part of a larger mindset.

Spokesman for Hells Angels, Rune Olsgården, says to NRK that he was not aware of payments to Gjensidige, and that the main men from the bombing attack have long been out of the club.

Corruption case at Siemens

Hells Angels and Gjensidige Insurance Company is no white-collar crime case. But it is a case of corporate responsibility to combat crime. A more typical example of white-collar crime and lack of corporate responsibility is the corruption case at Siemens. The German company faced a series of bribery and money laundering allegations in more than a dozen countries in 2004. In 2006, German police investigators raided Siemens headquarters in Munich and homes of leading executives. Police investigations revealed that Siemens had been bribing governmental officials to secure contracts and to gain favorable conditions for more than three decades. Eberl et al. (2015: 1209) argue that most of the executives involved "were clearly aware that they were violating the law, but they acted out of a sense of loyalty to and for the benefit of their company."

The severe violation of integrity at the organizational level at Siemens led to a substantial crisis of the organization's legitimacy and had strong negative effects on stakeholders' trust in the organization. To repair and restore trust in the organization, Siemens established a compliance program to detect corrupt practices, and they implemented corporate governance structures as well as accepted monitoring from external authorities.

Eberl et al. (2015) studied how Siemens tried to repair and restore trust. Their findings suggest that tightening organizational rules is an appropriate signal of trustworthiness for external stakeholders to demonstrate that the organization seriously intends to prevent integrity violations in the future. Their findings also suggest that such rule adjustments were the source of dissatisfaction among employees since the new rules were difficult to implement in practice.

Eberl et al. (2015) argue that these different impacts of organizational rules result from their paradoxical nature. To address this problem, they suggest managing an effective interplay between formal and informal rules.

In their document Corporate Social Responsibility Policy of Siemens (2014) and other documents, Siemens emphasizes the fight against corruption. Siemens supports the International Anti-Corruption Academy, which is dedicated to overcoming current shortcomings in knowledge and practice in the field of compliance and anti-corruption.

What is corporate responsibility?

This chapter discusses how combatting crime in general, and financial crime and white-collar crime in particular, is an integral part of corporate social responsibility, especially when crime finds its opportunity structure in the organization. White-collar crime originates and manifests itself in organizations. Organizations must carry responsibility for negative impacts on society, for example, when internal criminals are prosecuted and jailed at the expense of society.

To take on corporate social responsibility means to pay back to society. Pay-back is the opposite of causing costs to society. CSR is supposed to be a self-regulatory mechanism whereby a business monitors and ensures its active compliance with the spirit of the law, ethical standards, and national and international norms. CSR is a concept whereby companies integrate social and environmental concern in their business operations and in the interaction with their stakeholders on a voluntary basis (Ditlev-Simonsen, 2014).

CSR is receiving increased attention. Today, companies are expected to take on responsibilities beyond regulatory compliance and posting profits (Ditlev-Simonsen, 2014: 117):

> How companies engage the environment, human rights, ethics, corruption, employee rights, donations, volunteer work, contributions to the community and relationships with suppliers are typically viewed as components of CSR.

There are several links between CSR and crime prevention. One link is the company's responsibility toward society if crime occurs, as mentioned above. Another link is the effect of CSR on organizational members. Ditlev-Simonsen (2015) studied this effect in terms of affective commitment among organizational members from active CSR. Her study explored the relationship between employees' CSR perception and employees' affective commitment. Affective commitment is defined as an employee's duty or pledge to the company. Results indicate that CSR perception is a significant predictor of affective commitment, although how employees feel that the company cares about them has a stronger explanatory power on affective commitment.

CSR is about doing good. In the case of Gjensidige Insurance Company and Hells Angels, seven elements of doing good were mentioned: (1) being accountable: business responsibility to society, (2) compensating for negative impacts: business responsibility for society, (3) compensating for others' negative impacts: business responsibility for society, (4) contributing to societal welfare: business responsibility for society, (5) operating their business in an ethically, responsible, and sustainable way: business responsible conduct, (6) taking responsibility for society and the environment in broad terms, and (7) managing by business its relationships with society.

In total, these elements reflect an organization's active cooperation with values and attitudes in society. For example, anticorruption has been identified as a core value of corporate responsibility globally. CSR is demonstrated by activities based on assumed obligations to society. Stakeholders' expectations are to be met.

Ditlev-Simonsen and Midttun (2011) phrased the question: What motivates managers to pursue corporate responsibility? Branding, stakeholders, and value maximization were found to be key motivators. Branding is concerned with building a positive reputation and brand image. Stakeholders is about satisfying different stakeholders, while value maximization is concerned with creating long-term value for shareholders.

Failure in corporate responsibility

Corporate social responsibility is defined as a leadership task. Board members and chief executives in an organization have a particular responsibility to make sure that the organization is in compliance with laws and regulations, and that the organization makes contributions to society wherever relevant. Chief executives should make the organization accountable, compensate for negative impacts, contribute to societal welfare, operate the business ethically, take responsibility for society, and manage in relation with society.

But what happens then when such trusted persons in important leadership positions in business enterprises and other organizations abuse their positions for illegal gain? That is what white-collar crime is all about, either it is for personal gain or it is for company gain. Crime is the complete opposite of corporate social responsibility. Criminal activity is to abuse a privileged position for a purpose detrimental to CSR. White-collar crime is financial crime by privileged, powerful, and influential people when they occupy positions in business enterprises, public agencies, and political governance.

Osuji (2011) argues that corporate social responsibility is a relatively underdeveloped concept despite its increasing importance to corporations. One difficulty is the possible inexactness of CSR. Another is the apparent reluctance by regulatory authorities and policy makers to intervene in the area. Corporate involvement in unethical secrecy in cases of misconduct and crime has emerged as a component of CSR debate and agenda. In recent years, corporate operations and impact in areas such as criminal justice, human rights, and the environment have grown hand in hand with governmental and public concern for firm misconduct, and privatization of law enforcement and criminal justice (Schneider, 2006), particularly in relation to outsourcing of crime investigations to professional services firms. A critical question is how corporate misconduct and crime and the associated detection by financial crime specialists from professional services firms can be contextualized within the CSR agenda.

Stages of growth in corporate responsibility

In this section, we suggest that the powerful concept of stages of growth is extremely important in management research. Stages of growth models have been used widely in both organizational research and information technology management research. According to King and Teo (1997), these models describe a wide variety of phenomena. These models assume that predictable patterns (conceptualized in terms of stages) exist. The stages are (1) sequential in nature, (2) occur as a hierarchical progression that is not easily reversed, and (3) involve a broad range of organizational activities and structures.

Researchers have struggled for decades to develop stages of growth models that are both theoretically founded and empirically validated. Two decades ago, Kazanjian and Drazin (1989) found that the concept of stages of growth was already widely employed. Later, a number of multistage models have been proposed which assume that predictable patterns exist in the growth of organizations, and that these patterns unfold as discrete time periods best thought of as stages. These models have different distinguishing characteristics. Stages can be driven by the search for new growth opportunities or as a response to internal crises. Some models suggest that an organization progresses through stages while others argue that there may be multiple paths through the stages. Therefore, a stages of growth theory needs to allow for multiple paths through stages as long as they follow a unidirectional pattern.

Maturity models can have varying number of stages, and each stage can be labeled according to the issue at hand. Here we suggest the following four stages of growth for CSR as illustrated in Figure 8.1:

I. Business stage of profit maximization for owners within the corporate mission. At this basic maturity level, the company is only concerned with itself and its owners. In addition, the company seeks to please its customers so that they will continue to buy its goods and services. The sole responsibility corporations have is that of maximizing profits to shareholders while engaging in open and free competition, without deception or fraud (Adeyeye, 2011). To make decisions that serve other interests at the expense of shareholders would constitute a breach in trust and loyalty. It would be like taking money away from owners and resemble a kind of theft. According to this perspective, corporate executives do not have the right to behave like modern Robin Hood types, taking money from the rich and giving it to the poor.

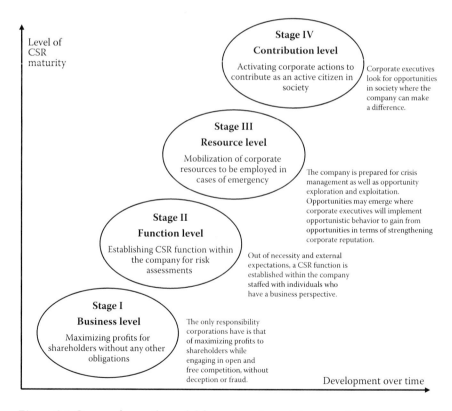

Figure 8.1 Stages of growth model for corporate social responsibility.

II. Function stage of establishing a function for corporate social responsibility in the company. At this second maturity level, business executives have understood that they need to address company relationships with the outside world in a professional manner. Out of necessity and external expectations, a CSR function is established within the company staffed with individuals who have a business perspective. The function here is to survey implications of business activities in the external environment; to develop intelligence to learn about external reactions to business practices; and to conduct risk assessments in terms of effects on corporate reputation. Here, Basu and Palazzo (2008) define corporate social responsibility as a process. The process implies that corporate leaders in the organization reflect over, and discuss, relationships with stakeholders and partners. The process also implies that corporate leaders identify their own and the organization's roles in relation to societal conditions and societal utility. This kind of reflection and discussion will cause them to endow their roles with relevant content and action.

III. Resource stage of resource mobilization for potential threats and opportunities. At this level, we find a complete, yet passive form of corporate social responsibility. It represents a reactive strategy where the company has mobilized resources for cases of emergency. The company is prepared for crisis management, as well as opportunity exploration and exploitation. Opportunities may emerge where corporate executives will implement opportunistic behavior to benefit from opportunities in terms of strengthening corporate reputation. CSR, at this level, is a concept that causes the company to integrate principles of social and environmental responsibility and induces engagement in the company's activities, both internally and externally. Two perspectives emerge from this definition. First, CSR implies a strong link to internal business processes; second, interactions with stakeholders and the society at large also require the involvement of stakeholders and the society at large, in terms of their relationships to the company (Zollo et al., 2009).

IV. Contribution stage of proactive involvement in society. At this final maturity level, corporate executives as well as all other organizational members perceive their business as part of a greater course in society. They adopt a comprehensive and active responsibility in both the local and the global society, and they look for opportunities in society where the company can make a difference. At this level of CSR, short-term loss to the company can be acceptable when weighed against the long-term good to society. CSR at this level is a long-term commitment to society (Mostovicz et al., 2009). Evidence is emerging that long-term citizen commitment on the part of the company by no means has to harm corporate profitability in either the short term or the long term.

One example might be the Norwegian insurance company Gjensidige. Gjensidige had a claim in the club house of Hells Angels (Gottschalk, 2013): while the claim involved a significant amount of money, it was impossible to retrieve, but the claim had a greater value in that it could nevertheless help both the municipality and the police in fighting organized crime in society (Gottschalk, 2013).

Convenience and corporate responsibility

As emphasized in this book's main perspective of convenience in white-collar crime, the judgment of CSR and its relevance must be conducted in a context. The contingent approach to CSR implies that what is needed in one context may neither be needed nor relevant in another context. Thus, the stage model developed in this chapter must be adapted to the relevant context before it can prove useful. The relevant context is white-collar crime.

It might be expected that the extent of white-collar crime will be large at Stage I and small at Stage IV. The argument would be that profit maximization is possible by both legal and illegal means, and profit maximization is all executives care about at Stage I. The argument for Stage IV would be that organizations contributing to the general welfare in society will never have criminals within them.

However, from a theoretical viewpoint, we may find a different pattern depending on the stages of growth. According to convenience theory, convenience occurs in the economical dimension, in the organizational dimension, and in the behavioral dimension. CSR does not really influence individuals in the behavioral dimension within the organization, and CSR does not really influence internal opportunities for financial crime. In fact, organizations at Stage IV may think so highly of themselves with high ethical standards and morale values, that they neglect controls and deny suspicions against any key persons in the organization. Knowing that they will not be suspected decreases their perceived likelihood of detection and thereby increases their willingness to commit crime. Organizations at Stage I, on the other hand, may be so well-organized and structured to reach business goals, so that deviant behavior is not possible or is quickly detected.

Therefore, to create a link between stages of growth in corporate social responsibility with prevention and detection of white-collar crime, there is a need to make explicit statements about combating crime at each stage:

1. Business stage of profit maximization for owners within the corporate mission. All means are acceptable to reach goals of profit maximization, including means that are on the wrong side of the law.
2. Function stage of establishing a function for corporate social responsibility in the company. White-collar crime is not an issue for the newly established function.

3. Resource stage of resource mobilization for potential threats and opportunities. Potential white-collar crime is perceived as a threat to the reputation of the organization. Resources are employed to reduce the degrees of freedom of privileged individuals in the organization, and proper controls are installed.

4. Contribution stage of proactive involvement in society. If the organization provided an opportunity for financial crime by enabling a white-collar criminal to commit offenses, then the enterprise will cover the costs of all correctional services and compensate for all other costs in society.

References

Adeyeye, A. (2011). Universal standards in CSR: Are we prepared? *Corporate Governance*, 11 (1), 107–119.

Asker and Bærum district court (2012). Case 12-066481MED-AHER/2, *Asker og Bærum tingrett*, 30.05.2012.

Basu, K. and Palazzo, G. (2008). Corporate social responsibility: A process model of sensemaking, *Academy of Management Review*, 33 (1), 122–136.

Borgarting (2009). Court of appeals case number LB-2008-90794-1. *Borgarting lagmannsrett (Borgarting Court of Appeals)*, 2009-04-27.

Ditlev-Simonsen, C.D. (2014). Are non-financial (CSR) reports trustworthy? A study of the extent to which non-financial reports reflect the media perception of the company's behaviour, *Issues in Social and Environmental Accounting*, 8 (2), 116–133.

Ditlev-Simonsen, C.D. (2015). The relationship between Norwegian and Swedish employees' perception of corporate social responsibility and affective commitment, *Business & Society*, 54 (2), 229–253.

Ditlev-Simonsen, C.D. and Midttun, A. (2011). What motivates managers to pursue corporate responsibility? A survey among key stakeholders, *Corporate Social Responsibility and Environmental Management*, 18, 25–38.

Drammen tingrett (2015). 15-002674ENE-DRAM, *Drammen tingrett (Drammen district court)*, 02.02.2015.

Eberl, P., Geiger, D. and Assländer, M.S. (2015). Repairing trust in an organization after integrity violations: The ambivalence of organizational rule adjustments, *Organization Studies*, 36 (9), 1205–1235.

Gottschalk, P. (2013). Limits to corporate social responsibility: The case of Gjensidige insurance company and Hells Angels motorcycle club, *Corporate Reputation Review*, 16 (3), 177–186.

Hegnar, T. (2014). Sviket mot Aschehoug (The Betrayal of Aschehoug), daily Norwegian business newspaper *Finansavisen*, Tuesday, January 14, p. 2.

Kazanjian, R.K. and Drazin, R. (1989). An empirical test of a stage of growth progression model, *Management Science*, 35 (12), 1489–1503.

King, W.R. and Teo, T.S.H. (1997). Integration between business planning and information systems planning: Validating a stage hypothesis. *Decision Science*, 28 (2), 279–308.

Kleppe, M.K. (2011). Banktopp dømt til tre års fengsel, *Finansavisen*, torsdag 22. December, pp. 6–7.

Lavigne, Y. (1996). *Hells Angels: Into the abyss*, New York: Harper Paperbacks, Harper Collins Publishers.

Mostovicz, I., Kakabadse, N. and Kakabadse, A. (2009). CSR: The role of leadership in driving ethical outcomes, *Corporate Governance*, 9 (4), 448–460.

Næss, A. and Ravn, L.K. (2013). Livsverket selges fra fengselet (Lifework sold from prison), daily Norwegian business newspaper *Dagens Næringsliv*, Friday, October 18, pp. 4–5.

Osuji, O. (2011). Fluidity of regulation-CSR nexus: The multinational corporate corruption example, *Journal of Business Ethics*, 103 (1), 31–57.

PwC (2014a). Hadeland Energi AS, Rapport—Gransking (Report of Investigation), PricewaterhouseCoopers, June 23.

PwC (2014b). Hadeland og Ringerike Bredbånd AS, Rapport—Gransking (Report of Investigation), PricewaterhouseCoopers, June 10.

Quinn, J. and Koch, D.S. (2003). The nature of criminality within one-percent motorcycle clubs, *Deviant Behavior: An Interdisciplinary Journal*, 24 (3), 281–305.

Rassel, J. and Komarnicki, J. (2007). Gangs ranked: Crazy Dragons head list of Alberta crime threats, *Calgary Herald*, Saturday, July 21.

Riisnæs, I.G. (2014). Hverken skyldig eller frikjent (Neither guilty or acquitted), daily Norwegian business newspaper *Dagens Næringsliv*, www.dn.no, published November 7.

Rostad, K. and Sletmoen, A.S. (2015). Har fått inn to millioner av Hells Angels (Has retrieved two millions from Hells Angels), website of the Norwegian public broadcasting corporation *NRK Hedmark og Oppland*, http://www.nrk.no/ho/har-fatt-inn-to-millioner-av-hells-angels-1.12515257, published August 25.

Schneider, S. (2006). Privatizing economic crime enforcement: Exploring the role of private sector investigative agencies in combating money laundering, *Policing & Society*, 16 (3), 285–312.

Siemens (2014), *Corporate social responsibility policy of Siemens Limited*, http://www.siemens.co.in/pool/about_us/sustainability/siemens-limited-india-corporate-social-responsibility-policy-december-2014.pdf.

Stavanger tingrett (2012), Court case 11-128794MED-STAV, *Stavanger tingrett* (Stavanger district court), November 15.

Zollo, M., Minoja, M., Casanova, L., Hockerts, K., Neergaard, P., Schneiderand, S. and Tencati, A. (2009). Towards an internal change management perspective of CSR: Evidence from project RESPONSE on the sources of cognitive alignment between managers and their stakeholders, and their implications for social performance, *Corporate Governance*, 9 (4), 355–372.

## chapter nine

Internal white-collar crime investigations

Convenience theory suggests that white-collar crime is stimulated when there is a need for profits, when the organization provides ample opportunities for misconduct, and when professionals in important and trusted positions find it acceptable to commit crime. In such organizations, suspicions of crime will occur more frequently than in organizations where people are less concerned with profits, where criminal opportunities are almost not present, and when the potential offender finds crime unacceptable.

When suspicion arises that crime has occurred, it can either be ignored or investigated. If the organization decides to investigate crime suspicions, then internal and/or external experts might get involved. Internal private investigations examine facts, sequence of events, and the causes of negative events as well as who is responsible for such events. Pending what hiring parties ask for, private investigators can either look generally for corrupt or otherwise criminal activities within an agency or company, or look more specifically for those committing white-collar crime. In other situations, it is the job of the private investigators to look into potential opportunities for financial crime to occur, so that the agency or company can fix those problems in order to avoid misconduct down the road.

Internal investigations include fact-finding, causality study, change proposals, and suspect identification. Recent years have seen an increasing use of private internal investigations in terms of the assessment of financial irregularities. The form of inquiry aims to uncover unrestricted opportunities, failing internal controls, abuse of position, and any financial misconduct such as corruption, fraud, embezzlement, theft, manipulation, tax evasion, and other forms of economic crime (ACFE, 2014; CFCS, 2014).

Characteristics of a private investigation include a serious and unusual event, an extraordinary examination to find out what happened or why it did not happen, develop explanations, and suggest actions toward individuals and changes in systems and practices. A private investigator is someone hired by individuals or organizations to undertake investigatory law services. They often work for attorneys in civil cases. A private investigator also goes under the titles of a private eye, private detective, inquiry agent, fraud examiner, private examiner, financial crime specialist, or PI (private investigator) for short. A private investigator does the detailed work to find the answers to misconduct and crime. Financial crime has become a major offense that clients hire private investigators to find the solutions to, in order to bring justice to the individuals affected, as defined by the client paying for the investigation.

Criminal investigation is a goal-oriented procedure for reconstructing the past. It is a method of creating an account of what has happened, how it happened, why it happened, and who did what to make it happen or let it happen. Criminal investigation is a reconstruction of past events and sequence of events by collecting information and evidence (Osterburg and Ward, 2014). An investigation is designed to answer questions such as when, where, what, how, who, and why, as such questions relate to negative events in the past. To reconstruct the past successfully in a professional manner, there is a need for knowledge management, information management, systems management, configuration management, and ethics management (Gottschalk, 2015a,b,c).

Internal private investigations typically have the following characteristics:

- Extraordinary investigation of suspicions by goal-oriented data collection
- Based on a mandate defined by and with the client
- Clarify facts, analyze events, identify reasons for incidents
- Evaluate systems failure and personal misconduct
- Independent, careful, and transparent work
- The client is responsible for implementation of recommendations

White-collar crime investigations are a specialized knowledge industry. Williams (2005) refers to it as the forensic accounting and criminal investigation industry. It is a unique industry, set apart from law enforcement, due to its ability to provide "direct and immediate responsiveness to client objectives, needs and interests, (unlike police) who are bound to one specific legal regime" (Williams, 2005: 194). The industry provides flexibility and a customized plan of attack according to client needs.

Investigations take many forms and have many purposes. Carson (2013) argues that the core feature of every investigation involves what we reliably know. The field of evidence is no other than the field of knowledge. There is an issue of whether we can have confidence in knowledge. A private investigator accumulates knowledge about what happened.

Police versus internal investigations

An investigation is an investigation, regardless of whether the investigator is employed by a police agency or a private firm. The goal is to uncover the facts in a particular situation. In doing so, the truth of the situation is the ultimate objective. However, an investigation by the police is going to start with a crime, or a suspected crime, and the end goal is going to arrest and successfully prosecuting the guilty person(s), or alternatively, dismissing the case because of innocence or lack of evidence. A private investigation is mainly after the facts, with the goal of determining how a negative event occurred, or the goal of determining whether the suspected action occurred at all. The goal might also be to prevent a situation from ever occurring in the first place, or to prevent it from happening again.

Police investigations differ from private investigations because they aim to convict a person of a crime or dismiss a person from the case, while internal investigations are used more to evaluate potential for economic crime to occur and to get rid of the issue internally rather than through the involvement of the police.

The roles of police officers and private investigators are different in the fact that they do not have the same powers. Police officers have strict rules that they have to follow within their department. They are responsible for following the rules and guidelines set before them by their law enforcement unit. Private investigators have more freedom to explore and conduct inquiries into suspected crime and criminals. However, the police officers' advantage is their ability to seize documents and subpoena the guilty party. The police have formal power in terms of law enforcement on behalf of society. While private police have less power in their work, they enjoy more freedom in how they do their work. Private investigators do not have the same powers as the police, and neither have to work according to strict guidelines such as the police.

The police are allowed to conduct special investigation activities such as intrusive inquiry, covert human operations, infiltration, surveillance, and covert recording of communications. The police may set up undercover enterprises, institutions, organizations, and units. During undercover questioning, law enforcement officers can mask their identity or purpose of the questioning. If not illegal, this kind of practice would be considered highly unethical in the private investigation business.

The criticism that comes with white-collar crime is the cost of policing fraud. When dealing with small internal frauds, "police would be called but often they did not offer help" (Brooks and Button, 2011: 307). The lack or number of limited resources has constrained the police force in dealing with fraud. The private sector has criticized the police for their lack of willingness to tackle the issue of investigating fraud, but it is sometimes out of their control when resources are not available to confront the issue. It is sometimes also a question of whether the police view fraud as a serious crime or if they have the capabilities in education and training to tackle economic crime (Button et al., 2007a,b).

Citizens might feel that the police lack commitment to their case and not report it. Their next step might be to report it to the private sector. This can result in problems in which fraud may be seen as a private matter and "can downgrade the seriousness of the offence as it does not require a public 'state' sanction, censure and condemnation and is hidden, and dealt with in-house in a secretive manner" (Brooks and Button, 2011: 310). People go to private investigators when they feel that the police will not take their issues seriously. However, the police still hold power when preparing an arrest and identifying whether a place needs to be searched for evidence. The police must be present when an unwanted search is being conducted on business premises or homes.

Private investigators also have the criticism of whether they have a bias toward the client that hires them to investigate the organization. They are the ones usually paid to do the investigation by the client to find something out of the ordinary. This can cause a bias when conducting their research. The private investigator might report in the client's favor because they are the ones paying for the investigation. The investigator might not want to go against the client that is paying for their service. This will result in a negative effect toward the other parties involved. Clients "may themselves attempt to influence investigations in order to limit lines of responsibility and produce narrow interpretations of incidents" (Williams, 2005: 199). There will be then "a constant tension between commercial imperatives and professional standards" in white-collar crime investigations (Williams, 2005: 199).

A private investigator can potentially challenge the rule of law by taking on all three roles of police investigator, public prosecutor, and court judge. This kind of privatization of law enforcement can represent a threat to the criminal justice system in democratic societies (Gottschalk, 2015a,b,c).

Private investigators may work alongside police detectives in order to collect evidence. Direct evidence is physical proof of an illegal act such as forensic samples such as hair, clothing fibers, or computer documents. Indirect evidence is collected through interviewing witnesses or potential accomplices, or through someone identifying the offender, for example in a photograph (Carson, 2013).

Reasons for private investigations

Criminal investigation is initiated when there is a need to study negative incidents and events that happened in the past. Contrary to the police, regulators, and other investigative agencies, forensic accounting and corporate investigation firms are able to conduct their investigations under a cloak of secrecy providing resolutions that are largely private in nature and which help to safeguard the client from embarrassment and unwanted publicity. Many companies want to deal with misconduct internally by resolving the matter by themselves. They want no publicity. They want to avoid courts, for example, because they do not want their shareholders, customers, or suppliers to see that misconduct and crime has occurred. Cases are resolved through informal means such as negotiated settlements and termination of an offending employee (Williams, 2014).

Corporations and other organizations value the possibility of secrecy, discretion, and control that private specialists bring to investigations. Openness could lead to problems such as reputational loss, which can have economic repercussions. While private investigations can consider secrecy, openness is a key characteristic of a public criminal justice procedure. Meerts (2014) argues that the reluctance of victim companies to report crime to the police because of fear of reputational damage is a well-researched subject. Reputational damage provides a motivation for a company to avoid publicity (Dupont, 2014: 272):

> The reputation of a company represents a valuable asset that can quickly become a liability when the erosion of customers' and suppliers' trust provokes a loss of competitiveness. Shareholders are also very receptive to such signals and several security managers explained how their performance was indirectly tied to their company's public valuation. The ambiguity that characterizes this risk category explains why contract security firms providing investigative and consulting services of all sort are routinely called in before the police—when the police is involved at all—in order to minimize external scrutiny and to maximize procedural control.

An important advantage of private investigations is legal flexibility. After an internal investigation, the client can choose from an array of legal alternatives and can decide which is best for the current case. Law enforcement, however, is more limited, generally working toward a criminal prosecution or taking no further action by dismissing the case. Minimizing and repairing damage is often the focus of private investigations, and thus other legal possibilities than those provided by criminal law are attractive. Employers often have nothing to gain by triggering a criminal justice procedure (Meerts, 2014).

Private sector investigative consultants conduct inquiries for their clients in cases of suspected corporate crime. Recent developments internationally when it comes to corporate criminal liability have led many business and government organizations to recruit consultants to develop internal compliance systems because the function of such systems is increasingly taken into account by prosecution authorities.

While public police are bound to the legal definitions of criminal conduct, corporate security is more flexible and can adapt to the definitions provided by their clients. Private investigators can focus exclusively on the occurrences pointed out as problematic by their clients. This means that private investigators can examine behavior harmful to their clients that is not criminal; and, conversely, that they can ignore behavior that is criminal but not damaging to their client (Meerts, 2014).

Internal investigations in private and public organizations serve important functions in society. They allow entities to discover misbehavior within management, make corrections, and define future conduct to assure compliance with laws, regulations, policies, and guidelines. Private investigations offer organizational solutions to organizational problems, while providing an incentive to corporations and public authorities to unmask misconduct. Internal investigations also allow corporations as well as other organizations to quietly examine allegations that may later prove to be wrong, without fear that disclosure will hurt the organization's or an individual's reputation (Green and Podgor, 2013).

Another reason for private internal investigations is that white-collar crime often is a difficult crime for police to handle. Police forces and their resources are frequently stretched thin, and mainly focused on potential terrorism, physical violence, and threats to the health of citizens. Successful prosecutions of white-collar crime are frequently knowledge and labor intensive, and a decision has to be made as to where people and man-hours are going to be allocated (Brooks and Button, 2011).

Investigative knowledge needs

Criminal investigation is based on a foundation of increasing knowledge over time, where knowledge is defined as information combined with interpretation, context, and reflection. A private investigation into financial crime suspicion needs to interpret and reflect on numbers in financial documents. One primary factor in financial documents that distinguishes fraud from error is whether the underlying action that results in the misstatement of financial accounts is perceived as intentional or unintentional. The ability to understand documents such as invoices, bank and other financial records as well as individuals who updated the records is a critical skill in financial crime and asset recovery work (CFCS, 2014).

Determining whether a crime has been committed necessitates an understanding of the criminal law and the elements of each criminal act (Osterburg and Ward, 2014). While a private investigator is not to conduct such a determination, he or she needs to understand the relevance of collected information as potential evidence. Penal law and criminal code are applied by the criminal justice system in roles of police investigators and prosecutors.

However, determining whether a negative event has occurred necessitates an understanding of misconduct as defined in the client organization as well as the elements of acts leading to the events. A private investigator needs to compare what is perceived as misconduct in the organization to what can be identified as acts leading to the negative event. The private investigator should neither compare acts to criminal law nor compare negative acts to personal opinions about what is wrong and what is right. Rather, the investigator should compare acts to what can be understood as client organization's guidelines and culture. For this reason the investigator should have knowledge of corporate structure and culture in the client organization.

Furthermore, investigators need to have knowledge to be able to identify perpetrators. Identifying perpetrators is as important in private investigations as in criminal investigation, with the distinct difference of misconduct versus crime perspectives. Finding out who did what is essential in almost all investigations. When people who know the perpetrator are unwilling or unable to provide information about the person, records and other forms of information may provide the answer as to a person's identity and activities.

Generally, a financial crime investigator needs to have the knowledge and training necessary to handle complex investigations. They need to have the skills necessary to reach intended objectives (Osterburg and Ward, 2014).

A financial crime specialist needs to have knowledge in a number of areas such as accounting, organization, management, finance, psychology, sociology, and criminology. Knowledge in such areas can be defined in terms of their level or depth:

a. Basic knowledge is knowledge of what has happened, it is know-what of a negative event.
b. Advanced knowledge is knowledge of how it happened, it is the know-how of a negative event. It is knowledge of modus operandi in financial crime.
c. Innovative knowledge is knowledge of cause-and-effects in terms of causality, it is know-why of a negative event.

According to the knowledge-based view of the firm, knowledge is a scarce resource, and the ability to manage it determines an organization's competitiveness. Law firms, auditing firms, and other consulting firms employing financial crime specialists have to invest in knowledge management initiatives to improve their access to the dispersed knowledge of their employees (Beck et al., 2014).

Knowledge management can be defined as a systematic, organizationally specified process to acquire, organize, and communicate individual knowledge so that others may make use of it (Beck et al., 2014). Knowledge management is concerned with knowledge sharing and knowledge creation in organizations. Knowledge management activities include creation, acquisition, identification, storage, sharing, and application of knowledge (Heisig, 2009). Knowledge sharing is defined as the exchange between two or more parties of potentially valuable knowledge.

Crime disclosure by whistleblowers

A city manager told us that corruption in procurement happens every day and that when he first started with the town, the FBI was already investigating the public works director and a purchasing director. We asked him how the FBI knew to investigate, and he said it was someone inside the organization or maybe people just talking outside of work. That is the difficulty in the detection—you really have to depend on people within the organization to blow the whistle. Auditors could also be relevant, but they might only be called in after a complaint or report has been filed.

In the database of 405 convicted white-collar criminals in Norway, whistleblowers are not registered as a source of detection. Journalists are at the top of the detection list. It is very likely that many, probably most, of the media work was initially based on tips from insiders. Whistleblowers as the main source of initial information was probably the case also for internal auditors and police investigators. It might be argued that more than half of all detected white-collar criminals in Norway were revealed by whistleblowers.

In the United States, it is possible to make money by blowing the whistle. A whistleblower can get a share of the retrieved and recovered sum of money. In 2014, the Securities and Exchange Commission (SEC) paid $30 million in a whistleblower award. It was the largest award thus far, and a reporter wrote: "Blowing the whistle is increasingly worth big bucks." The SEC did not identify the tipster, where he or she is from, or the case this award was tied to. Andrew Ceresney, director of the SEC's enforcement division, said in a statement that "this whistleblower came to us with information about an ongoing fraud that would have been very difficult to detect" (Ensign, 2014). The Office of the Whistleblower at SEC (www.sec.gov/whistleblowers) is authorized by congress to provide monetary awards to eligible individuals who come forward with high-quality original information.

Public whistleblowers are not entitled to awards. Stieger (2012) argues that offering monetary rewards to public whistleblowers represents a proposal for attacking public corruption at its source. He suggests offering a carrot: if a public official reports a bribe offer, leading to the conviction of the offering party, the state will pay the reporting official the full amount of the offered bribe. By tying the amount of the reward to the amount of the bribe, any financial incentive the official would have to take the bribe is removed.

According to Kaplan et al. (2011), employee tips are the most common form of initial fraud detection, suggesting that employees frequently are aware of fraud before others professionally charged to unveil fraud, such as internal and external auditors. The willingness of employees, who learn about fraud, to report this information, varies with several factors. For example, if the executive, to whom misconduct should be reported, is not trusted, employees will tend not to report. Whistleblowing decisions are dependent on information, trust, security, predictability, self-confidence, job security, and organizational culture in general.

Johnson (2005) has the following definition of whistleblowing:

> Whistleblowing is a distinct form of dissent consist-
> ing of four elements: (1) the person acting must be
> a member or former member of the organization
> at issue; (2) his or her information must be about
> nontrivial wrongdoing in that organization; (3) he
> or she must intend to expose the wrongdoing, and
> (4) he or she must act in a way that makes the infor-
> mation public.

Vadera et al. (2009) has the following definition of whistleblowing:

> Whistleblowing is the disclosure by organizational
> members (former or current) of illegal, immoral,
> or illegitimate practices under the control of their
> employers, to persons or organizations that may be
> able to effect action.

Atwater (2006) defines whistleblowing as an act by which an indi-
vidual reveals wrongdoing within an organization to those in positions of authority or to the public, with hopes of rectifying the situation.

Vadera et al. (2009) identified the following characteristics of whistleblowers and whistleblowing:

- Federal whistleblowers were motivated by concern for public interest, were high performers, reported high levels of job security, job
  achievement, job commitment, and job satisfaction, and worked in
  high performing work groups and organizations.
- Anger at wrongful activities drove individuals to make internal reports to management. Retaliation by management shifted

individuals' focus away from helping their organizations or victims and toward attaining retribution.

- Whistleblowing was more likely when observers of wrongdoing held professional positions, had more positive reactions to their work, had longer service, were recently recognized for good performance, were male, were members of larger work groups, and were employed by organizations perceived by others to be responsive to complaints.
- Whistleblowing was more frequent in the public sector than in the private sector.
- Whistleblowing was strongly related to situational variables with seriousness of the offense and supportiveness of the organizational climate being the strongest determinants.
- Inclination to report a peer for theft was associated with role responsibility, the interests of group members, and procedural perceptions.

Zipparo (1999) identified the following two main factors which deter public officials from reporting corruption:

- Concern about not having enough proof
- Absence of legal protection from negative consequences

One of the more successful whistleblowers is Michael Lissack. He worked as a banker at the Smith Barney brokerage. In 1995, he blew the whistle on a fraudulent scheme, known in municipal financing as "yield burning." Dr. Lissack filed a whistleblower lawsuit against more than a dozen Wall Street firms under the False Claims Act. In April 2000, 17 investment banks agreed to pay approximately $140 million dollars to settle charges that they defrauded the federal government by overpricing securities sold in connection with certain municipal bond transactions. The U.S. government has recovered more than $250 million as the result of Dr. Lissack's whistleblower action. His allegations have brought on more than a dozen civil and criminal investigations by the SEC, IRS, and the U.S. Department of Justice. Dr. Lissack has written editorials about whistleblowing for the *New York Times* and the *Los Angeles Times* and has been profiled in many international publications, including the *Wall Street Journal*, the *Financial Times*, *Fortune*, *Business Week*, the *Economist*, and *USA Today* (www.whistleblowerdirectory.com).

In 2001, Sherron Watkins, an employee in the American energy company Enron, notified her chief executive officer Kenneth Lay about a perceived accounting scandal. Watkins did so hoping Lay would act. He did not, and was later arrested due to his involvement in the wrongdoing because she blew the whistle (Bendiktsson, 2010).

Negative consequences after whistleblowing, suffered by some whistleblowers, are labeled retaliation. Retaliation implies to take an undesirable action against a whistleblower, who reported wrongdoing internally or externally, outside the organization. Retaliation can be defined as taking adverse action against an employee for opposing an unlawful employment practice or participating in any investigation, proceeding, or hearing related to such a practice (Bjørkelo and Matthiesen, 2011).

Thus, receivers of complaints and reports have two issues to consider when dealing with whistleblowers as an information source. First, not all that is said and not all accusations from a whistleblower are necessarily true. Therefore, information from a whistleblower has to be carefully checked and verified. Second, a whistleblower may be in danger of retaliation, making it a requirement for receivers to protect the whistleblower. Report receivers have to make sure that a whistleblower contributing to an investigation does not experience negative consequences.

The National Whistleblowers Center (NWC) in the United States lists a number of whistleblowers (www.whistleblowers.org). A few of them blew the whistle because of public procurement corruption. An example is Bunnatine Greenhouse who stood alone in opposing the approval of a highly improper multibillion dollar no bid contract to Halliburton for the reconstruction of Iraq. In retaliation for her courage she was removed from her position as the highest-ranking civilian contracting official of the Army Corps of Engineers. On June 27, 2005, she testified to a congressional panel, alleging specific instances of waste, fraud, and other abuses and irregularities by Halliburton with regard to its operation in Iraq since the 2003 invasion. Vice President Dick Cheney had been the CEO of Halliburton. Criminal investigations into Halliburton were opened by the U.S. Justice Department, the Federal Bureau of Investigation, and the Pentagon's inspector general. These investigations found no wrongdoing within the contract award and execution process. On July 25, 2011, the U.S. District Court in Washington, DC approved awarding Greenhouse $970,000 in full restitution of lost wages, compensatory damages, and attorney fees.

The Whistleblower Directory (www.whistleblowerdirectory.com) is a comprehensive database showcasing individuals who reported financial crime. An example is Jim Alderson who worked as an accountant for Quorum Health Services in Montana and a Chief Financial Officer at the Whitefish hospital. In 1992, he blew the whistle on the hospital's fraudulent bookkeeping practices, wherein reimbursements were routinely sought after filing fraudulent cost reports with Medicare. In retaliation for his whistleblowing disclosure, Alderson was fired. He filed a whistleblower lawsuit against his former employer, Quorum Health Services, and its former owner, Hospital Corp. of America. Five years after Alderson filed the lawsuit, the federal government joined the case. In October 2000, Quorum settled the case. Under the False Claims law, Alderson received $11.6 million dollars and Quorum paid a fine of $77.5 million dollars.

Janet A. Garrison and Herb F. Hyman were procurement professionals who blew the whistle. During the course of their employment with public entities in Florida, they uncovered unethical procurement practices. They then became whistleblowers. In their jobs as government purchasers, both Garrison and Hyman believe that they are entrusted by the public to spend taxpayer dollars wisely and fairly. Each individual also notes that codes of ethics govern their membership in professional procurement associations, as well as their certifications: Thus, Garrison and Hyman felt it was their public and professional duty to report ethics breaches that clearly violated our nation's laws or specific procurement statutes. However, their efforts to "do the right thing" met with unanticipated outcomes, ranging from the mixed reactions of others to a complex maze of ongoing legal proceedings (Atwater, 2006).

Janet A. Garrison's whistleblowing experience occurred when she worked as a purchasing analyst for the Florida Department of Education (DOE). Back in 2003, she was asked to help develop a solicitation for privatizing about 174 jobs in DOE's Office of Student Financial Assistance (Atwater, 2006).

For Herb F. Hyman, procurement manager with the Town of Davie, FL, his whistleblowing experience related to the purchasing practices of the Town Administrator, Christopher J. Kovanes. Hired by the Town Council as a contract employee, Kovanes was the town's top leader. Thus, Kovanes was Hyman's boss (Atwater, 2006).

Another whistleblower was already mentioned, involving white-collar corruption in public procurement. In the case of Acar investigation presented later in this book, Yusuf Acar was unveiled by means of whistleblowing from the office of the chief technology officer (Sidley, 2010: 28):

> It was instead the cooperation of a confidential informant that led to the discovery of the fraud.

Miceli et al. (2009) suggest that employees can be encouraged to report wrongdoing both before concerns are expressed and once concerns are expressed. Before concerns are expressed, employees can be encouraged in development of moral identity and moral agency, in creating a tough antiretaliation policy that permits disciplining or dismissing employees who retaliate against whistleblowers, and in disseminating the policy through the intranet, in orientation materials, and elsewhere. After concerns are expressed, employees can be encouraged to focus on the wrongdoing alleged in the complaint and not on the complainant, to investigate reports fully and fairly, and to take swift action when the complainant is well-founded.

In a study of corruption in public procurement in the European Union, Wensink and Vet (2013) found that approximately 40% of fraudulent activities are detected by a whistleblower alert. They recommend to further invest in good functioning systems for whistleblowers, including proper protection of whistleblowers. Legislation on whistleblowing as well as protection of whistleblowers are areas that are not well regulated yet.

Some potential whistleblowers are reluctant to blow the whistle because they adhere to the loyalty-betrayal paradox. They consider whistleblowing an act of treachery against the organization. The loyalty-betrayal paradox leads to a pro-organizational behavior defined by a dedication to the ingroup and reflects such values as patriotism, self-sacrifice, and allegiance. In the name of loyalty, individuals will sacrifice themselves to save their group members (Fehr et al., 2015).

Privatization of law enforcement

Ever since Schneider (2006) wrote his classic article on privatizing economic crime enforcement, the potential threat to criminal justice from private rather than public investigation, prosecution, and sentencing of individuals in white-collar crime cases has steadily increased. In our context of private investigations, we apply the term private policing to capture similarities and differences with law enforcement (Gottschalk, 2016). Private policing of economic crime can be detrimental to an open and democratic society where the rule of law is to be transparent. Privatization of law enforcement and criminal justice, as is currently a trend in many countries, represents a potential threat to democratic societies as all powers toward citizens in a state should be organized and managed by public authorities under democratic government control, and not by private business firms (Gottschalk, 2015b).

Privatization of criminal justice seems not uncommon in Norway. Offenses are not reported to the police. In the Norwegian survey by Transparency International, 40% of respondents agreed with the statement that crime is not reported because companies have decided to treat such matters internally (Renaa, 2012).

A typical example of privatization is mentioned by Williams (2005: 195):

> Barring an informal resolution in which the suspect voluntarily agrees to leave the company based on specific conditions, such as repayment of misappropriated assets, one of the most common legal avenues pursued in these cases is termination with cause. This falls under the auspices of employment and labor relations law.

Stenning (2000) found that the division of responsibilities for policing between public and private authorities has become increasingly blurred. Similarly, Hoogenboom (2006) found that the blurred boundaries between public and private spheres has created confusions and inefficiencies in areas such as intelligence.

Brooks and Button (2011) suggest a hybrid solution between private investigators and the police. If a suspect in a private investigation does not cooperate with private fraud examiners and the suspicion and evidence of white-collar crime is overwhelming, then the matter is turned over to the police.

Disclosure of investigation reports

The rule of law and criminal justice is secured in constitutional states by public prosecution and courts that are open to everyone to observe (Gottschalk, 2016). If there are suspicions of violations of criminal laws in a country, it is important that information about suspects becomes known to public authorities such as police investigators and public prosecutors. Disclosure of investigation reports is a must in cases of criminal offenses. However, organizations find all kinds of reasons why they do not disclose their findings to the police (Gottschalk, 2015a):

1. *Control.* One reason is that the client organization loses control over the subject matter. By hiring examiners from an auditing firm or law firm, the client organization pays for the investigation and is owner of the investigation report.
2. *Reputation.* If it becomes known that the police are investigating the case, it could lead to negative publicity and financial loss. For example, law-abiding employees who are attractive on the labor market could choose to leave. Qualified external candidates could choose not to apply.
3. *Exclusion.* As long as the company is under investigation by the police, the company may be put on hold for contracts in both the public and private sectors.
4. *Penalty.* Reaction against the company may be a reason for not going to the police. The company hopes it can keep the matter hidden and thus not lose money as they would have to pay a potential fine. Generally, the consequences of going to the police are considered greater than keeping the matter hidden.
5. *Protection.* Shielding both individuals and the organization from police investigation is yet another reason for not disclosing evidence of white-collar crime to the police.
6. *Passivity.* Police often demonstrate passivity when approached about possible offenses. Many cases are dismissed without investigation.

A survey by Norway Security Council (2014) shows that 75% of companies that responded to the survey agreed with the statement that crime is not reported because the police usually dismiss the case without proper investigation.

7. *Effort.* In the same survey, 65% of respondents agreed with the statement that crime is not reported because it takes too much time and effort. The police will ask for all kinds of documentation and access to computers.

8. *Failure.* Just like a private investigation can fail to establish the facts so can police investigations fail to find the truth about a negative event. If police investigations are expected to end up in nothing, why bother involving the police, some organizations may certainly argue.

9. *Trifle.* The organization considers what happened to be an insignificant issue. White-collar offenders operate with relative impunity because of widespread apathy in both private and public contexts.

10. *Competence.* Investigating white-collar crime suspicions requires highly specialized expertise, which is often not available in the police at the time a potential financial crime is reported to law enforcement.

11. *Capacity.* There is an inability of the state to unilaterally cope with the rising tide of economic crime due to limited resources.

12. *Bargaining.* Plea bargaining is available to a varying degree in different countries. Where this option is limited or nonexistent, people will be even less reluctant to report suspicions of white-collar crime to the police.

Competence of private investigators

Private internal investigators for hire are in the business of examining facts, sequence of events, and the causes of negative events, as well as who is responsible for such events (Gottschalk, 2016). Pending what hiring parties ask for, private investigators can either look generally for corrupt or otherwise criminal activities within an agency or company, or look more specifically for those committing white-collar crime. In other situations, it is the job of the private investigators to look into potential opportunities for financial crime to occur, so that the agency or company can fix those problems in order to avoid misconduct down the road.

Private investigators exercise substantial legal powers, even if not the constitutional powers we associate with public police (Stenning, 2000). Private detectives are invited in by corporations on their terms and when they deem it appropriate. Police detectives have strict rules that they have to follow within their department. They are responsible for following the rules and guidelines set before them by their law enforcement unit.

Private investigators have more freedom to explore and conduct inquiries into suspected crime and criminals.

The competence of financial crime specialists and fraud examiners is varying to an extent that it represents a threat to the rule of law, privacy, and democracy. Some private investigators seem very professional, while others are not, as illustrated by the lifting of the cloak on a largely hidden world of investigations showing some of the key aspects of the cases, the key events, and the key results. Especially lawyers seem to make many mistakes in private investigations, since they are not trained detectives.

The institute of counter fraud specialists (ICFS) was founded as a result of the United Kingdom government's initiative to professionalize public sector fraud investigation. The institute exists to further the cause of fraud prevention and detection across all sectors of the UK and abroad. The membership of the ICFS is made up of accredited counter fraud specialists who have successfully completed the government's professionalism in security training (Button et al., 2007a,b). In the accredited counter fraud specialist handbook by Tunley et al. (2014) mandatory elements of the accreditation are covered.

While the government in the United Kingdom took the initiative and is involved in the requirements to and training of fraud specialists, it is all left to the private sector in the United States. Both ACFS (2014) and CFCS (2014) are voluntary programs by practitioners. In addition, the U.S. training seems to be much more recipe oriented, where normative messages on what investigators should do dominate their manuals. There seems to be a lack of academic link to research and evidence related to private investigation performance.

In the United Kingdom, the brief overview by Button et al. (2007a,b) illustrates the innovative development of partnerships between counter fraud agencies and universities in developing life-long learning routes that lead to professional qualifications. Button et al. (2007b) argue that the CFS has become the most common type of fraud investigators in the United Kingdom.

Gill and Hart (1997) argue that to achieve professional status, investigators have to lift their competence to quite different levels. This is a particular challenge in countries such as Norway, where people are not required to undergo any form of training in order to set up as private investigators.

Limits by investigation mandate

The client defines a mandate for the investigation, and the investigation has to be carried out according to the mandate. The mandate tells investigators what to do. The mandate defines tasks and goals for the investigation.

The mandate is an authorization to investigate a specific issue or several specific issues by reconstructing the past (Gottschalk, 2015b).

The mandate can be part of the blame game, where the client wants to blame somebody while at the same time divert attention from somebody else (Datner, 2011; Eberly et al., 2011; Farber, 2010; Hein, 2014; Hood, 2011; Keaveney, 2008; Lee and Robinson, 2000; Slyke and Bales, 2013). Some are too powerful to blame (Pontell et al., 2014). The mandate can be part of a rotten apple or rotten barrel approach, where attention is either directed at individuals or at systems failure (Ashforth et al., 2008; Gonin et al., 2012; Keaveney, 2008; O'Connor, 2005; Punch, 2003). Anchoring of suspicion can be unintentionally or purposely misplaced in the mandate.

A badly formulated mandate can be misleading for investigators and also represent possible avenues for opportunistic behaviors by investigators. Rather than getting to the core of the matter, an investigation may end up avoiding touching any inflamed issues. Rather than spending resources on difficult issues, investigators may end up solving the simple issues, thereby completing the assignment quickly and making a business profit on the project. Investigators can take advantage of positions of professional authority and power as well as opportunity structures (Kempa, 2010).

Empirical sample of investigation reports

Given the secret nature of private internal investigations, we decided to search for investigation reports that are publicly available. While a report does not represent the investigation process, it documents the investigation outcome. We wanted to obtain a representative sample of private internal investigation reports for our research into privatization of law enforcement, disclosure of investigation reports, competence of private investigators, and limits by investigation mandate. Unfortunately, almost all such reports tend to be secret and never disclosed for research purposes.

Therefore, our research methodology was simply to use what we could find. Some reports we found by searching on the Internet, but most reports we found based on ideas and tips from knowledgeable insiders. During 2014, we were able to detect and retrieve 32 investigation reports (Gottschalk, 2016).

Our sample is neither representative of all potentially available reports nor representative of all reports that internal investigators have written. However, we will argue that the reports represent an interesting diversity that indeed can provide insights into our four research topics.

Table 9.1 lists all 32 obtained internal investigation reports. Cases are listed alphabetically by the name of the client organization that was investigated. For example, Adecco is a company running nursing homes, and it also is in the business of cleaning services. Suspicion occurred in the

Table 9.1 Characteristics of reports from financial crime specialists
in private investigations

#	Case	Investigator	Suspicion	Pages
1	Adecco *Nursing and cleaning services business*	Wiersholm law firm	Exploitation of work force in nursing home in terms of low wages and inhuman working hours	22
2	Ahus *Public hospital*	PwC auditing and consulting firm	Buying expensive geographical information system services	15
3	Briskeby *Football stadium*	Lynx law firm	Over charging for construction work at football stadium	267
4	Eckbo *Family foundation*	Dobrowen and Klepp lawyers	Executives in ideal foundation for personal gain	119
5	Fadderbarna *NGO for children*	BDO auditing and consulting firm	Excessive administration costs in NGO	46
6	Forsvaret *Army*	Dalseide judge	Suspected corruption at procurement of information technology	184
7	Furuheim *Church foundation*	Dalane and Olsen lawyers	Executives in church foundation for personal gain	164
8	Gassnova *Carbon capture and storage*	BDO auditing and consulting firm	Irregular procurement procedures by employees	27
9	Hadeland and Ringerike Bredbånd *Hadeland and Ringerike Broadband, communication company*	PwC auditing and consulting firm	Embezzlement by chief financial officer	32
10	Hadeland Energi *Hadeland Energy, utility company*	PwC auditing and consulting firm	Embezzlement by chief financial officer	25

(Continued)

Table 9.1 (Continued) Characteristics of reports from financial
crime specialists in private investigations

#	Case	Investigator	Suspicion	Pages
11	Halden ishall *Sports Ice Arena*	KPMG auditing and consulting firm	Excessive cost overrun in reconstruction	121
12	Halden kommune *City of Halden*	Gjørv and Lund lawyers	Manager in department of planning and construction suspected of corruption	46
13	Kraft & Kultur *Power utility company*	Ernst & Young auditing and consulting firm	Chief executive officer manipulated financial results	31
14	Kragerø Fjordbåtselskap *Shipping company*	Deloitte auditing and consulting firm	Chief executive suspected of abuse of company funds	109
15	Langemyhr *Construction company*	PwC auditing and consulting firm	Fraud by overbilling city work in hours	26
16	Lindeberg *Nursing home*	Kommune-revisjonen public auditing	Outside authority of personnel	92
17	Lunde Group *Transportation company*	Bie law firm	Fraud and tax evasion for 30 million US dollars	86
18	Moskvaskolen *Norwegian school in Moscow*	Ernst & Young auditing and consulting firm	Private living expenses for dean covered by school	52+23
19	Norges Fotballforbund *Football association*	Lynx law firm	Football players changing clubs without clubs paying transfer money	48
20	Norsk Tipping *Public betting firm*	Deloitte auditing and consulting firm	Financial relationships between employees and external firm	61

(*Continued*)

Table 9.1 (Continued) Characteristics of reports from financial
crime specialists in private investigations

#	Case	Investigator	Suspicion	Pages
21	Oslo Vei *Road construction company*	Kvale law firm	Chairman and CEO suspected of fraud after bankruptcy	53
22	Romerike Vannverk *Public water supply*	Distrikts-revisjonen public auditing	Chief executive suspected of corruption and embezzlement	555
23	Samferdselsetaten *Public transportation*	PwC auditing and consulting firm	Suspicion of kickbacks from taxi owners for licenses	88
24	Spania *City of Oslo project in Spain*	PwC auditing and consulting firm	Abuse of public money spent on friends in Spain to build a local hospital for Norwegians	92
25	Stangeskovene *Private forest property*	Roscher and Berg lawyers	Board members controlling share sales	94
26	Sykehuset Innlandet *Hospital*	Davidsen and Sandvik lawyers	Chief executive suspected of employment violations	15
27	Terra *Cities investing in bonds*	PwC auditing and consulting firm	Outside authority of city management	52
28	Troms Kraft *Power supply company*	Nergaard consultant	Accounting manipulation in subsidiary and illegal political party support	663
29	Tyrkia *City of Stavanger project for Turkish children*	PwC auditing and consulting firm	Smuggling of adopted children out of Turkey financed by the city of Stavanger	14
30	Undervisningsbygg *School maintenance agency*	Kommune-revisjonen public auditing	Fraud by property managers in the City of Oslo	36
31	Verdibanken *Religious bank*	Wiersholm law firm	Investment fraud by bank executive	5

(Continued)

Table 9.1 (Continued) Characteristics of reports from financial
crime specialists in private investigations

#	Case	Investigator	Suspicion	Pages
32	Videoforhandlere *Video film distributors and dealers*	BDO auditing and consulting firm	Subsidies paid to video publishers	20

Source: Derived from Gottschalk, P. (2016). *European Journal of Policing Studies*, 3 (3), 292–314.

media that the work force in the nursing home were working too long hours; that they received below minimum wage compensation; and that working conditions were inhuman. The company was accused of violating the Working Environment Act to increase its profits. Private investigators from the law firm Wiersholm were hired by Adecco to investigate the matter, and investigators wrote a 22-page report about their findings.

Our research technique is archival study in the form of content analysis of the reports listed in the table, where reports ranged from 5 pages to 555 pages, as listed in the last column. We conducted a review of each report in terms of each report's communication on our four critical issues in private investigations.

The first issue is privatization of law enforcement, where we looked for consequences for individuals without involvement from the criminal justice system. The second issue is disclosure of investigation reports. While all these investigation reports were eventually disclosed, it was sometimes after a struggle by the media and others. The third issue is competence of private investigators, where we identified names of involved investigators and their formal and practical background. The fourth and final issue is limits by the investigation report, where we did a comparison and ranking of the mandates in terms of their openness versus closeness relative to the matter at hand. This is a very subjective procedure, which can have different outcomes. However, it was an expert assessment based on subject knowledge.

A sample of 32 private investigation reports from Norway is presented again in Table 9.2. They can be evaluated in terms of start, process, result, and impact. Quality can be determined by the mandate and motivation for the examination, the professional examination process, investigation results, as well as consequences of the investigation. Here we focus on these reports by evaluating how key issues in private investigations were dealt with by financial crime specialists in the 32 investigations. Our four key issues are privatization of law enforcement, disclosure of investigation reports to the police, competence of private investigators, and limits by investigation mandates.

Table 9.2 Key issues in private investigations

#	Private investigation case	Privatization of law enforcement	Disclosure of investigation report	Competence of private investigators	Limits by investigation mandate
1	Adeco *Nursing and cleaning services business* Wiersholm law firm	Violation of labor laws for employees working too long hours	Denied disclosure for research, only summary available	Lawyers without investigative focus	Limited to possible violations of working environment legislation
2	Ahus *Public hospital* PwC auditing and consulting firm	Fraud by vendor, paid back without prosecution	Posted on Ahus hospital web site	Forensic accounting with investigative focus	Limited to transactions with vendor
3	Briskeby *Football stadium* Lynx law firm	Suspected fraud never investigated	Posted on Hamar municipality web site	Lawyers with investigative focus	Mandate revised during investigation
4	Eckbo *Family foundation* Dobrowen and Klepp lawyers	Misconduct in assets, but no crime	Posted on Oslo city web site	Lawyers without investigative focus	Limited to asset mis-appropriation
5	Fadderbarna *NGO for children* BDO auditing and consulting firm	Individual fired, but never prosecuted	Accepted disclosure for research	Auditors with investigative focus	Limited to accusations
6	Forsvaret *Army* Dalseide judge	Individual fired, but never prosecuted	Posted on defense ministry web site	Auditors with bureaucratic approach	Limited to corruption suspicions

(Continued)

Table 9.2 (Continued) Key issues in private investigations

#	Private investigation case	Privatization of law enforcement	Disclosure of investigation report	Competence of private investigators	Limits by investigation mandate
7	Furuheim *Church foundation* Dalane and Olsen lawyers	Two persons sentenced to prison	Accepted disclosure for research	Lawyers with investigative approach	Open investigation of management issues
8	Gassnova *Carbon capture and storage* BDO auditing and consulting firm	No misconduct or crime	Accepted disclosure for research	Auditors with formalistic approach	Limited to procurement processes
9	Hadeland og Ringerike Bredbånd *Hadeland and Ringerike Broadband, communication company* PwC auditing and consulting firm	CFO sentenced to prison, CEO and chairman left after massive media pressure	Disclosed after massive media pressure, obtained from local newspaper for research	Auditors with formalistic approach without investigative focus	Limited to facts, legal issues, and internal controls
10	Hadeland Energi *Hadeland Energy, utility company* PwC auditing and consulting firm	CFO sentenced to prison, CEO and chairman left after massive media pressure	Disclosed after massive media pressure, obtained from local newspaper for research	Auditors with formalistic approach without investigative focus	Limited to transactions and legal issues

(Continued)

Table 9.2 (Continued) Key issues in private investigations

#	Private investigation case	Privatization of law enforcement	Disclosure of investigation report	Competence of private investigators	Limits by investigation mandate
11	Halden Ishall *Sports Ice Arena* KPMG auditing and consulting firm	Misconduct without consequences	Obtained from Halden municipality for research	Auditors with passive approach	Limited by small investigation budget
12	Halden kommune *City of Halden* Gjørv and Lund lawyers	Misconduct without consequences	Obtained from Halden municipality for research	Lawyers with passive approach	Limited to accusations by two whistleblowers
13	Kraft & Kultur *Power utility company* Ernst & Young auditing and consulting firm	CEO prosecuted by the police	Disclosed after massive media pressure, obtained from newspaper for comments	Auditors with forensic accounting approach	Open investigation of board members' knowledge roles
14	Kragerø Fjordbåtselskap *Shipping company* Deloitte auditing and consulting firm	Fired CEO never prosecuted	Posted on Kragerø municipality web site	Lawyers without investigative focus	Limited to conflicts between board and management
15	Langemyhr *Construction company* PwC auditing and consulting firm	Contract terminated, but case dismissed in court	Obtained from City of Oslo for research	Financial crime specialists trusting outside single judgment	Limited to Labor Inspection Authority's accusations

(Continued)

Table 9.2 (Continued) Key issues in private investigations

#	Private investigation case	Privatization of law enforcement	Disclosure of investigation report	Competence of private investigators	Limits by investigation mandate
16	Lindeberg *Nursing home* Kommunerevisjonen public auditing	Labor laws violated, but no public prosecution	Posted on web site by radical party in Oslo municipality	Passive investigation	Limited to control of formal procedures
17	Lunde Group *Transportation company* Bie law firm	Public prosecution based on bankruptcy report	Obtained for research from bankruptcy lawyer	Active investigation by bankruptcy lawyer	Complete bankruptcy report, no limitations
18	Moskvaskolen *Norwegian school in Moscow* Ernst & Young auditing and consulting firm	Rector fired and reported, but case dismissed by the police	Obtained for research from Skedsmo high school	Passive investigation of documents and failed interviews	Limited to consequences for suspected individuals
19	Norges Fotballforbund *Football association* Lynx law firm	Misconduct but no crime	Obtained from newspaper asking for comments	Active investigation prevented by client	Limited access to data
20	Norsk Tipping *Public betting firm* Deloitte auditing and consulting firm	Misconduct but no crime	Posted on company web site	Passive legal investigation of relationships	Limited to individual financial dispositions
21	Oslo Vei *Road construction company* Kvale law firm	Misconduct and crime, but no police investigation	Disclosed by bankruptcy lawyer for research	Bankruptcy lawyers avoided crime focus	Only focusing on bankruptcy issues

(Continued)

Table 9.2 (Continued) Key issues in private investigations

#	Private investigation case	Privatization of law enforcement	Disclosure of investigation report	Competence of private investigators	Limits by investigation mandate
22	Romerike Vannverk *Public water supply* Distriktsrevisjonen public auditing	CEO and others sentenced to prison	Posted on web site by Romerike public district	Combined legal and forensic accounting	No limitations
23	Samferdselsetaten *Public transportation* PwC auditing and consulting firm	Removed executive without prosecution	Obtained from City of Oslo for research	Formal investigation procedure	Limited to accusations against named individuals
24	Spania *City of Oslo project in Spain* PwC auditing and consulting firm	Displaced executive without prosecution	Posted on Oslo City web site	Forensic accounting without investigative interviews	Superficial investigation because of cost constraints
25	Stangeskovene *Private forest property* Roscher and Berg lawyers	Investigation report failed as evidence in court	Obtained from one shareholder for research	Detailed transaction review without other investigative sources	Limited to shares handled by the board
26	Sykehuset Innlandet *Hospital* Davidsen and Sandvik lawyers	Misconduct but no crime, no consequence	Posted on hospital web site	Legal assessment without other perspectives	Limited to accusations by whistleblowers

(Continued)

Table 9.2 (Continued) Key issues in private investigations

#	Private investigation case	Privatization of law enforcement	Disclosure of investigation report	Competence of private investigators	Limits by investigation mandate
27	Terra *Cities investing in bonds* PwC auditing and consulting firm	Misconduct but no crime, mayor resigned	Obtained from city mayor	Financial crime specialists without responsibility focus	Limited to roles in failed investments
28	Troms Kraft *Power supply company* Nergaard consultant	Misconduct but no crime, board members left	Disclosed after massive media pressure, obtained from journalist asking for comments	Management review rather than investigation	Unlimited and unfocused investigation of too many issues
29	Tyrkia *City of Stavanger project for children* PwC auditing and consulting firm	Investigators failed to find out what had happened in Turkey	Obtained from City of Stavanger	Failed to interview main information source	Limited to transactions within a law firm
30	Undervisningsbygg *School maintenance agency* Kommunerevisjonen public auditing	Several internal and external persons sentenced to prison	Posted on Oslo City web site	Failed to detect more crime, that was later revealed by police investigation	Limited to a formal review and audit

(Continued)

Table 9.2 (Continued) Key issues in private investigations

#	Private investigation case	Privatization of law enforcement	Disclosure of investigation report	Competence of private investigators	Limits by investigation mandate
31	Verdibanken *Religious bank* Wiersholm law firm	Misconduct, but not crime, one executive dismissed	Obtained from executive in the bank	Lawyers without investigative skills	Limited to legal assessment of accusations in the media
32	Videoforhandlere *Video film distributors and dealers* BDO auditing and consulting firm	Misconduct, but not crime, no consequence	Obtained from victim of the investigation	Lawyers without investigative skills	Limited to review of subsidy payments and routines

Source: Derived from Gottschalk, P. (2016). *European Journal of Policing Studies*, 3 (3), 292–314.

The column for disclosure in the table lists how investigation reports were obtained for this research. It is important to keep in mind that these were the only ones successfully obtained. A number of other reports were denied insight. In addition, and probably the largest number, are all those private investigation reports that we as researchers do not know about.

The first key issue is privatization of law enforcement in the third column in the table. We find that several suspects were subject to accusations in investigation reports without any possibility to defend themselves. Employers used reports to fire them, or suspects left because of media pressure and other circumstances created by the internal investigation. They were defenseless after receiving blame from private investigators in their reports. "Individual fired, but never prosecuted," "fired CEO never prosecuted," "rector fired and reported, but case dismissed by the police," and "CEO and chairman left after massive media pressure" are clear examples of privatization of law enforcement with no application of the criminal justice system. For these individuals, there were negative consequences—they lost their jobs—without any fair trial. Others experienced negative consequences from private investigations as well, such as "contract terminated, but case dismissed in court," "removed executive without prosecution," "displaced executive without prosecution," "mayor resigned," and "one executive dismissed." However, there are also several examples, where suspects have been taken care of by the criminal justice system, such as "two persons sentenced to prison," "CFO sentenced to prison," and "CEO and others sentenced to prison."

The second key issue in the table is disclosure of investigation reports. Since these reports were the only ones we were able to access, they were all disclosed to the media and to research, but some were disclosed after massive media pressure. An example is the Hadeland and Ringerike investigation (case #9), where the report was "disclosed after massive media pressure, obtained from the local newspaper for research." Some reports were easily obtainable, such as "posted on Kragerø municipality web site," "posted on web site by radical party in Oslo municipality," "obtained for research from Skedsmo high school," "obtained from newspaper asking for comments," and "posted on company web site."

The third key issue in the table is competence of private investigators. The business of private investigators seems dominated by lawyers. This can be inappropriate, as an investigation is mainly concerned with reconstructing the past, where legal knowledge is less important compared to investigative knowledge, financial knowledge, and knowledge of business administration. Furthermore, many investigations can best be characterized by passivity, as investigators mainly studied what was presented to them by their clients. Examples include "auditors with passive approach," "lawyers with passive approach," and "lawyers without investigative focus."

The fourth and final issue is limits in the investigation mandate. We find bias in most of the cases, such as "limited to consequences for suspected individuals," "limited to individual financial dispositions," "limited to accusations against named individuals," and "limited to transactions within a law firm." The latter example of limitations to a law firm should help the City of Stavanger as a client for the investigation to avoid being blamed by PwC.

References

ACFE (2014). *Report to the nations on occupational fraud and abuse, 2014 global fraud study*, Austin, TX: Association of Certified Fraud Examiners.

Ashforth, B.E., Gioia, D.A., Robinson, S.L. and og Trevino, L.K. (2008). Re-reviewing organizational corruption, *Academy of Management Review*, 33 (3), 670–684.

Atwater, K. (2006). Whistleblowers enforce procurement ethics, *American City & County*, published October 23, http://americancityandcounty.com/mag/whistleblowers-enforce-procurement-ethics.

Beck, R., Pahlke, I. and Seebach, C. (2014). Knowledge exchange and symbolic action in social media-enabled electronic networks of practice: A multilevel perspective on knowledge seekers and contributors, *MIS Quarterly*, 38 (4), 1245–1270.

Bendiktsson, M.O. (2010). The deviant organization and the bad apple CEO: Ideology and accountability in media coverage of corporate scandals, *Social Forces*, 88 (5), 2189–2216.

Bjørkelo, B. and Matthiesen, S.B. (2011). Preventing and dealing with retaliation against whistleblowers, in: Lewis, D. and Vandekerckhove, W. (Eds.), *Whistleblowing and democratic values*, London, U.K.: International Whistleblowing Research Network.

Brooks, G. and Button, M. (2011). The police and fraud investigation and the case for a nationalized solution in the United Kingdom, *The Police Journal*, 84, 305–319.

Button, M., Frimpong, K., Smith, G. and Johnston, L. (2007a). Professionalizing counter fraud specialists in the UK: Assessing progress and recommendations for reform, *Crime Prevention and Community Safety*, 9, 92–101.

Button, M., Johnston, L., Frimpong, K. and Smith, G. (2007b). New directions in policing fraud: The emergence of the counter fraud specialists in the United Kingdom, *International Journal of the Sociology of Law*, 35, 192–208.

Carson, D. (2013). Investigations: What could, and should, be taught? *The Police Journal*, 86 (3), 249–275.

CFCS (2014). *CFCS certification examination study manual*, 4th ed., Miami, FL: Certified Financial Crime Specialist, Association of Certified Financial Crime Specialists.

Datner, B. (2011). *The blame game—How the hidden rules of credit and blame determine our success or failure*, New York: Free Press.

Dupont, B. (2014). Private security regimes: Conceptualizing the forces that shape the private delivery of security, *Theoretical Criminology*, 18 (3), 263–281.

Eberly, M.B., Holley, E.C., Johnson, M.D. and Mitchell, T.R. (2011). Beyond internal and external: A dyadic theory of relational attributions, *Academy of Management Review*, 36 (4), 731–753.

Ensign, R.L. (2014). SEC to pay $30 million whistleblower award, its largest yet, *The Wall Street Journal*, published September 22, http://www.wsj.com/articles/sec-to-pay-30-million-whistleblower-award-its-largest-yet-1411406612.

Farber, N.E. (2010). *The blame game—The complete guide to blaming—How to play and how to quit*, Minneapolis, MN: Bascom Hill Publishing Group.

Fehr, R., Yam, K.C. and Dang, C. (2015). Moralized leadership: The construction and consequences of ethical leader perceptions, *Academy of Management Review*, 40 (2), 182–209.

Gill, M. and Hart, J. (1997). Exploring investigative policing, *British Journal of Criminology*, 37 (4), 549–567.

Gonin, M., Palazzo, G. and Hoffrage, U. (2012). Neither bad apple nor bad barrel: How the societal context impacts unethical behavior in organizations, *Business Ethics: A European Review*, 21 (1), 31–46.

Gottschalk, P. (2015a). *Fraud examiners in white-collar crime investigations*, Boca Raton, FL: CRC Press, Taylor & Francis.

Gottschalk, P. (2015b). *Investigating financial crime—Characteristics of white-collar criminals*, Hauppauge, NY: Nova Science Publishers.

Gottschalk, P. (2015c). *Internal investigations of economic crime—Corporate case studies and regulatory policy*, Boca Raton, FL: Universal Publishers.

Gottschalk, P. (2016). Private policing of financial crime: Key issues in the investigation business in Norway, *European Journal of Policing Studies*, 3 (3), 292–314.

Green, B.A. and Podgor, E. (2014). Unregulated internal investigations: Achieving fairness for corporate constituents, *Boston College Law Review*, 54 (1), 73–126.

Hein, M. (2014). *The blame game*, www.heinsights.com/.../theblamegamev2.doc.

Heisig, P. (2009). Harmonisation of knowledge management—Comparing 160 KM frameworks around the globe, *Journal of Knowledge Management*, 13 (4), 4–31.

Hood, C. (2011). *The blame game—Spin, bureaucracy, and self-preservation in government*, Princeton, NJ: Princeton University Press.

Hoogenboom, B. (2006). Grey intelligence, *Crime, Law and Social Change*, 45, 373–381.

Johnson, R.A. (2005). Whistleblowing and the police, *Rutgers University Journal of Law and Urban Policy*, 1 (3), 74–83.

Kaplan, S., Pope, K.R. and Samuels, J.A. (2011). An examination of the effect of inquiry and auditor type on reporting intentions for fraud, *Auditing: A Journal of Practice & Theory*, 30 (4), 29–49.

Keaveney, S.M. (2008). The blame game: An attribution theory approach to marketer-engineer conflict in high-technology companies, *Industrial Marketing Management*, 37, 653–663.

Kempa, M., Carrier, R., Wood, J. and Shearing, C. (2009). Reflections on the evolving concept of 'private policing,' *European Journal on Criminal Policy and Research*, 7, 197–223.

Lee, F. and Robinson, R.J. (2000). An attributional analysis of social accounts: Implications of playing the blame game, *Journal of Applied Social Psychology*, 30 (9), 1853–1879.

Meerts, C. (2014). Empirical case studies of corporate security in international perspective, in: Walby, K. and Lippert, R.K. (Eds.), *Corporate security in the 21st century—Theory and practice in international perspective*, Hampshire, Houndmills, U.K.: Palgrave Macmillan, pp. 97–115.

Miceli, M.P., Near, J.P. and Dworkin, T.M. (2009). A word to the wise: How managers and policy-makers can encourage employees to report wrongdoing, *Journal of Business Ethics*, 86, 379–396.

Norway Security Council (2014). *Moerketallsundersoekelsen (Shaddow numbers survey)*, Norwegian Business Association Security Council, http://www.nsr-org.no/om-nsr/.

O'Connor, T.R. (2005). Police deviance and ethics.In part of web cited, MegaLinks in Criminal Justice. http://faculty.ncwc.edu/toconnor/205/205lect11.htm, retrieved on 19 February 2009.

Osterburg, J.W. and Ward, R.H. (2014). *Criminal investigation—A method for reconstructing the past*, 7th ed., Waltham, MA: Anderson Publishing.

Pontell, H.N., Black, W.K. and Geis, G. (2014). Too big to fail, too powerful to jail? On the absence of criminal prosecutions after the 2008 financial meltdown, *Crime, Law and Social Change*, 61 (1), 1–13.

Punch, M. (2003). Rotten orchards: "Pestilence," police misconduct and system failure. *Policing and Society*, 13, (2) 171–196.

Renaa, H. (2012). *Norges integritetssystem—Ikke helt perfekt? (Norway's integrity system—Not quite perfect?)*, Oslo, Norway: Transparency International, www.transparency.no.

Schneider, S. (2006). Privatizing economic crime enforcement: Exploring the role of private sector investigative agencies in combating money laundering, *Policing & Society*, 16 (3), 285–312.

Sidley (2010). Report of investigation regarding procurement practices at the office of the chief technology officer of the District of Columbia, Sidley Austin LLP, July 14, DRAFT, 60 pages, http://assets.bizjournals.com/cms_media/washington/pdf/Sidley%20Report.pdf.

Slyke, S.R.V. and Bales, W.D. (2013). Gender dynamics in the sentencing of white-collar offenders, *Criminal Justice Studies*, 26 (2), 168–196.

Stenning, P.C. (2000). Powers and accountability of private police, *European Journal of Criminal Policy and Research*, 8, 325–352.

Stieger, C.J. (2012). Offering monetary rewards to public whistleblowers: A proposal for attacking corruption at its source, *Ohio State Journal of Criminal Law*, 9 (2), 815–829.

Tunley, M., Whittaker, A., Gee, J. and Button, M. (2014). *The accredited counter fraud specialist handbook*, Chicheester, UK: Wiley & Sons.

Vadera, A.K., Aguilera, R.V. and Caza, B.B. (2009). Making sense of whistleblowing's antecedents: Learning from research on identity and ethics programs, *Business Ethics Quarterly*, 19 (4), 553–586.

Wensink, W. and Vet, J.M. (2013). *Identifying and reducing corruption in public procurement in the EU*, PwC, Ecorys, and Utrecht University, PwC EU Services, Belgium,ec.europa.eu/.../identifying_reducing_corruption_in_public_proc.

Williams, J.W. (2005). Governability matters: The private policing of economic crime and the challenge of democratic governance, *Policing & Society*, 15 (2), 187–211.

Williams, J.W. (2014). The private eyes of corporate culture: The forensic accounting and corporate investigation industry and the production of corporate financial security, in: Walby, K. and Lippert, R.K. (Eds.), *Corporate security in the 21st century—Theory and practice in international perspective*, Hampshire, Houndmills,U.K.: Palgrave Macmillan, pp. 56–77.

Zipparo, L. (1999). Factors which deter public officials from reporting corruption, *Crime, Law & Social Change*, 30 (3), 273–287.

chapter ten

The case of the Betanien investigation

Are Blomhoff (born 1952) was a priest and the CEO at diaconal institution Betanien Foundation. The foundation runs nursing homes, kindergartens, and other social institutions in Norway. In addition, it is in charge of a nursing home for retired Norwegians in Spain. Blomhoff frequently visited the nursing home in Spain and bought himself an apartment in the neighborhood. He opened a bank account for himself in a local Spanish bank and started to transfer some Betanien money to his private bank account in Spain. The embezzled money paid for his housing expenses as well as wild parties, where he paid local prostitutes to join his parties. Two junior employees at Betanien tried to blow the whistle on Blomhoff, but nobody on the board of directors believed their accusations of wrongdoings on the part of the priest and chief executive. Therefore, Blomhoff's embezzlement could continue for many years. Finally, someone on the board of directors believed the whistleblowers, and the board hired fraud examiners from BDO to investigate the matter. BDO investigators found evidence of several million Norwegian kroner embezzled by Blomhoff, and he was later sentenced to 3 years in prison by a district court (Drammen Tingrett, 2015).

Are Blomhoff was a respected Methodist pastor decorated by King Harald in Norway. Blomhoff headed the church-funded Betanien Foundation in the city of Bergen that ran a local hospital, a college, a day care center, and a nursing home in Spain. In late 2013 he was defrocked and charged with one of the largest cases of serious fraud in a religious organization in Norway. Blomhoff's massive fall from grace started earlier that year, after two whistleblowers informed the board on the Betanien foundation of financial irregularities concerning its nursing home operation in Spain. Blomhoff was charged with siphoning off 14.6 million NOK ($2.4 million) from the nursing home's bank account. Blomhoff had authority over the Spanish bank account that regularly received funding from the foundation in Norway. Blomhoff allegedly used the account as his own personal wallet, and used the bank card tied to the account for personal use over a period of at least seven years. When first confronted with the suspected swindle, he admitted to siphoning off funds. Betanien's board reported him to the police when the extent of the fraud became known, and he was arrested (Helgheim and Moe, 2014).

BDO investigation at Betanien

Betanien is one of the cases in the table of private investigations in Norway (Case 4). Two internal whistleblowers informed a senior manager about personal credit card misuse of corporate credit cards by the chief executive officer. The whistleblowers thought the chairperson of the foundation had close ties to CEO Blomhoff and potentially participated in the misconduct, so they did not inform him. This was in August 2012. The chairperson learned about the CEO fraud in December of that year. He waited until after Christmas, and then he confronted the CEO with the allegations. The CEO admitted to embezzlement, but could not tell how much it was. The board immediately dismissed the CEO from his position in January 10, 2013, and the chairperson initiated an investigation that resulted in the identification of a total embezzlement amount of 12 million NOK (about $2 million). Investigators presented this conclusion from the private investigation to the chairperson in March 2013. The board had several meetings during the spring and summer of 2013, but waited until November 2013 to report the criminal case to the police. The board reported to the police a total of 14 million NOK in embezzlement suspicion.

In February 2014, the chairperson initiated a second private investigation by auditing firm BDO (2014a) that identified more embezzlements, making the total add up to 20 million NOK (about $3 million). Investigators presented this conclusion from the second private investigation to the chairperson in January 2014. The chairperson waited until October 2014 to report the case to the police.

BDO (2014a) charged the Betanien Foundation 2.5 million NOK (about $350,000) for the second investigation. The first as well as this second investigation report were kept secret. Only an anonymized and revised summary of the second report to the Betanien foundation was made available to the media and researchers on June 27, 2014. The anonymized and revised summary was produced based on a request from the chairperson at Betanien.

Financial crime specialist Kristian Thaysen was the responsible partner at the auditing firm BDO for the Betanien investigation. BDO carried out its investigation from February until June 2014.

Investigators from BDO were given the following mandate from Betanien (BDO, 2014a):

1. Examine and assess uncovered financial irregularities committed by the general manager, including time and extent of fraud.
2. Examine and assess whether further financial misconduct has been committed by the general manager.
3. Examine and assess whether others in the foundation are involved in or contributed to fraud.

4. Examine and assess the foundation's internal control systems, especially regarding the control of general manager.
5. Examine and assess the board's handling of the case.
6. Examine and assess the board efforts in securing claims against the general manager.
7. Examine and assess whether foundation employees or trustees have undertaken criminal and/or indemnifying actions that lead to eligibility for replacement.

BDO obtained and reviewed a large number of documents from various sources including the Betanien Foundation in Norway, Fundacion Betanien in Spain, Fundacion Betanien's accountant in Spain, banks in Norway and abroad, as well as accessible public records. Interviews with 16 individuals were conducted. The former general manager did not want to be interviewed by investigators from BDO. He responded to some questions from BDO in writing. BDO went through electronically stored information (among others, e-mail) about the former general manager and about another employee in the foundation. BDO had access to police criminal documents for the case on behalf of the foundation as the aggrieved party.

The private investigation was to a large extent focused on following illegal monetary flows, including the purpose of examining whether there were more hidden and unknown assets that could potentially be returned to the foundation. The investigation was made difficult by lacking access to detailed information and documentation from Spanish banks. One reason for the difficulties was that a number of mergers of Spanish banks had occurred. Another reason was inadequate archival systems in Spanish banks. A third reason was that some transactions in the embezzlement case were more than 10 years old and thus exceeded the statutory retention for banks.

Normally, electronically stored information such as e-mail correspondence is a valuable source of information in private investigations. Missing backup of electronically stored information and some other circumstances caused BDO to state that they could not exclude the possibility that information and documentation of significant importance either was lost or destroyed.

BDO investigation report

The first private investigation was initiated on January 29, 2013 and completed on March 21, 2013. The second private investigation by BDO (2014a) was initiated in February 2014 and completed on June 27, 2014. It is a summary of the second investigation report that is made publicly available and described in the following.

BDO found evidence of more than the initial 12 and then 14 million NOK. They concluded that the former general manager had acquired wrongful funds from the foundation for a total of 21 million NOK from 2000 to 2012. He gained most of this amount when money was transferred from the foundation's bank to accounts in Spain.

BDO (2014a) was asked in the mandate to examine and assess seven issues that they replied to in their investigation report.

1. Financial irregularities of 21 million NOK were uncovered. Some of the bank accounts in Spain were only used by the former general manager, and these bank accounts were neither part of the foundation's accounting in Norway nor part of the accounting in Spain.
2. Financial misconduct by the general manager of 21 million NOK included both funds transferred as well as refund of private travel expenses and purchase of a house in Spain financed by the foundation.
3. Others were not involved. BDO did not find indications that others than the former general manager had committed financial crime. Other persons in the Betanien Foundation in Norway, in the Fundacion Betanien, and the accountant in Spain had transferred money to bank accounts that was solely at the discretion of the general manager after instructions from him, without being aware that something was wrong.
4. Internal control systems appear to be of the same quality as systems found in comparable organizations. This implies that the internal control is not sufficiently based on a documented (written chronicled) risk picture where there is a systematic and documented correlation between risk and established controls.
5. The board could have handled the case differently in several respects. First, all board members should immediately have been informed. Second, the board should have reported the case much earlier to the police. Third, the board should not have signed a consulting agreement with the dismissed general manager. Fourth, the board should immediately have closed all access to email and computer systems when the general manager was dismissed. Fifth, and finally, a safe with potentially valuable information went missing because the board did not report the case to police before the offender was informed about the case against him.
6. The board's efforts in securing claims against the general manager were insufficient. For example, no efforts had been made to secure funds by mortgaging properties owned by the former general manager.
7. Foundation employees and trustees had not undertaken criminal and/or indemnifying actions that lead to eligibility for replacement.

Liability presupposes that a financial loss has been encountered for the foundation and that there is a basis for liability (e.g., negligence) by whoever is liable.

The BDO (2014a) investigation report by financial crime specialist Kristian Thygesen is a summary of 10 pages. Most of the pages discuss what the board did and should have done. Although the report suggests there is no legal liability for the board or no responsibility to pay compensation to the foundation from the board, investigators are quite critical of the way the case had been handled. Christian Hysing-Dahl, chairperson of the board, did not resign from his position. He was still chairperson in 2014, but resigned in 2015.

While this research had only access to a summary of the investigation report of 10 pages, the court had access to the complete report. In court documents, the following information can be found from the complete investigation report (Drammen Tingrett, 2015: 3–4):

> The accused issued an unreserved confession in court. The correctness of his confession is strengthened by other information in the case, including the comprehensive investigation report from BDO dated June 27, 2014. The report is included as document 08.04 in police documents. The report from BDO contains in section 3.2 (pages 17–41) a detailed review of what is referred to as "additional economic fraud" and is forming basis for post II in the indictment. A summary of economic misconduct can be found in section 3.3.6 (pages 74–77). From this summary on page 74 is cited:
>
> > Based on the documentation that BDO had access to, the Foundation has had three bank accounts for different time periods in Spain that have not been part of the Foundation's accounts. These bank accounts have been at the disposal of Are Blomhoff. Based on the transactions that have been carried out on these bank accounts, it seems that withdrawals from these bank accounts after funds had been transferred from the Foundation (either directly or indirectly) have been spent by Are Blomhoff on "whatever he wished." BDO has not identified that persons other than Are Blomhoff have made or given instructions regarding withdrawals from these bank accounts. BDO thus

assumes that those amounts that have been transferred to these bank accounts have been used by
Are Blomhoff.

Are Blomhoff has in his explanations to BDO,
the police and the court confirmed that this is a
correct representation, but that a certain portion
of these withdrawals nevertheless concerned the
Foundation in such a way that he could have registered it as expenses of the Foundation or Fundacion
Betanien. In the interrogation report included in
the police documents as document 05.04, he has
estimated that this amounts to a few hundred thousand, but he has not been able to quantify it more
exactly.

In the report from BDO a table can be found
(Table 24) with a summary of the amounts, which
BDO believe that the accused has used for purposes
that do not concern the Foundation Betanien or
its Spanish branch Fundacion Betanien. It follows
from the table that in the period from 2005–2012 a
total of 1.992.093 Euro were removed, equivalent
to NOK 16.215.637, from the so-called maintenance
account. In the police notice to the prosecutor dated
December 1, 2014, it appears that the police as a
basis for the indictment have assumed this monetary amount, and then based on the accused's statements have deducted NOK 400.000.

Moreover, it appears from the summary on
page 76 that in the period from 2005–2012, Are
Blomhoff was refunded a number of travel expenses
and other costs twice, both from the foundation in
Norway and the foundation in Spain. Double reim-
bursement amounts to approximately NOK 557.000.

CEO priest prosecution in court

The case against Are Blomhoff was scheduled as a confession verdict in
Drammen District Court outside Oslo. His defense attorney was Per-Erik
Gåskjenn. The prosecutor in Bergen had concluded the case and for-
warded it to a prosecutor in Drammen (Buanes, 2015a).

When the confession case was prosecuted in Drammen District Court
on Tuesday, January 27, 2015, daily Norwegian newspaper *Bergens Tidende*
wrote that the prosecutor demanded "four years in prison for priest," the

priest "misappropriated 15 million," and that most of the money "went to parties with prostitutes" (Buanes, 2015b):

> Prosecutor's punishment proposal is prison for four years. In this lies a confession discount of between nine months and one year, said police attorney Anders Johnsen in Drammen District Court.
>
> The former priest and Betanien director Are Blomhoff met Tuesday morning in court to get a confession verdict. Here he admitted embezzling 15.8 million and fraud of around 550.000 kroner by receiving refund for expenses already repaid. Most of the embezzled amount was spent on large parties that he arranged in Spain, where he hired prostitutes. Blomhoff had already admitted to an issue in the indictment that was concerned with purchase of sexual services abroad. Other party participants did also have sex with the women. Prosecutor Johnsen reminded that the Betanien Foundation has a Christian mission statement.
>
> It is difficult to get further away from this purpose than Blomhoff has spent this money, said Johnsen.
>
> In addition to prison for 4 years, the prosecutor required a reimbursement of 18.8 million croner to the Betanien Foundation. This corresponds to the embezzled amount, plus interest. The claim is not disputed by Blomhoff. Besides where the money went, the prosecutor says that the amount must count as aggravating when sentencing. Embezzlements occurred in the period from 2005 to 2012.
>
> We also learned that he did not stop his offenses of his own free will, but after it was detected. He has over a period of eight years acted with criminal intent, said Johnsen.
>
> Defense attorney Per Erik Gåskjenn argued that Blomhoff had to get a milder treatment. During his presentation in court the attorney meant it was most relevant to refer to a previous sentence of two and a half years in prison.
>
> Our contention is that he must be treated in the mildest possible way. The court must also be able to

assess whether any part of the verdict can be condi-
tional, Gåskjenn said.

He acknowledged immediately after he was
confronted with the criminal offenses, and has
afterwards done what he can to expedite the matter so that it should get a complete clarification, says
Gåskjenn.

The defense attorney argued that there was no reason to punish a
white-collar criminal in a religious organization more severely than others. We return to the issue of white-collar criminals in religious organizations later in this chapter.

If a defendant admits to all charges in court, then a confession procedure is normally applied in the Norwegian criminal justice system. It is
similar to the plea bargain in the United States, where the prosecutor and
defendant enter an agreement based on the assumption that the defendant will plead guilty to charges. However, in the Norwegian system the
defendant does not necessarily plead guilty in return for a more lenient
sentence. Rather, a defendant may plead guilty in return for a short court
hearing, where details of the case are not exposed to the public.

CEO priest conviction in court

The district court sentenced Are Blomhoff to prison for 3 years. The judge
in Drammen Tingrett (2015) wrote an eight-page verdict, where the following discussion is included:

The accused is to be sentenced for gross embezzlement and fraud against his former employer
Foundation Betanien, as described in the indictment. In addition, he is to be sentenced for having acquired for himself and others sexual acts for
remuneration. It is embezzlement and fraud, as
described in the indictment, which has the most
serious impact on the imprisonment assessment.
The court agrees with the prosecutor that these conditions must be seen combined, and then be based
on the total amount of 16.3 million kroner.

It revolves around a very large amount, and the
court finds that, as the prosecutor, it is aggravating
that it has being going on for a long time period
of 8 years, and that his actions did not come to an
end before he was detected. The accused has thus

expelled a permanent criminal intent. The accused has had a trusted position where he served as a senior manager in a large commercially driven foundation, and he has thus exploited the trust that was shown to him.

It is also aggravating that the accused attempted to hide his misconduct by producing fake vouchers when auditors in Norway, in connection with the audit of the trust's accounts for 2011, asked the Spanish accountant to provide an overview of amounts that were received from the foundation in Norway. Furthermore, the court finds it aggravating that money partly has gone to finance purchases of sexual services, an action that is punishable for Norwegian citizens even when it is committed in countries where it is legal.

As a mitigating circumstance, the court refers to the confession that has been of importance both for the investigation as well as for the legal implementation. The accused is entitled to a confession discount. The court finds only to a limited extent grounds for considering the personal burden it has been to be an accused in this case. It is clear that the case has been given substantial attention both internally in the foundation as well as in the media. The court finds that this has been a large burden for the accused, but this is still within what must be expected in a case like this. (…)

Are Blomhoff, born 1952, is sentenced for violation of Penal Code §255, violation of Penal Code §270, as well as §271 and §202a to 3—three—years in prison.

It is interesting to note that the judge to a large extent based the sentence on the private investigation report by citing parts of the report in the verdict document. One reason is that the police in Bergen included parts of the private investigation report in police documentation submitted to the prosecutor. The police are supposed to conduct an independent investigation and not trust evidence provided by others without carrying out its own inquiries. Police district Hordaland where Bergen is the main city, has its own unit for combating financial crime. But in this case the local police might have gained more insight by asking for support from the national criminal investigation service (Eidsvik et al., 2015).

Religious white-collar criminals

Are Blomhoff was a respected Methodist pastor and managing director of the Betanien Foundation. He was sentenced to prison for embezzlement and fraud against the foundation. Based on the Betanien case, it is relevant to phrase the following questions: Is there too much trust, too much freedom, too much individual authority, too little skepticism, and too little control of the financial side in religious organizations? Is trust often betrayed in terms of white-collar crime in religious institutions (Fleckenstein and Bowes, 2000)? According to Owens and Shores (2010), most white-collar crime incidents are exploitations of trust, which can be fostered by a shared religious identity between the victim and the perpetrator. Are social religious networks an attractive arena for white-collar criminals (Shores, 2010)? Is the moral of not acting illegally blinded from a chance perspective when an attractive opportunity arises? Do shared religious beliefs lead to less acceptability of white-collar crime (Corcoran et al., 2012)? Many questions are asked and can be put forward concerning white-collar criminals in religious organizations (Gottschalk, 2015).

In the sample of 390 convicted white-collar criminals in Norway from 2009 to 2014, as presented later in this book, very few of them were associated with or committed their crime linked to a religious organization. Nevertheless, the subsample of six religious white-collar criminals is worth exploring in terms of their characteristics and to what extent they may be different from the majority of white-collar criminals. In addition to Blomhoff, two were convicted in another church foundation case, one was convicted in a bank that managed religious people's and institutions' money, and two were convicted in a bishop family.

Corcoran et al. (2012) found that shared religious beliefs and the importance of God in one's life are negatively related to the acceptability of white-collar crime. Religious belief was found to be associated with lower acceptance of white-collar crime and certain types of religious contexts condition this relationship. These effects, however, weaken in religious contexts characterized by belief in an impersonal or amoral God, as do the effects of religious social relationships and belonging to a religious organization (Gottschalk, 2015).

Owens and Shores (2010) examined the importance of social and spatial distance in the case of Bernard Madoff, the perpetrator of one of the largest white-collar crime cases in U.S. history. Their study shows that residents of countries in which there were stronger Jewish networks were more likely to be victimized by Madoff. Shores (2010) found that Jewish Americans form an ethnic group sharing a common religion, religious language, a history composed of stories of events, a homeland, and oppression. Many Jewish Americans also share a common heritage as many of their ancestors emigrated from central and east parts of Europe.

Additionally, there are many population clusters of Jewish Americans, in particular in cities throughout the United States.

In 1990, the comptroller of the Catholic Diocese of Buffalo was charged with the embezzlement of $8 million of money belonging to the Diocese. He was subsequently convicted and served several years in state prison. It was a newspaper story that revealed that he had purchased church property at less than market value and had used the church's tax exemption for his own purchases. It was revealed that his wife bought 36 acres of land for half the price of what the Diocese paid for it 25 years previously (Fleckenstein and Bowes, 2000).

Heaton (2006) phrased the question: Does religion really reduce crime? He found no empirical evidence for the proposition that religion has a deterrent effect on crime, although sociologists and criminologists have long recognized the potential links between religious belief and delinquent behavior. One theory, labeled hellfire hypothesis, posits that religion deters criminal behavior by increasing the costs of delinquency through the fear of punishment in the afterlife. Works that are more recent have emphasized the role of religious bodies as reference groups against which individuals frame behavior.

Hofmann et al. (2014) studied morality in everyday life. They repeatedly assessed moral or immoral acts and experiences in a large (N = 1252) sample using ecological momentary assessment. Moral experiences were frequent and manifold. Religious and nonreligious participants did not differ in the likelihood or quality of committed moral and immoral acts.

A discussion of Hofmann et al.'s (2014) research results in the Norwegian religious newspaper *Vårt Land* ("Our Country") revealed that most people who were interviewed agreed with the findings. When religious people get an opportunity to commit crime, they will basically act the same way as nonreligious people. Some may consider whether they will be paid in heaven, or whether they should take what they can on earth. Some may argue that it is the will of God, and therefore they can violate the law. Some religious individuals portray themselves as more moral than others (Arnesen, 2014).

I commented to journalist Arnesen (2014: 31) on the topic of religious persons:

> When you have the opportunity to commit economic crime, there are many who are considering whether they should wait until they get paid in heaven, or take their share on earth. There are surprisingly many people who do the latter, says Gottschalk.

A general characteristic of white-collar criminals in general and in religious networks in particular is the betrayal of trust. When we are not sure, we tend to give the other the benefit of the doubt. Fleckenstein and Bowes (2000) argue that the immediate problem for a religious organization is the different perceptions of trust. Relationships are rooted in ideals, values, and services. When trust is violated, some are led to question their trust in God who these organizations claim to serve. Such negative experiences have led many to place their trust elsewhere, thereby abandoning their faith (Gottschalk, 2015).

The low fraction of this religious category of offenders, only 1 1/2 percent of 390 white-collar criminals sentenced to prison in Norway, who betrayed trust based on shared religious beliefs, is an indication either of an unwillingness among religious individuals to commit immoral deeds or of less detection and reporting to the police of misconduct and crime.

Are Blomhoff was not the only religious white-collar suspect who was enjoying media attention in the city of Bergen in Norway in 2014 and 2015. A father and a son who were active in a church also received attention. The police suspected them of white-collar crime. The son was a pastor in a church as well as employed in the Norwegian military. Father and son were indicted for having swindled the military of several million Norwegian kroner. The father was accused of setting up a fake company from which the son bought and paid for fake services to the military (Valland, 2015).

I commented to journalist Valland (2015: 11) on the topic of religious persons:

> If someone were to notify that a religious person
> has done something wrong, the person who is noti
> fied will not believe it, says Gottschalk.

An example of a religious person suspected of white-collar crime is Major John Lee Cockerham. He was prosecuted for orchestrating the largest single bribery scheme against the military since the start of the Iraq war. According to prosecutors, the 41-year-old officer, with his wife and sister, used an elaborate network of offshore bank accounts and safe deposit boxes to hide nearly $10 million in bribes from companies seeking military contracts. Major Cockerham was active in the New Friendship Baptist Church. The congregation in the church celebrated Cockerham's last promotion with a parade. At his son's baptism, he told fellow worshipers that he hoped to instill in his children the values he had wrested from his hardship. He and his 17 siblings grew up without electricity and running water. Crockerham was sentenced to 17 1/2 years in prison for accepting bribes from Army contractors (Thompson and Schmitt, 2007).

Comments from the chairman of the board

Christian Hysing-Dahl was chairperson at Betanien Foundation during and after the embezzlement case of CEO Are Blomhoff occurred. He had read the case presentation above and made a number of comments in an email on March 24, 2015:

- The summary report by BDO (2014b) tells what happened, page 4 and onward is about the board's handling of the case.
- Here is what happened: Two whistleblowers informed a board member on August 14, 2012. The board member immediately informed me. I met one of the whistleblowers the same day. Then we had to investigate quietly to see if there was any foundation for the allegations. I was discouraged to go into the email account of Blomhoff without informing him. The whistleblowers were very concerned not to inform him. They were afraid of him. We thus chose to mirror his emails and search on via an auditor to see if we could disclose embezzlement. We thought that would be possible within the ordinary audit for accounting year 2012. Then we might detect and reveal the embezzlement without him becoming suspicious about who had blown the whistle. I agreed with the whistleblowers on this procedure. In November 2012, email was presented to me that revealed Blomhoff. I then decided to look into his email without informing him. We found evidence. We removed him from his position on January 10, 2013, after confronting him with our findings. We then started to investigate what had happened with help from external fraud examiners. We then found that the embezzlement was much larger. In June 2013, we had a good overview, and then we should have reported him to the police. We did report him until November 1, 2013. According to our notes the embezzlement was then approximately 15 million Norwegian kroner carried out from 2005 to 2013.
- The whistleblowers did all the time express skepticism toward reporting him to the police. The board had a meeting with both whistleblowers on October 8, 2013. They then expressed their opinion that they did not wish a police report.
- After the police report, we initiated the second private internal investigation. This investigation also looked at the earlier period starting in 2000, which caused the estimate for embezzlement to rise to 21 million Norwegian kroner.
- You have access to a summary report of 10 pages. That is the publicly available summary. The complete report has 150 pages. It has been given to the police, the Norwegian Foundation Authority, and the leadership at the Methodist Church who are responsible for

appointing board members in the Betanien Foundation. The complete report is not made public because it names a number of persons including the whistleblowers. That the report is kept secret from the public is in accordance with advice from the Foundation Authority.

- I am not familiar with information the whistleblowers had contact with a journalist. I consider it unlikely.
- Why did we not report the case earlier to the police? I do not blame the whistleblowers. It was meant mainly as case information. I have no proof of it except the direct question in the board meeting on October 8, 2013, where they said that they were not in favor of a police report.
- The board considered negative consequences and concluded on disclosure to the police at the board meeting on October 25. We considered negative consequences like fear of losing contracts from our clients and internal negative effects of public prosecution.
- I cannot tell you about the internal discussions on the board. The conclusion is that a unanimous board decided to report the case to the police.

In April 2015, Christian Hysing-Dahl resigned from the position of chairperson of the board at the Betanien Foundation.

References

Arnesen, H. (2014). Jasså, du trodde troen gjorde deg mer moralsk? (Oh, you thought your faith made you more morale?), daily Norwegian religious newspaper *Vårt Land* (Our Country), Saturday October 11, pp. 30–31.

BDO (2014a). Gransking av Stiftelsen Betanien Bergen (Examination of the Foundation Betanien Bergen)—Anonymisert og revidert sammendrag (Anonymised and revised summary), auditing firm BDO, Oslo, Norway, 10 pages.

BDO (2014b). Rapport til Norges idrettsforbund (Report to the Norwegian Sports Federation)—Faktautredning av enkelte opplysninger i boken "Fotballagenten" (Facts study of certain information in the book "The Football Agent"), BDO, Oslo, Norway, PowerPoint presentation, 4 pages.

Buanes, F. (2015a). Prest tilstår underslag (Priest admits to embezzlement), daily Norwegian newspaper *Aftenposten*, Saturday, January 10, p. 14.

Buanes, F. (2015b). Krever fire års fengsel for prest (Asks four years prison for priest), daily Norwegian newspaper *Bergens Tidende*, www.bt.no, published January 27.

Corcoran, K.E., Pettinicchio, D. and Robbins, B. (2012). Religion and the acceptability of white-collar crime: A cross-national analysis, *Journal of the Scientific Study of Religion*, 51 (3), 542–567.

Drammen Tingrett (2015). Drammen tingrett (Drammen district court), 15-002674ENE-DRAM, February 2, 2015.

Eidsvik, Ø.L., Nicolaisen, C., Torheim, Ø., Christophersen, R., Bleikelia, M. and Kvamme, L. (2015). Tror politimesteren er omdiskutert (Thinks the chief of police is debated), daily Norwegian newspaper *Bergens Tidende*, Tuesday, February 10, p. 5.

Fleckenstein, M.P. and Bowes, J.C. (2000). When trust is betrayed: Religious institutions and white collar crime, *Journal of Business Ethics*, 23 (1), 111–115.

Gottschalk, P. (2015). *Fraud examiners in white-collar crime investigations*. Boca Raton, FL: CRC Press, Taylor & Francis.

Heaton, P. (2006). Does religion really reduce crime? *Journal of Law & Economics*, 49 (1), 147–172.

Helgheim, S.V. and Moe, T.A. (2014). Mener direktøren underslo for over 20 millioner (Claims director embezzled for over 20 million kroner—3 million US dollars), *NRK*, www.nrk.no, downloaded October 1.

Hofmann, W., Wisneski, D.C., Brandt, M.J. and Skitka, L.J. (2014). Morality in everyday life, *Science*, www.sciencemag.org, 345 (6202), 1340–1343.

Owens, E.G. and Shores, M. (2010). *Informal networks and white collar crime: Evidence from the Madoff scandal*, Social Science Research network, www.pars.ssm.com, 54 pages.

Shores, M. (2010). Informal networks and white collar crime: An extended analysis of the Madoff scandal, www.dspace.library.cornell.edu, 71 pages.

Thompson, G. and Schmitt, E. (2007). Graft in military contracts spread from base, *The New York Times*, September 24, http://www.nytimes.com/2007/09/24/world/middleeast/24contractor.html?_r=1&.

Valland, G. (2015). Svindel-tiltalt er pastor i menighet (Fraud-accused is pastor in church), daily Norwegian newspaper *Bergens Tidende*, Saturday, February 14, p. 11.

Conclusion

The convenience perspective introduced in this book argues that white-collar crime is committed out of convenience. When financial trouble occurs or when easy extra profit is detected, then white-collar crime can be an attractive option. Convenience implies that financial crime is a rational choice (economical dimension), an available opportunity (organizational dimension), and an acceptable action (behavioral dimension).

White-collar crime is very different from and is also perceived as very different from street crime. In fact, many do not consider offenders as criminals. Social conflict theory illustrates how complicated it is for the ruling class to punish one of their own. Many people think of crime in terms of violent acts. White-collar crime never involves violence.

This book has made a contribution to our understanding of white-collar crime by explaining the phenomenon using an integrated approach for convenience. The organizational dimension has been neglected by many scholars since Sutherland (1940) coined the term. The organizational roles importance was reiterated in this book by emphasizing power and influence in roles held by privileged, trusted, and prominent professionals.

Convenience theory suggests that crime magnitude and frequency can only be reduced and will only decline if future costs of convenience increase. Costs of convenience include detection, prosecution, and punishment in terms of prison sentence. Costs of convenience may also include negative media attention, job loss, financial ruin, family breakup, loss of friends, and depression.

This book was not about prevention of white-collar crime. However, we know from experience what does not work. From the detection statistics in this book, we know that auditors, who are supposed to control correctness and legality of accounting, seldom detect financial crime. Law enforcement such as the police hardly ever detects financial crime. They are policing violent crime. We know that compliance is mainly window dressing and seldom implemented. Ethical guidelines are expected to be followed by others, but not necessarily by self.

We know from experience what works. We know that whistleblowing works, both whistleblowing to journalists and whistleblowing to government authorities. Whistleblowing internally seems not to work properly, since whistleblowers tend to suffer from negative reactions because of their own whistleblowing further down the road. We know that victims of financial crime, such as employers and banks, tend to detect financial crime to some extent.

Convenience theory tells us that subjective detection probability—the belief that you will get caught—determines the extent of white-collar crime. If a potential offender believes that he or she will be detected and not get away with it, then crime is no longer a convenient option to the offender.

Hence, the question arises how to make privileged and trusted individuals believe that they will be detected and end up in jail if they break the law. This question is best left open to future research.

But it is worth mentioning that governments regularly attempt to address the question. One example is in the United States in 2015, where Attorney General Loretta E. Lynch issued new rules on prosecuting corporate executives (Apuzzo and Protess, 2015):

> Stung by years of criticism that it has coddled Wall Street criminals, the Justice Department issued new policies on Wednesday that prioritize the prosecution of individual employees—not just their companies—and put pressure on corporations to turn over evidence against their executives.
>
> The new rules, issued in a memo to federal prosecutors nationwide, are the first major policy announcement by Attorney General Loretta E. Lynch since she took office in April. The memo is a tacit acknowledgment of criticism that despite securing record fines from major corporations, the Justice Department under President Obama has punished few executives involved in the housing crisis, the financial meltdown and corporate scandals.
>
> "Corporations can only commit crimes through flesh-and-blood people," Sally Q. Yates, the deputy attorney general and the author of the memo, said in an interview on Wednesday. "It's only fair that the people who are responsible for committing those crimes be held accountable. The public needs to have confidence that there is one system of justice and it applies equally regardless of whether that crime occurs on a street corner or in a boardroom."

Though limited in reach, the memo could erase some barriers to prosecuting corporate employees and inject new life into these high-profile investigations. The Justice Department often targets companies themselves and turns its eyes toward individuals only after negotiating a corporate settlement. In many cases, that means the offending employees go unpunished.

References

Apuzzo, M. and Protess, B. (2015). Justice Department sets sights on Wall Street executives, *The New York Times*, published September 9, http://mobile.nytimes.com/2015/09/10/us/politics/new-justice-dept-rules-aimed-at-prosecuting-corporate-executives.html?_r=2&referrer.

Sutherland, E.H. (1940). White-collar criminality, *American Sociological Review*, 5, 1–12.

Index